The First Seven Ecumenical Councils (325-787)

Their History and Theology

by

Leo Donald Davis, S.J.

A Michael Glazier Book
THE LITURGICAL PRESS
Collegeville, Minnesota

Cover: Constantine the Great Mosaic—Haghia Sophia, Istanbul

Cover design by David Manahan, O.S.B.

Typography by Richard Smith.

8   9   10

Library of Congress Cataloging-in-Publication Data

Davis, Leo Donald.
   The first seven ecumenical councils (325-787) : their history and
theology / by Leo Donald Davis.
      p.   cm.
   Reprint. Originally published: Wilmington, Del. : M. Glazier,
c1983.
   "A Michael Glazier book."
   Includes bibliographical references and index.
   1. Councils and synods, Ecumenical—History.   2. Church history-
-Primitive and early church, ca. 30-600.   3. Church history—Middle
Ages, 600-1500.   4. Theolgoy, Doctrinal—History—Primitive and
early church, ca. 30-600.   5. Theology, Dorctrinal—History—Middle
Ages, 600-1500.   I. Title.
BR200.D34   1990
262'.514—dc20   90-38449
                                                      CIP

Table of Contents

"Nobody will ever write a history of Europe that will make any sort of sense, until he does justice to the Councils of the Church, those vast and yet subtle collaborations for thrashing out a thousand thoughts to find the true thought of the Church. The great religious Councils of the Church are far more practical and important than the great international treaties which are generally made the pivotal dates of history ... For in almost every case the international peace was founded on a compromise; the religious peace was founded on a distinction—the enunciation of a principle which has affected, and still does affect, the general state of mind of thousands of Europeans from admirals to applewomen."

—G.K. Chesterton

Preface

The early councils of the Church became the subject of my serious study when some years back I was asked to introduce students to their history and theology at Weston School of Theology, Cambridge, Massachusetts. Very soon I discovered that there was an inexhaustible wealth of source material, monographs and periodical literature on every aspect and in all major languages. However, I soon found too that no one had yet ventured to gather all this together in a convenient form and in English. Even though several short histories in English had appeared at the time of Vatican II, none of them did justice to the political tumult and theological speculation that gave rise to these extraordinary gatherings. The present book is an attempt to fill that void. Our study makes no pretence as originality; others have written elsewhere all that is contained in these pages.

The historical and theological story of the seven first ecumenical councils is of paramount and perennial interest to Christians. Their importance to Christian belief and practice is evident in the fact that the Orthodox churches of the East and the main line Protestant churches of the West accept only these seven as truly ecumenical expressions of Christian faith.

An introductory chapter furnishes a brief outline of the political and cultural world in which the Church was born. Each subsequent chapter is centered on one council, setting it in its historical background, indicating the positions of various theologians whose disagreements brought about a

9

crisis of faith which the Church, through its assembled bishops, then attempted to end by reexamining its traditional interpretation of Scripture. Unfortunately for the peace of the Church these conciliar decisions often resulted in further controversy, calling in turn for another council. As a sub-theme I have tried to indicate the growing authority of the Papacy within the developing structure of the Church and the difficulties that the East had with the Bishop of Rome's understanding of his authority. To guide the student through the mass of historical detail I have added chronologies at the end of each chapter, and to provide an opportunity for further reading, a selection of books in English; and I have confined footnotes to the essential minimum.

I have taught the contents of this book to various student audiences—undergraduates, seminarians and graduates, and I trust that students and others will profit from this study.

I owe a debt of gratitude for various kinds of help to the following: The Reverend John Coventry, S.J., Master of St. Edmund's Hall, Cambridge, England, for the opportunity to spend a sabbatical year in his college; The Very Reverend Vincent J. Beuzer, S.J., sometime rector of the Jesuit Community, Spokane, Washington, for making funds available for a sabbatical year; Dr. John W. Rettig, professor and chairman of the classics department of Xavier University, Cincinnati, for reading the manuscript; Weston School of Theology, Cambridge, Massachusetts, for the chance to teach there as visiting professor and to use the riches of the libraries in that area; Ms. Sharon Prendergast, director of interlibrary loans of Crosby Library, Spokane, for tracking down many of the books included in the bibliographies; Mrs. Eunice Staples for her accurate and prompt typing of the manuscript; The Reverend Jack Heim, S.J., for technical assistance and encouragement; Ms. Oona Hanratty, for helping correct the proofs.

Leo Donald Davis, S.J.
Florence, Italy • January 1, 1987

1

Introduction

1. The Roman Empire

By the time the first ecumenical council opened at Nicaea in 325, Rome as a city had flourished for a thousand years, and as an Empire, regarded as eternal and universal, had dominated 50-60 million inhabitants of the Mediterranean littoral and western Europe for over three hundred. Augustus Caesar (27 BC to AD 14), grand-nephew of Julius, had ended the civil wars which disrupted the five hundred year old Roman Republic and united the state in a new constitutional system, the Dyarchy, dual government by the First Citizen and the Republican Senate and magistracies. Emperors following Augustus were chosen from his family, proclaimed by Senate and Army, until the death of Nero in 68. Nero's overthrow by the palace guard and subsequent suicide led to the famous year 69, the year of the four emperors, when the Army and its leaders learned that emperors could be made elsewhere than in Rome. But with the accession of the general Vespasian, the Empire entered a period of peace and prosperity lasting until the murder of the emperor Commodus in 192. The civil war which followed shook the foundations of the state. The victor in the civil war, Septimius Severus (193-211), as he lay dying, revealed to his sons the secret of the empire: "Enrich the army and despise the rest." In the next forty years there were twelve official emperors, not one of whom died in his bed. After 253 emperors rose and fell in every part of the empire with such fateful rapidity that it is almost impossible to count them.

To political instability was added the constant threat of foreign invasion. The Germanic tribes of Franks and Alamanns menaced the Rhine frontier, while the Goths surged against the Lower Danube. Periodically the Germans broke through the frontier and ravaged the West. In the East the Persians underwent a national revival under a restored dynasty and a renewed religious faith, Zoroastrianism. Persian armies swept into Syria, and in 260 even the Emperor Valerian himself was taken prisoner.

The maintenance of the army and the ravages of war, civil and foreign, strained the Roman economy beyond its limits. As costs mounted, taxation remained almost stable. Instead of reforming the cumbersome tax system, the emperors resorted to depreciating the currency. The coinage degenerated in appearance and in content of precious metal; in the early third century, the well minted silver denarius was valued at 1250 per pound of gold; by 301 it had become a silver washed lump of bronze rated at 50,000 to a pound of gold.

Paradoxically, the sector of the population most affected was the civil service and the army dependent on their wages. Since taxes were not increased, salaries could not be raised and inflation gnawed away at the real value of their income. Soldiers augmented their pay by looting; civil servants by increased fees for services and by outright corruption. The government granted increasingly frequent bonuses to the army and civil service, arbitrarily exacted from the Senate and the town councils. In addition, the government issued free rations and uniforms to both classes, requisitioning them from an already heavily burdened public.

The devastation of civil war and foreign invasion combined with wholesale requisition of crops and cattle were ruinous to Roman agriculture. Peasants deserted the land for work in the towns or for lives of brigandage. By the late third century, abandoned lands were affecting government revenue, and the decurions, the hereditary members of the town councils, were declared collectively responsible for maintaining the previous levels of taxation. Even more disastrously, these twin scourges of devastation and requisition resulted in frequent famine which in turn made the population more susceptible to epidemics. All these factors seem to have combined to shrink the population from the late third century on.

Amid these calamities, the traditional order of society was disrupted. At the top of the social scale, many of the wealthy and stubbornly pagan senatorial families, who held the ancient republican offices, governed the provinces and commanded the armies, were killed off or ruined in the frequent changes of emperors. Many either sought to evade holding expensive magistracies or were barred from office by suspicious emperors. The knights, upperclass businessmen, who traditionally supplied officers to the army and officials to the civil service, found their order thrown open to the lower ranks of the army who aspired to careers as generals, governors and even emperors. The decurions or town councillors, the well-to-do middle class property owners who managed and maintained the cities, began to evade their increasingly burdensome duties. Since the Empire was in fact a great federation of self-governing cities, the dying civic loyalty of the decurions threatened the whole administrative and financial structure of the Empire. At the bottom of the social scale the army, which supplied as well the lower grades of the civil service, no longer attracted the sons of veterans who normally supplied the largest number of voluntary recruits to its ranks. The old order was shaken. Concludes A.H.M. Jones: "Now the sense of *noblesse oblige* was failing among the aristocracy, the spirit of civic patriotism was fast vanishing in the middle class, the discipline of the troops was decaying, and there was nothing to take their place."

2. Imperial Organization

In 284, the Emperor Numerian, leading his army home from a campaign against Persia, was found dead in his litter.

The legions promptly acclaimed the commander of the imperial body guard, Valerius Diocles, emperor, under the name Diocletian. Thirty-nine years old at his accession, he was a man of humble origin, the son of an ex-slave clerk from the mountains of what is today Yugoslavia, a favorite recruiting ground for the Roman army. With a force of character which dominated his able colleagues and with a genius for careful administration, he would reign for twenty years, 284-305, and die peacefully in retirement in 313. Under his rule the Dyarchy of First Citizen and Senate established by Augustus Caesar would give way to the Dominate, an out-and-out military dictatorship. The emperor was in fact the supreme fount of law, though theoretically bound by the law. Diocletian surrounded his person, now clad in gold and jewels, with the elaborate Persian court ceremonies. Everything associated with him became sacred as he ruled under the protection of Jupiter. He was addressed as "Lord and God." All prostrated themselves when entering his presence. All stood while he remained seated during imperial consistories (a term which later passed into papal practice to describe the formal meetings of the pope and his cardinals). All this pomp had the practical effect of exalting the emperor above the ambitious generals from whose ranks Diocletian had so recently risen.

Soon after his accession, Diocletian recognized the need for expanding the administration to govern an empire beyond the control of a single individual. He named Maximian, another Illyrian general of peasant origin, augustus of the West, a name now become a technical term for a senior emperor. From his nomadic court, often in residence at Nicomedia, Diocletian ruled the East directly and continued to dominate his colleague in the West. In 293 he further sub-divided the administration, naming Constantius Chlorus, father of the future emperor Constantine who would summon the Council of Nicaea, caesar or junior emperor for the West, and Galerius, caesar for the East. These two were to learn their jobs from their seniors and in due time replace them. But the Empire remained a legal whole, divided only for administrative purposes. In a further reorganization of the administration which would leave its mark on the Church's organization, Diocletian divided the existing provinces, formed of cities and their hinterland into 100 new provinces, separating civil from military duties. Provinces were further grouped into 13, later 15, dioceses administered by vicars. Dioceses were further grouped together into prefectures: Gaul, comprising modern England, France, Spain and Morocco; Italy, including northern Africa, Italy, northern Yugoslavia and Austria; Illyricum, comprising Bulgaria, Romania, Macedonia and Greece; the Orient, stretching from Thrace around the Levant to Egypt.

Though the empire had been badly shaken, the emperor still ruled through a vast and well-ordered administration which gave him authority which would bewitch the Christian bishops once he was no longer their dreaded persecutor. Beside each emperor stood the pretorian prefects, in effect prime ministers who supervised the vicars of the dioceses and the governors of the provinces, acted as supreme court of appeal, army chief of staff, adjutant and quartermaster general, and oversaw the state arms factories and vast network of roads. Among the chief ministers, the quaestor acted as attorney general; the master of offices supervised the imperial secretariate, the foreign office, and the state messengers, often used as inspectors and secret police; two Counts of Finance managed the state revenues and the imperial estates. Three chief secretaries saw to the voluminous correspondence of the court, chief of whom was the master of memory who as chief legal counsel drafted legislation. A lesser administrative official, the Grand Chamberlain, a eunuch, could often exercise great political power as his supervision of the court and palace brought him into close contact with the emperor.

Each of the 100 provinces had its governor with a staff of 100 subordinates flanked by a count in the interior provinces and a duke on the frontier who commanded the military. Over the governors presided 13, later 15, vicars with staffs of 300. The city of Rome itself and later Constantinople were administered by Prefects of the City who headed the Senate, managed the city government, police, water supply, food supply and markets. There were in all about 30,000 civil servants, now dressed in uniforms and regarded as extensions of imperial power.

The army, raised by Diocletian to about 500,000-600,000 men, whose backbone was the heavy infantry legion of 1000 flanked by light foreign infantry and cavalry squadrons, was divided into a stationary force on the frontier and mobile divisions held in reserve for emergencies. The emperors in the East wisely kept command of the armies dispersed among five masters of the soldiers. The emperors in the West fatefully allowed the commands of infantry and cavalry to coalesce into one Master of Both Services who became the emperor's rival and soon his master as well.

The vitality of this vast governmental machine was shown by the financial reforms instituted by Diocletian. He introduced the indiction, a system whereby the tax structure of the empire was revised every 15 years. Land was evaluated according to quantity and quality and divided for tax purposes into jugera, theoretically the amount of land required to support one peasant family. Each year a governmental budget was drawn up and taxes pro-rated on each jugerum to be collected by the decurions under supervision of the governors. Taxes rose to one-third of the farmer's gross product.

But it was a sluggish vitality at best, for Diocletian attempted to impose a freeze on the prices of the principal commodities for sale in the public markets, a measure promptly bypassed by dealings in the black market. More ominously, workers were frozen into the guilds of workers providing services essential to the state, bakers, shoemakers, arms smiths and the like. In the cities, the decurions were locked into their order; in the countryside, the peasants became coloni, bound to the land they worked. More and more little men looked to wealthy and powerful patrons to protect them from the rigors of law and taxation. The mobs of the cities found an outlet for their repressed political aspirations in cheering for their favorites in the chariot races held in the great circuses.

In 305 Diocletian abdicated and persuaded his reluctant

colleague in the West, Maximian to do likewise. Whereupon he retired to his vast and still existent palace in Split, Yugoslavia, where he devoted his last years to growing prize cabbages. In the East Galerius succeeded as augustus with the brutal Maximin Daia as caesar. In the West, Constantius Chlorus became augustus with Severus as caesar. After a century of disorder, the transition of supreme power seemed to have been accomplished peacefully. Unfortunately for Diocletian's well-laid plans, Constantine, son of Constantius Chlorus, and Maxentius, son of the retired Maximian, passed over in the succession, sulked in the background.

WEST	EAST
Maximian, Augustus, retired 305	Diocletian, Augustus, retired 305
Constantius Chlorus, Caesar	Galerius, Caesar
Constantius Chlorus, Augustus, died 306	Galerius, Augustus, died 311
Severus, Caesar, killed by Maxentius, 306	Maximin Daia, Caesar
Maxentius and Constantine, Augusti from 306	Maximin Daia and Licinius, Augusti
Constantine defeated Maxentius 312	Licinius defeated Maximin Daia 313

Constantine defeated Licinius, 324, ruled as sole Augustus till 337

3. *Paganism and Christianity*

Religious belief within this far-flung empire ranged from a lofty but nebulous pantheism to primitive animism. The Romans were traditionally tolerant of the beliefs of others, willing to allow a wide diversity as long as believers supported the state and did not outrage the Roman sense of decency. The ancient gods of the Roman people led by Jupiter the Thunderer and his consort Juno naturally held pride of place. Once they had conquered the Greek city states, the Romans could easily find that Zeus and Hera exercised equivalent functions in the Greek pantheon. Thus the wealth of Greek literature saturated with religious belief could be used to enrich the rather unimaginative theology of the Romans. But the great high gods of the Romans and Greeks were the austere patrons of the state and evoked little personal emotional response from the masses. Nonetheless the great literature which they inspired had a charm which long captivated the minds of Roman intellectuals. Many came to see the gods as reflections of the power and perfections of one supreme deity and the beautifully expressed stories about them as mere allegories. The cult of the deified emperor also served to bolster the authority of the state. Few probably really believed the living emperor divine; certainly few prayed to him, and by the fourth century the imperial cult had been secularized to such an extent that it represented little more than the respect due to powerful heads of state.

Beside the exalted traditional gods of old Rome swarmed an army of more exotic deities. In the great dim temples of the Valley of the Nile, the Egyptians still worshipped their age-old zoomorphic gods, cats sacred to Bastad, Horus the falcon, Souchos the crocodile, Apis the bull and their like elaborately embalmed after their death. In Syria and North Africa the crowds revered the local Baals and Ashtoreths with fertility rites and ritual prostitution turning the rivers red with the blood of the sacrificed Adonis. To the north of Syria the citizens of Emesa honored the sacred stone which the sun god had sent from heaven. Throughout Asia Minor the dominant gods under a variety of names were the Great Mother and her son and consort, in whose honor frenzied devotees castrated themselves. Farther west in Illyricum the unconquered sun was the focus of devotion. In the Celtic lands of Europe the pious worshipped the gods and goddesses of spring, river, and forest, and above all the sun. All of these gods became closely associated with villages and towns and took on particular characteristics in the jealous local cults. Sometimes they were identified with the gods of the Greek and Roman pantheon, and Baal often wore the mask of Zeus or Jupiter.

In the great towns the more cosmopolitan middle and lower classes and some of the aristocracy, emotionally dissatisfied with the gods of the state and with little taste for philosophical reflection, turned to the mystery religions. Through secret rites of exotic ancient oriental flavor, the devotee was initiated into their theology, purified and assured of some form of life after death. The worship of the Phrygian Great Mother with her sacred black stone and eunuch priests was introduced in Rome during the stress of the Second Punic War (218-201 BC). At first, the orgiastic rites of the cult, which included frenzied self-mutilation and castration, led to its being confined to one temple on the Palatine Hill, but later it spread throughout Italy. Somewhat later the cult of Isis, the earth mother, her consort Serapis and their son Horus reached Rome from Egypt. The devotees of Isis participated in an annual rite celebrating the death of Serapis and his resurrection through the efforts of Isis. A more recent import from Asia Minor was the cult of Mithras who had slain the bull of darkness and safeguarded heavenly light and truth for humankind. Washed by the blood of a slaughtered bull and fed with a sacramental meal of bread and wine, the devotee absorbed the vigor of the sacred bull and was promised eternal life.

All these exotic deities and cults point up the basically religious nature of the period. People were intensely interested in winning the favor of higher forces amid the difficulties of human life. They sought to placate the gods and win their favor through magic and foresee the future through astrology. They longed for assurance of happiness in an afterlife better than they had known in the material prison of this world. Their religions offered no program of social justice, no hope of bettering the world in which they lived. So they clung to this great ill-organized ramshackle system, voluntarily maintaining without central authority the temples and priests that served the communities of initiates in every village and town. Except in Egypt there was no professional priesthood; local dignitaries were elected annually to serve as priests along with their other public duties. But paganism was all pervasive: the Senate opened its deliberations by burning incense at the Altar of Victory; magistrates and soldiers sacrificed to the gods as part of their public duties; the theater, athletics, the race track, were all parts of celebrations in honor of gods; above all, education was founded on the great classics that contained the divine mythologies.

It was in this world of thought and devotion that Christianity was born and developed. The Christian Church too had its Savior-God who died and rose from the dead. Its devotees came to share the life of Christ through the rites of baptism which initiated them into divine life and of the Eucharist which sustained it. The Christians voluntarily organized their communities and supported their priests. They appealed to the same urban middle and lower classes as the mystery religions, at first scarcely touching the aristocracy and the peasants. But they resolutely refused to worship the gods of their neighbors, regarding them as demoniacal forces. They would have no part in the sacred rites which the pagan regarded as essential to the maintenance of divine favor. They avoided too the spectacles in theaters and athletic contests held in honor of the gods. They were wary of even dining out in an age when most meat for sale had come from the temple sacrifices (1 Cor. 10:23-30). Military and civil service they avoided because they involved oaths and duties their religion could not countenance. This avoidance of customs regarded as natural by their pagan neighbors soon earned for them a reputation as enemies of the human race.

Yet Christianity had a social ethos that appealed to many. The Christians were profoundly cosmopolitan. Their faith transcended all local boundaries; they were professedly a non-nation. They were also profoundly egalitarian. There was to be among them no Greek, no Jew, no slave or free (Gal 3:28; Col 3:11). In Rome in the early third century, as Peter Brown points out, "the Church included a powerful freedman chamberlain of the emperor; its bishop was a former slave of that freedman; it was protected by the emperor's mistress, and patronized by noble ladies." The Christians also formed strong local communities led by a bishop assisted by priests, deacons and deaconesses which were conscious of common bonds among all similar communities. Their literature is full of expressions of peace, unanimity, concord, charity, society, community which reveal an underlying sense of "communio," a bond based on a common faith and love. Christians of the local community were conscious of unity among themselves and their bishop; bishops expressed their sense of unity with other bishops by constant written communication and meetings. Communio was more than a union of common purpose. The Christian community was called together by Christ and based on faith in him and sacramental union with him. This consciousness found expression in the drawing up of lists of bishops who were on good relations with one another, in letters of recommendation granted to travelers assuring other communities of their sincere adherence to the Church, in the custom of inviting visiting bishops to preside at the Eucharist of the host communities. Communio was a powerful force that bound the local community and its bishop together in an organic unity, set it off from the pagan world surrounding it, and united it with its fellow communities throughout the Roman world. Moreover, the Christians expressed their communio practically by taking care of their own. In times of emergency the Christian clergy was often the only group capable of organizing the food supply and burying the dead. By 250 the Church in Rome was supporting 1500 poor and widows. In 254 and 256 the Churches of Rome and Carthage sent large sums of money to Africa and Cappadocia to ransom Christian captives from the bands of barbarian invaders. It was perhaps above all this sense of community which attracted to the ranks of the Church the Roman citizen lost as an individual in a vast impersonal empire, whose ancient cities had lost his allegiance.

The aspect of communio most apposite for our purpose is the frequent consultation of bishops among themselves as embodiments of the communities over which they presided. The bishops could read in the Acts of the Apostles of the method of the apostolic church in dealing with the first great crisis of the Church: to what extent must a Gentile convert take upon himself the obligations of Judaism. Peter and Paul met with the leader of the Jerusalem community, James, and resolved the dispute as it seemed good to them and the Holy Spirit, largely freeing Gentile Christians of the burdens of Judaic law borne by their Jewish Christian confreres (Acts 15). There is no record of subsequent councils of bishops until the outbreak of Montanism, which had its origin in the teachings of Montanus who taught from 156 to 172 in Phrygia, always a center of religious fanaticism. In the face of the increasing institutionalization of the Christian Church, Montanus taught the apocalyptic outpouring of the Holy Spirit on the Church in a Heavenly Jerusalem soon to appear and already begun through the prophets and prophetesses of the sect, who developed an ascetic rigorism opposed to what they regarded as the lax rules of marriage, fasting and penitential discipline. Ordinary Catholics were regarded as psychics or "animal men" while Montanists were pneumatics, spirit-filled. The issue before the bishops was not a theological aberration but a new discipline. They must determine the locus of the action of the Holy Spirit—the prophets and prophetesses of the new provisional Montanist sect living in the expectation of the apocalypse, or the wider, permanent, institutional Church presided over by the bishops. In 175 the earliest known council of bishops and laymen was called to deal with the problem of Montanism and by 200 a series of Asiatic councils had condemned the sect.

Conciliar methods of government had proved their worth; in 190 Pope Victor ordered a series of councils to resolve the dispute over the manner of calculating the date of Easter since East and West differed on the issue. Recorded councils met in Pontus, Palestine, Syria and Osrohene without resolving the issue to the Pope's satisfaction. In a Roman council of 250-51, 60 Italian bishops met under the presidency of the bishop of Rome. From the 220's on in Africa the calling of councils was a well developed custom much used by Cyprian, bishop of Carthage (248-258), to resolve the problems arising out of the persecution of the Christians;

in the Council of Carthage of 256-257, 87 African bishops were present. There is little record of councils in Gaul and Spain, but at the Council of Elvira in c. 306, important for its 87 severe disciplinary canons, 33 bishops from southwest Spain were in attendance presided over by Ossius, bishop of Cordoba who would be active in conciliar activity throughout his long life (257-357). Few councils are recorded in Egypt where the bishop of Alexandria dominated ecclesiastical affairs. At a council in Antioch in 252, called to deal with problems in the aftermath of the severe Decian persecution, bishops of Syria, Palestine, Cappadocia and even the bishop of Alexandria were in attendance. Again at Antioch in 264-68 councils were called to deal with the theological aberrations of Paul, eccentric bishop of Samosata. In 314 at Ancyra 12 to 18 bishops from Asia Minor and Syria met to establish penitential discipline for those who had denied the faith in the recent persecution. Even this incomplete list is evidence enough that the council, a meeting of bishops to resolve theological and disciplinary disputes among the faithful, had a long history behind it before the Council of Nicaea.

There is evidence to show that the deliberative procedures of the Roman Senate left their mark on the collective deliberations of the Christian bishops. Bishops adopted for many of their councils the official senatorial formulae of convocation. Like the Senate the council was a deliberative assembly, each bishop having equal rights in its discussions. Like the imperial magistrate who presided over the Senate, the principal bishop first read out a program designed to keep discussion to the point at issue. The assembled bishops were then interrogated and each offered his *sententia,* his official response. A final vote was usually not necessary, for the *sententiae* most often issued in unanimity, the result of previous negotiation. The unanimous decision was circulated among the faithful in a synodal letter. Bishops then felt themselves bound to abide by the decisions thus promulgated. Constantine would later find the Church governed by procedures with which he was familiar.

4. Church and State

Since the reign of the emperor Nero (54-68), who foisted the blame for the famous burning of Rome on to the Christians, the very name Christian was enough to involve its bearer in the toils of the Roman courts. In addition, the refusal of the Christians to swear allegiance to the gods of the state and to a divine emperor raised governmental suspicion about the political loyalty of the Church. It soon became clear to the Roman authorities that the Christians were not just a Jewish sect and therefore not protected by the laws which granted a generous but expensive measure of toleration to that stubbornly monotheistic race. Popular feeling as well supported the official suspicion of the Christians. In the eyes of the pagan masses the Christians were atheists who did not worship the traditional gods. They were suspected of sexual license as they celebrated their "love feasts." They were cannibals because they ate the flesh of the Son of Man and drank His blood. In the second century the emperor Trajan's reply to the anxious request of Pliny, governor of Bithynia in Asia Minor, for instructions on how to handle the increasingly numerous Christians in his area throws light on the government's attitude toward the Christians. "They are not to be sought out; but if they are accused and convicted, they must be punished—yet on this condition, that who so denies himself to be Christian, and makes that fact plain by his action, that is, by worshipping our gods, shall obtain pardon in his repentance, however suspicious his past conduct may be. Papers, however, which are presented unsigned ought not to be admitted in any charge, for they are a very bad example and unworthy of our time."

Until 250, persecution was sporadic and unofficial. But in that year, in an effort to stem the general decline, the emperor Decius sought to appease the gods by dealing with the atheistic Christians. The precision and efficiency of his measures reveal the power of the state even in the turmoil of the third century. At a given date, throughout the Empire, all were ordered to sacrifice to the gods under the eye of government officials and receive certificates attesting to this fact. In 257 the emperor Valerian ordered the arrest of all Christian senators and knights and the execution or deportation of the bishops and priests hitherto arrested. At this time thousands of Christians apostatized or procured fraudulent certificates of pagan orthodoxy, creating grave problems for the penitential discipline of the Church. But for all his piety, Valerian was defeated and murdered in the East by the invading Persians. His successor Gallienus in 260 called off the persecutions, released the imprisoned clergy and even restored its buildings and property to the Church.

It was in the late third century, an era relatively free of persecution, that the Church came to terms with Greco-Roman culture. Under the influence of men like Justin Martyr (100-165) in the West and more especially Origen of Alexandria (185-254) in the East the Christian Church found that it could identify with the culture, outlook and needs of the average well-to-do civilian. From being a sect ranged against or alongside of Roman civilization, Christianity had become a Church prepared to absorb a whole society. As Peter Brown observes, "This was probably the most important *aggiornamento* in the history of the Church; it was certainly the most decisive single event in the culture of the third century. For the conversion of a Roman emperor to Christianity, of Constantine in 312, might not have happened—or, if it had, it would have taken on a totally different meaning—if it had not been preceded for two generations by the conversion of Christianity to the culture and ideals of the Roman world." By the early fourth century a council of Spanish bishops ruled on the conditions according to which Christians might hold municipal offices and even the high priesthood of the imperial cult. For the Christian apologists of the early fourth century like Lactantius (250-320), Christianity was the sole guarantee of Roman civilization. Only by being confirmed by Christian revelation could the best traditions of classical philosophy and ethics be saved from the ravages of the barbarians. Only the Christian God could save the Empire from destruction.

Peace between Church and State, however, was not to last. About 298 as Diocletian and his caesar Galerius were sacrificing to obtain the omens, the soothsayers were unable to find the usual marking on the victims' livers after repeated attempts. The chief soothsayer then denounced the Christian officials present as responsible for the failure by crossing themselves as protection against the demons. Outraged, Diocletian ordered the entire court—soldiers and civil servants—to sacrifice. Then the relatively tolerant Diocletian, probably at the instigation of the more fanatically pagan Galerius, broadened his attack on the Christians in 303. Christians were ordered to surrender their sacred books and their churches were to be destroyed. A detachment of troops promptly demolished the church of Nicomedia which stood in sight of the imperial residence. The next day all Christians were deprived of their rank. The hardy Christian who tore down the edict was executed by prolonged torture. After two fires broke out in the palace, a second edict was proclaimed ordering the arrest of all bishops and priests. When the arrested clergy overcrowded the Roman prisons, never designed for long-term confinement, the emperor in a third edict ordered them released after being forced to offer sacrifice to the gods. In 304, Diocletian, in a fourth edict, resorted to the tactic Decius had used 50 years before: all citizens were ordered to sacrifice and obtain certificates recording their act. Implementation of the four edicts varied throughout the Empire. In the West the caesar Constantius Chlorus published the first edict but confined his efforts to the destruction of the churches. There is no evidence that the second or third or even the severe fourth edict was even promulgated in the West. Relatively few died in this persecution, but thousands underwent arrest and torture, while all Christians suffered from insecurity and the insults of the pagans.

In 305, Diocletian, who had been in ill health, resigned along with his co-augustus of the West, Maximian. As Constantius Chlorus became new augustus of the West, he asked Galerius, new augustus of the East, to send him his son Constantine. Now about twenty, Constantine was the son of Helena, ex-barmaid wife of Constantius Chlorus, who had divorced her in 293.

For the last twelve years he had been living at Diocletian's court, ostensibly pursuing his education, actually as a hostage for his father's good conduct. Galerius agreed but the next day changed his mind and attempted to halt Constantine's journey to the West. But Constantine moved fast, disabling the horses of the imperial posting stations, effectively thwarting his pursuers. He joined his father in northern Gaul and accompanied Constantius to Britain to campaign against the Picts. In 306 at his father's death at York, he was acclaimed augustus by the legions. His claims were recognized only in Britain and Gaul. Reluctantly, the eastern augustus Galerius finally recognized him as caesar, but raised Severus as augustus of the West. Later in 306, Maxentius, son of the retired augustus Maximian, was acclaimed augustus at Rome. With his father's help he rallied Africa and Spain to his cause and defeated and executed Severus, the legitimate augustus. To cement an alliance with Constantine, Maximian offered him his daughter. Constantine promptly married her. After Maximian quarreled with his son, Maxentius, he fled to Constantine, against whom he soon rebelled and was executed. Vainly Galerius in the East made Licinius augustus of the West, who succeeded in holding Illyria while the remainder of the West was still divided between Constantine and Maxentius.

5. Constantine the Great

The Christians of the West, from 306, found themselves free from persecution under the more tolerant rule of Constantine and Maxentius. In the East, however, the caesar Maximin Daia renewed the persecution, forcing all again to sacrifice. The next year he began sending obstinate Christians to work in the mines and quarries of Egypt and southern Palestine, blinding their right eyes and cutting the tendons of their left legs. In this brutal policy the augustus Galerius cooperated until stricken ill in 311. In that year, in agony from cancer of the bowels, he declared toleration for the Christians and induced Maximin Daia to acquiesce. As

Galerius lay dying, the mutilated Christians were allowed to return to their homes. Soon, however, Maximin Daia returned to the attack by indirect means. He encouraged the various cities of the East to denounce Christians and drive them from their homes. He launched an attempted reform of the pagan cults by appointing a high priest in each city to supervise worship and keep an eye on the Christians. But by 312 the executions began again, and during this final storm Lucian the influential theologian of Antioch was martyred.

In 312 Maxentius prepared to move against Constantine and Licinius to make himself master of the West. But Constantine attacked rapidly and quickly reduced all of northern Italy. He then turned south toward Rome where Maxentius feverishly prepared for a siege. As Constantine approached with inferior forces, Maxentius unwisely sallied out of the Flaminian Gate toward the north. Constantine decisively defeated him and he died in the crush of his army retreating into Rome across the Milvian Bridge. Now that he was master of the West, in October, 312, an obliging Senate acclaimed the young Constantine senior augustus.

In the same year in the East, Licinius moved against Maximin Daia, who began to relax his persecution of the Christians in the face of a triple threat—his defeat by the Christian king of Armenia, famine and plague which ravaged his domains, the hostility of Licinius. Maximin retired to southern Asia Minor, but when Licinius forced a crucial pass, he killed himself. Licinius, master of the East, met Constantine at Milan where they resolved their differences and compromised on a common policy toward the Christians: the property of the church was to be returned and full liberty of worship permitted.

The inscription on the great arch erected in Rome by the orders of the Senate to commemorate his triumph reveals a curious fact about Constantine's victory: "To the Emperor Caesar Flavius Constantine, the Greatest, the Pious, the Fortunate, Augustus, because by the prompting of the Divinity and the greatness of his soul, he with his forces avenged the commonwealth with just arms both on the tyrant and all his factions, the Senate and people of Rome dedicated this triumphal arch." The pagan Senate makes no mention of the gods; they refer only to a vague divinity, knowing that Constantine believed the ancient gods had no part in his victory. In fact, Constantine's victorious army had borne on their shields the strange device of a Greek chi set over a rho, the first letters of the name Christos. Constantine believed wholeheartedly that he had won the West through the mercy of the Christian God.

Authors have long been divided about Constantine's religious beliefs at the time of his victory, his decree of tolerance to the Christians and afterward. Some have regarded him simply as a political opportunist without religious conviction who sought to win the Christians to his side to strengthen his hold on the Empire. Others have seen him as a religious syncretist, recognizing all religions, again to strengthen his political power. Today, most would admit that Constantine was sincere about his rather confused faith in the Christian God at the time of his victory at the Milvian Bridge and gradually grew in the knowledge of his new faith, always believing that a common orthodox faith was necessary for the preservation of a unified Empire.

When proclaimed emperor in 306 by the legions at York in Britain in succession to his father Constantius Chlorus, he was like his father a solar syncretist, worshipping a solar divinity under the name of Apollo. His religious outlook gradually gave way to a philosophic monotheism and reverence for the divine spirit by whom the universe was governed and whose symbol was the sun. But even at this stage he must have known of Christianity. His father had not implemented the persecution of Christians in those parts of the empire under his jurisdiction, and one of his sisters bore the Christian name of Anastasia (Resurrection). As Constantine moved toward the decisive battle at the Milvian Bridge outside of Rome which would give him control of the West, he underwent some sort of religious experience; his biographers speak of his seeing a cross in the sky and a subsequent dream explaining that under this sign he would conquer. Whereupon he put a Christian emblem on his legions' shields, and conquer he did. Then in 313 he and his co-emperor in the

East, Licinius, proclaimed religious toleration throughout the Empire. Though he avoided baptism, retained until his death the pagan title pontifex maximus, and allowed pagan symbolism on his coinage down to 320, from 312 on there is clear evidence that he had growing faith in Christ and favored the Christian Church. By 313 he was making large contributions to the Church in Africa, and at Rome had begun a series of great churches, putting the Lateran Palace at the bishop's disposal and heavily endowing these institutions. By law the clergy were exempted from onerous public functions; wills in favor of the Church were permitted, and slaves could be freed in the Christian churches. Still these privileges were already those of pagan priests and institutions. Even the declaration of the first day of the week as a day of rest was ambiguous, since it was both the day of Christ's resurrection and the day sacred to the sun. By 315-316 Christian ideas began to modify the harshness of the Roman civil law itself: crucifixion was abolished; concubinage outlawed; children protected; branding on the face forbidden; and laws against celibacy repealed.

Constantine had learned, too, the Church's methods of dealing with internal problems from his attempts to settle the Donatist schism which grew out of an African controversy over the validity of sacraments conferred by clerics who had lapsed into paganism or turned over Christian books and vessels to the pagan authorities during the persecutions. Since the Donatists refused to recognize such sacraments and demanded baptism and ordination anew while the Catholics recognized them as valid, the African Church underwent a bitter and long-standing schism. When the case was first presented to him in 314, Constantine applied the Roman juridical procedure by setting up a court of investigation and judgment by a commission of bishops. Militiades, bishop of Rome, with great presence of mind, turned the court into an ecclesiastical synod by including a number of Italian bishops. But the bishops never questioned the emperor's right to intervene. Once Constantine had learned of the Church's procedure, he followed it in subsequent dealings with the Donatists and would follow it again in the case of the Arians.

6. Chronology

27 BC-AD 14	Augustus Caesar.
68	Death of Nero.
175	First recorded church council.
192	Death of Commodus and beginning of political disorder.
250	First general persecution of Christians.
284-305	Diocletian reorganized Empire.
303	Diocletian's persecution of Christians.
306	Constantine proclaimed emperor.
312	Constantine seized Rome.
313	Edict of Toleration.
324	Constantine became sole emperor.
325	Council of Nicaea.

7. Select Bibliography

The institutional structure of the Roman Empire is detailed in A.H.M. Jones, *The Decline of the Ancient World* (London, 1961). A short reliable secular history of the period is Glanville Downey, *The Late Roman Empire* (New York, 1969). Peter Brown, *The World of Late Antiquity, A.D. 150-750* (London, 1971), in word and picture beautifully captures the spirit of the age. The story of the Church's adaptation to the Roman world is told in R.A. Marcus, *Christian-*

ity in the Roman World (New York, 1974). The standard
histories of the Early Church are Louis Duchesne, *The Early
History of the Christian Church,* 3 vols. (London, 1909) and
Hans Lietzmann, *A History of the Early Church,* 4 vols.
(London, 1961). The persecutions of the Christians are
authoritatively analyzed in W.H.C. Frend, *Martyrdom and
Persecution in the Early Church* (Garden City, 1967). The
changes in religious sentiment are described in E.R. Dodds,
Pagan and Christian in an Age of Anxiety (Cambridge,
1965) and A. Momigliano, ed., *The Conflict between Paganism and Christianity in the Fourth Century* (Oxford, 1963),
There is a good brief biography of Constantine in A.H.M.
Jones, *Constantine and the Conversion of Europe* (London,
1948); the controversies surrounding his conversion are
treated in John W. Eadie, ed., *The Conversion of Constantine* (New York, 1971). F. Dvornik, *Early Christian and
Byzantine Political Theory,* 2 vols. (Washington, 1966) deals
fully with the question of church and state, and his "Emperors, Popes and General Councils," *Dumbarton Oaks Papers,*
6 (1951), 1-23, advances the thesis that the procedure of the
early councils was modeled on that of the Roman Senate.
Ludwig von Hertling, *Communio* (Chicago, 1947) analyzes
the bonds of union in the early church. A sound one-volume
history of the Church is W.H.C. Frend, *The Rise of
Christianity* (Philadelphia, 1984).

2

Council of Nicaea I, 325

1. The Trinitarian Problem and Proposed Solutions before Nicaea

The problem which would confront the bishops assembled at Nicaea had long been the basic question confronting all previous Christian theologians. It was not simply whether Jesus is God. For in the pagan milieu of the early Church, any mysterious power could be endowed with attributes of divinity as Paul and Barnabas found to their horror when the Lycaonians attempted to offer sacrifice to them after their cure of a cripple (Acts 14:8ff). The problem was, as G. L. Prestige defines it, "how within the monotheistic system which the Church inherited from the Jews, preserved in the Bible, and pertinaciously defended against the heathen, it was still possible to maintain the unity of God while insisting on the deity of one who was distinct from God the Father."

By the fourth century a bewildering array of solutions had been offered to the problem. As Bernard Lonergan remarks, "The abundance and variety of the material, unless it be drawn together in a manner that displays a pattern or order, are more likely to obfuscate than to illuminate the mind, to cloud the issue rather than clarify it." It is largely his pattern which will be used to order the various solutions to the trinitarian problem proposed before the Council of Nicaea.

As the post-apostolic Church emerged from the Jewish world, Judaeo-Christianity still fashioned its solutions from images drawn from the Old Testament and the apocalyptic literature. The heretical Ebionites of the second century, to cite only one group out of many, continued to insist on the observance of Jewish law and custom. For them Jesus was the elect of God and a true prophet, but they denied His virgin birth and eternal pre-existence. The Son was created as one of the archangels who rule over the other angels and over creatures of this world. This heavenly archangel descended upon Jesus the man. His primary mission in coming to earth was to end the Old Testament priesthood. Jesus earned His name of Christ by fulfilling the Law, and the Law not Jesus Himself remained the true way to salvation.

Judaeo-Christianity, as a cultural form, went beyond the deficient theology of groups like the Ebionites and left its imprint, the use of Old Testament images to describe Christ, on many more orthodox Christian thinkers. For the Jews the "name" meant normally more than a mere name in our modern sense, but the person, power, and nature of the one named; it meant for the Jews what "being" meant for the Greeks. So for the Jews the name of God is glorious; through the name mankind is delivered; one trusts in the name of God. The author of the mysterious Shepherd of Hermas who wrote at Rome perhaps as early as AD 96 adopts this terminology to develop his theology. The name of the Son of God is great and incomprehensible; it implies complete transcendence and pre-existence of the invisible part of Jesus, the only-begotten Son, who sustains the whole cosmos as the foundation and support of creatures who bear His name. The name is present too in Christians as a result of their baptism and confession of faith. The name of the Son of God is the only door, the only entrance to salvation for those who receive His name. Thus by the use of the name, the author of the Shepherd of Hermas established a distinction within God and somewhat vaguely allowed the foundation of a trinitarian or at least binarian belief. Yet God not the Son founded the Church; it is God not the Son who comes at the Last Judgment.

Another way used by those influenced by Jewish ideas to express the significance of the Son was to identify Him with the Law, the Torah taken in its active sense as God establishing laws. Justin Martyr (d. 165) calls Christ at the same time Law and Covenant: "It was prophesied that Christ, the Son of God, was to be an eternal law and a new covenant for the whole world." Christ is Law and Covenant in His existence, in His all-embracing divine reality which is present in the man Jesus in the world.

Another more popular attempt to express the transcendence of Christ was "angel Christology," the designation *Christos angelos.* This is a useful way to hint at Christ's function in the economy of salvation, but it came soon to be recognized as quite insufficient to express His true nature. For the Jews the angel Michael was the supreme leader of the heavenly host. This position the Shepherd of Hermas assigned to the Son of God but with a difference. "Have you seen," the Shepherd asks, "the six men and the glorious and great man in their midst? The glorious man is the Son of God and those six are the glorious angels who support him on right and left. Of these glorious angels none can enter the presence of God without him. Whoever does not receive his name will not enter the kingdom of God." For the Shepherd the Son of God is like Michael but more; for He is the way to God even for the angels. The point of all this is that the Judaeo-Christian mentality was content merely to illustrate the doctrine of the New Testament concerning Jesus Christ and His relation to God the Father by images drawn from the Old Testament and the apocalyptic literature without fashioning these often profound insights into a coherent explanation.

But new problems arose as Christianity encountered Hellenistic speculation, moving, as Lonergan remarks, "from a cast of mind which saw a chosen race meeting its God, conceived as a person, in the concrete events of history to an intellectualized outlook that created a world of theory which directed and controlled the world of practical common sense." Christian Gnostics of the second and third centuries elaborated a system of knowledge purporting to answer the questions whence we came, what we have become, whither we are heading. Within their various systems they had, as Christians, to account for Father, Son and Holy Spirit. Their attempt has been called pseudo-symbolic speculation: speculation because they dealt with ultimate questions; pseudo-symbolic because they personified abstract ideas, mingling them in with sensible representations. The Valentinians, followers of Valentinus who taught at Rome and Alexandria in the mid-second century, to resolve the ancient Greek problem of the one and the many, began by postulating a supreme Father, unbegotten and perfect, who had by his side Silence, the thought of the Father. From this primal couple, Mind and Truth, Word and Life, Man and Church flow out successively, by a process akin to that whereby thought proceeds from mind or desire from will. From this first group of eight proceeds in turn a group of ten and then another of twelve, so there are at last thirty divine entities or aeons, half of whom are male, half female, forming the divine order or pleroma and bridging the abyss between the single source and the realm of multiplicity. But the lowest of the thirty aeons, Wisdom, yearns illicitly to understand the Father and thus gives birth to Desire. In order to rectify this primal disorder, Mind and Truth produce Christ and the Holy Spirit to instruct the aeons about their proper relation to the Father. Formless Desire, offspring of Wisdom, meanwhile gives rise further to matter and psyche, whereupon Christ impresses form upon Desire who then gives rise to spirit or pneuma. Wisdom then proceeds to fashion the Demiurge or Creator, equivalent to God of the Old Testament, out of psychic substance. From matter and psyche, the Demiurge forms heaven and earth and the creatures inhabiting it. Among these creatures, the Demiurge fashions carnal man and breathes into him his own psychic substance. But Desire secretly plants spirit as well into certain men. This spiritual element yearns for the Father, and salvation consists in liberation of spirit from the lower psychic and carnal elements of the human constitution to ascend to the Father. The Savior Jesus provides the means of salvation through his revelation of the workings of the system. Merely carnal men, however, cannot be saved; psychic men can be saved with difficulty through knowledge and imitation of Jesus; spiritual men need only apprehend the teaching of Jesus to be saved. All of this fantastic system is supported by an equally fantastic exegesis of the Scriptures where it is regarded as lying hidden. Irenaeus of Lyons (fl. 180) provided an example of this sort of exegesis; he said, according to the Gnostics, the thirty aeons are signified by the thirty years of the Lord's hidden life; the group of twelve aeons, by the fact that Jesus at the age of twelve disputed with the doctors of the Law in the temple; the group of eighteen aeons, by the eighteen months which Jesus supposedly spent among His disciples after His resurrection. As Lonergan observes, this system is related to theology as alchemy to chemistry or legend to history.

Yet it contains certain conceptions of great value to scientific theology. One of these is the process of emanation; aeon proceeds from aeon as human thoughts and desires proceed from mind and will. This idea has a long future ahead of it in the history of trinitarian thought. A second conception is that of consubstantiality. What is emitted is of the same nature (*homoousion*) as that which emits it. So the Demiurge breathes into the soul which is earthly, material, irrational and consubstantial with the beasts something which is consubstantial with himself, the spirit of life which forms the soul into living soul. This conception, purged of material overtones, will be the key to the later pronouncements of the Council of Nicaea, yet unwelcome to many because of its connnection with the various Gnostic systems.

These systems are clearly dualistic, opening a chasm between spirit and matter. Matter is not the creation of the ultimate God but the result of primal disorder and fall, formed into creatures by a Demiurge or Creator equivalent to the God of the Old Testament. The historical dimension of the material world is totally disregarded. The spiritual element yearns to be freed from matter to ascend to its true home among the aeons, helped along by a series of mediators. The means whereby the spiritual element frees itself from material entanglement is knowledge of the system and its workings. This knowledge is revealed by Jesus, an aeon distinct from the aeon Christ, who dwelt in a man but left him before the crucifixion. One Jesus Christ is divided into the aeons, Christ and Jesus, and a man upon whom the aeon Jesus descends.

The second century heretic, Marcion, has some kinship with Gnostic ideas, though he did not adopt their mythical speculations about the aeons. A native of the Black Sea region, he broke with the Church in Rome in 144. Raised a Christian, he rejected the Old Testament because in his view its legalism and strict justice conflicted with the grace and love of the New. Of the New Testament, he accepted only the Gospel of Luke, purged of its Hebrew conceptions, and ten Pauline Epistles. Theologically, he concluded that there must be two gods, a lower creator identified with the God of the Old Testament, and the Supreme God made known by Christ. He is similar to the Gnostics only in the fact that he distinguished between the Gods of Old and New Testament.

The theologian who attempted the first full-scale refutation of the Gnostic systems was Irenaeus of Lyons. Probably from Smyrna in Asia Minor, he crossed the Mediterranean to settle at Lyons in Gaul (France). Carrying out a mission for the Church of Lyons at Rome, he thus was in contact with theological views in major centers aross the Roman world. About 180 he became bishop of Lyons where he wrote his principal work, *Against the Heresies.* He took great pains to insist that the God of the Old Testament, the God of the Gospels, and the God attainable through reason are all one and the same God. The first article of our faith, he said, is "God the Father, increate, unengendered, invisible, one and only Deity, creator of the universe." The world has only one creator identical with the God proclaimed in the Old Law and the Gospels. That there is only one God is a fact ascertained by reason: "Either there must be one God who contains all things and has made every creature according to His will, or there must be many indeterminate creators or gods.... But in this case we shall have to acknowledge that none of them is God. For each of them ... will be defective in comparison with the rest, and the title 'Almighty' will be reduced to naught." Since God is rational, added Irenaeus, He created whatever was made by His Word. It is the Word who establishes things, bestows reality on them, the Spirit who gives them order and form. In addition, according to the economy of our redemption there are both Father and Son. If anyone asks how was the Son produced by the Father, Irenaeus answered that no man understands that production or generation or may describe it. But the Father begat and the Son was begotten. Thus God has been declared through the Son who is in the Father and has the Father in Himself. Since whatever is begotten of God is God, the Son is fully divine; the Father is God and the Son is God. It was the preexistent Word who became incarnate, and Irenaeus applied again and again the formula one and the same to the Lord Jesus Christ to rebut the Gnostic distinction between the aeons Jesus and Christ. Only if the Word is fully divine and entered fully into human life, earthly and historical, could redemption be accomplished. Jesus Christ then is truly God and truly man, summing up in Himself the whole sequence of mankind, sanctifying it and inaugurating a new, redeemed human race. In order to control the fanciful exegesis practiced by the Gnostics, Irenaeus appealed to the canon of written scriptures and their authoritative interpretation by the bishops who are the lineal successors of the Apostles and the particular locus of the action of the Holy Spirit.

Admirably balanced though Irenaeus' system is, it has its problems. The Word is God's immanent rationality which He extrapolates in creation and redemption; the Word is co-eternal with the Father, but as a person He does not seem to have been eternally generated from the Father. Nor are Father and Son precisely equal; what is invisible in the Son is the Father, said Irenaeus, and what is visible in the Father is the Son. But Irenaeus did yeoman service for the early Church in refuting the Gnostic distinction between the Supreme God and the lower Creator God, between Jesus and the Christ.

Other currents within Christian theology would accept the one God of the Old Law and the Gospels but would explain His relation to Jesus Christ in different ways. On one hand, the Adoptionists answered the questions about Jesus by arguing that He was a mere man in whom God dwelt in a special way. On the other, were the Monarchians, a general term for those who stressed the unity of God in such a fashion that they acknowledged the divinity of Christ but denied His distinction from the Father.

The earliest Adoptionist of which we have record seems to have been a second century shoemaker of Byzantium teaching at Rome, Theodotus by name. For him Jesus was merely man, though born of a virgin according to divine will. When Jesus was baptized in the Jordan, He did not become God but received the power to work miracles, for a spirit, the heavenly Christ, descended upon Him and dwelt within Him. The condemnation of Theodotus by Victor of Rome (d. 198) did not prevent one of his disciples, Theodotus the Banker, from alleging that Jesus was even inferior to Melchizedek, since the latter is fatherless, motherless, without genealogy, whose beginning and end is neither comprehended nor comprehensible.

A far more troublesome advocate of Adoptionism than these amateur lay theologians was Paul of Samosata who was bishop of the great metropolis of the East, Antioch in Syria, from 260 to 268. He seems, to say the least, to have been a bizarre sort of bishop, allied with Queen Zenobia of Palmyra who controlled Antioch at this time. He went about attended by a large cortege of body-guards, consorted freely with unmarried women, and preached to his tumultuous congregation while clapping his hands and stamping his feet from a high throne erected in his cathedral. He reasoned that "the Word is from above, Jesus Christ is man from hence; [Mary] gave birth to a man like us, though better in every way, since He was of the Holy Spirit." Apparently, he did not say that Father, Son and Holy Spirit are one and the same, but gave the name God to the Father who created all things, that of Son to the mere man and that of Holy Spirit to the grace which dwelt in the Apostles. The Logos, the expression of God's immanent rationality, descended upon the man, Jesus, born of Mary, but their mode of union was simply a coming together. The Logos did not enter into substantial union with the man, for this would compromise the dignity of the Logos. It was Jesus' moral progress that won for Him the title Son of God. It seems that Paul applied the term *homoousios* to the relationship of the Logos to God the Father. According to Athanasius he used it in a *reductio ad absurdum* arguing that the Logos and the Father could not be consubstantial, using the word in its material sense, as two pennies are consubstantial because both are of the same substance, copper. If consubstantiality were true of Father and Son, Athanasius said Paul reasoned, there must then be an antecedent substance of which both would partake, a manifest absurdity. Perhaps more correctly, Hilary of Poitiers says that Paul claimed that the Logos was *homoousios* with the Father, that is He was identical with the Father, one and the same as the Father, opposing the contention of his episcopal accusers that the Word was a substance (*ousia*), that is, a real entity distinct from the Father. The bishops assembled in Antioch in 268 deposed him and condemned both his adoptionist teaching and his use of consubstantial. Again, as in the case of the Gnostics, *homoousios* was tainted by objectionable connotations for the orthodox because of its connection with the condemned Paul.

A second group of theologians would admit the divinity of Christ but deny His distinction from the Father. This particular view afflicted the Church at Rome in the late second and early third centuries. That this was the view of Praxeas who taught at Rome is known only through the writings against him of Tertullian (d. 220). It has been suggested with some plausibility that the name Praxeas, Busybody, was Tertullian's pseudonym for Callistus, Bishop of Rome (217-222), who was, as we shall see, concerned to protect the divine unity. At any rate, said Tertullian, "He is such a champion of one Lord, the Almighty, the creator of the world that he makes a heresy out of unity. He says that the Father himself came down into the virgin, himself was born of her, himself suffered, in short himself is Jesus Christ."

This view that the Father himself suffered on the Cross earned for its advocates the title Patripassians, Father-sufferers. Teaching, too, at Rome and opposed by Hippolytus (d. 235) was Noetus of Smyrna who alleged that "Christ was the Father himself, and that the Father himself was born, suffered, and died." However, the theologian who gave his name most prominently to this view was Sabellius, a native of what is today Libya, where his teaching would linger for some time after his death. Sabellius came to Rome during the pontificate of Zephyrinus (199-217) where he later enjoyed the confidence of Callistus (217-222), was opposed by Callistus' arch-rival Hippolytus, and where he was in the end condemned by the previously friendly pontiff. Hippolytus reports that Sabellius said the Logos himself is the Son who is given, too, the name Father, but there is only one undivided spirit who is God; Father and Logos are one and the same. The Spirit, clothed with flesh in the virgin, is one and the same as the Father. What is visible, namely the man, is the Son, but the Spirit who descended upon the Son is the Father. It was the Father who deified the flesh and made it one with Himself, so that Father and Son, one person, suffered together. Sabellius also used the analogy of the one sun which can be distinguished into form, light and warmth; so in the one God, form is the Father, light the Word, warmth the Holy Spirit. Possibly, he may have employed the Stoic idea of the expansion of the primal One, the Father, by a process of development projecting Himself as Word for the purpose of creation and redemption and as Spirit for inspiration and the bestowal of grace. Though Sabellius was condemned by Callistus and became in the minds of its adversaries the principal proponent of the Monarchian viewpoint, the theologians of the West would continue to be more preoccupied than those in the East with safeguarding the unity of the Godhead while rejecting strict Monarchianism.

Callistus of Rome himself was accused by Hippolytus of condemning the arch-heretic Sabellius only to dispel rumors of his own sympathy with the heresy. Unfortunately, this accusation was colored by Hippolytus' hatred of Callistus, whose election as bishop of Rome dashed his own hopes for the office and led him into schism as the first anti-pope. Indeed, Callistus whole-heartedly insisted on the divine unity, the single Godhead being the indivisible spirit pervading the universe. He admitted the distinction of Father and Word, the Word being the pre-temporal element which became incarnate, the Son being the historical figure, the man. But the Son was not one thing and the Father another, nor was the Word another thing alongside the Father. Yet since the Father was the unique divine spirit, Callistus spoke of him as identical with the Word and even as becoming incarnate, but in his view the Father only co-suffered with the Son. Callistus was clearly in sympathy with the Monarchians, but aware of the difficulties of their position, he groped inadequately for some form of compromise. Others would seek to do greater justice to the reality and distinction of the Three within God's being.

But distinction was sometimes achieved only at the price of subordinating the Son to the Father as in the case of the great African theologian, Tertullian (d. c. 220), a pagan-born lawyer who broke with the mainstream Church in 207 to join the rigorist, prophetic sect of the Montanists. In his work against the Monarchian Praxeas, Tertullian reasoned that the Word of God is not empty and hollow like the sound uttered by a human being. Since it proceeds from so great a substance, God Himself, it too must be a substance. But of what sort? The mistake of the Gnostics, argued Tertullian, was that they separated their emanations from their source so that an aeon could not know its father. But Tertullian himself would not separate the Son or Word from the Father. The Word alone knows the Father and reveals the Father's mind and heart; it is the Father's will that He manifests, having known it from the beginning. The Word is in the Father, was always with God, never separated from the Father, was never other than the Father. This Tertullian explained in images: God brought forth the Word as the root brings forth a shoot; the spring, a stream; the sun, a ray. Each of these proceeds from a source, yet shoot is not separated from root, nor stream from spring, nor ray from sun. Each pair remains conjoined, undivided, coherent. In such fashion the Father and the Word are two, yet the Word is never separated from the Father. Moreover, just as the fruit comes from root and shoot, river from spring and stream, point of light from sun and ray, so there is a third, the Spirit, with Father and Word. But God is one because the three elements are conjoined and cohere; nothing is separated from its source. "The mystery of the divine economy," said Tertullian, "should be safeguarded, which of the unity makes a trinity, placing the three in order not of quality but of sequence, different not in substance but in aspect, not in power but in manifestation; all of one substance, however of one quality and of one power, because the phases, the aspects, the manifestations are all of the one God, in the name of the Father and the Son and the Holy Spirit." He further explained the divine monarchy by an analogy with human monarchy: "If he who is monarch has a son, and if the son is given a share in the monarchy, this does not mean that the monarchy is automatically divided, ceasing to be a monarchy. For the monarchy belongs principally to him by whom it was communicated to the son, and being exercised by two who are so closely united with each other, it remains a monarchy." In fine, the unity of rule among a plurality of rulers guarantees the unity of the monarchy.

Western theologians were greatly indebted to Tertullian for enriching theological vocabulary with new terms, none more important than "substance" and "person." For Tertullian, substance connoted the divine essence, that which God is, with emphasis on its concrete reality. "God," he said, "is the name for the substance, that is, the divinity." Hence, when he speaks of the Son as being of one substance with the Father, he means that they share in the same divine nature, and since the Godhead is indivisible, they are of one identical being. Person, the Latin *persona*, originally meant an actor's mask or face, then role, and finally individual with the stress on the external aspect. Thus for Tertullian person meant the concrete presentation of an individual, and when applied to Father, Son and Holy Spirit, meant the otherness or independent subsistence of the Three within the unity of the divine substance.

Though a step forward in trinitarian thought, it is clear that Tertullian's view is still somewhat immersed in the sensible. Spirit is for him really only attenuated matter, and imagination so pervaded his thinking that he could explain the unity of the divine substance in terms of a kind of organic continuity and of concord within a human monarchy. His view of Father and Son as of one quasi-material substance is different from the consubstantiality (*homoousion*) that will form the basis of Nicaea's pronouncements. To this difficulty in Tertullian's thought are added certain notions contradicting his fundamental view. "There was a time," he said, "when there was no Son to make God a Father." Immanent in God from all eternity, the Word came forth from God as Son, making God a Father, for the purpose of creation and redemption. His thought clouded by sensible imagination Tertullian could say, "the Father is the whole substance, whereas the Son is something derived from it." In his struggle to express diversity within unity, Tertullian ends by subordinating the Son to the Father.

To an even more marked degree this same difficulty appears in the thinking of Hippolytus of Rome, opponent of the Monarchians Noetus and Sabellius and first anti-pope in opposition to Callistus, who died a martyr in 235. For him the generation of the Word was a progressive development, the Word appearing as Son only at a time determined by the Father. Hippolytus described the process thus: while existing alone, God yet existed in plurality, for He was not without reason, wisdom, power and counsel. Determining to create the universe, He begat the Word through whom all things come to be. God next made the Word visible, uttering Him and begetting Him as Light of Light, in order that the world might see Him in His manifestation and be capable of being saved. Thus there appeared another beside God Himself, but there are not two Gods, but only Light from Light, Word coming from God as water from a fountain or as a ray from the sun. This is the Word which came into the world and was manifested as Son. Prior to His incarnation, the Lord was not yet perfect Son, although He was the perfect, only begotten Word. He was manifested as perfect Son of God only when He took flesh. Moreover, the generation of the Word was a free act like creation itself. Hippolytus' trinitarian thought has a more primitive air about it than does Tertullian's, but there is some of the same immersion in sense categories and a more marked stress on the voluntariness of the generation of the Son from the Father and on the subordination of the Word to God.

Following Hippolytus' line of thinking was Novatian, a morally rigorous yet brilliant Roman priest who led a schism as anti-pope against the morally more moderate Pope Cornelius (251-253), yet died a martyr in 257. Since he was the first theologian in Rome itself to write in Latin, his work is important in revealing the sophistication of western theological vocabulary. According to Novatian, since the Son is begotten of the Father, He is always in the Father, otherwise the Father would not always be Father. Yet the Father is antecedent to the Son, and because the Son is in the Father and is born of the Father, He must be less than the Father. At a time willed by the Father, the Son, whose name is Word, proceeded from the Father and all things were made through Him. Yet the unity of God is assured because the Son does nothing of His own will and renders due submission to the Father in all things. By His obedience He shows that the Father, from whom He drew His origin, is one God. To describe this unity of God, Novatian conceived a kind of circular movement whereby the power of divinity transmitted to the Son is directed back to the Father. "Hence all things are laid at His feet and delivered to Him who is Himself God, but, since He refers back to the Father everything that is subjected to Him, He returns to the Father the whole authority of the divinity; and so the Father is the one true, eternal God, from whom alone the power of the divinity comes, which He transmits and extends to the Son. Because, being turned back into the Father, the Son shares His substance, the Son is also God, for to Him the divinity has been extended; nevertheless, the Father is the one God; for in stages, by a backward flow, the majesty and the divinity, given by the Father to the Son, is turned back by the Son Himself and returns to the Father." To some extent as well,

Novatian anticipated the later doctrine of mutually opposed relations that found the diversity of persons within the divine unity. "...The Son is indeed a second divine person, God proceeding from God, but this does not mean that the Father is no longer the one God. If the Son had not been born, but, like the Father, had known no birth, then they would both be equal, alike in all things, and thus there would be two gods." Powerful though Novatian's thinking is, it still remains entangled in subordinationism.

Sabellianism too was at this time troubling the Egyptian Church, and Dionysius, formerly head of the great catechetical school of Alexandria and now bishop there (248-265), made an attempt to combat it. His attempt was an unfortunate foreshadowing of the teaching of Arius. He wrote: "...that the Son of God is a work of God, a thing that was made, not by his own nature God, but other than the Father in respect of His substance; as the farmer is different from the vine, and the carpenter is different from the bench he makes. For since He is a thing that was made, He did not exist before He was made." Dionysius exemplifies the concern of the East to do greater justice to the distinction and reality of the Three within the One than did the Sabellians or even the other orthodox theologians of the West. He spoke of three substances (hypostases), that is, three distinct subsistent beings in the Godhead. But when reproached for this, he objected that other statements of his were overlooked and that, in fact, he had added "that a plant coming from a seed or root was different from that whence it sprang and yet was absolutely of one nature with it." Dionysius, the Bishop of Rome (259-268), intervened in the dispute between his namesake of Alexandria and the Sabellians to set both on the right path. The Bishop of Rome rebuked the Sabellians who say that the Son is the Father and those who preach in some sort three Gods, dividing the sacred Monad into three substances foreign to each other and utterly separate. Though Dionysius of Alexandria was not mentioned by name, it is clear that he was the one referred to. "For it must needs be," said the Bishop of Rome, "that with the God of the Universe the Divine Word is united, and the Holy Spirit must repose and dwell in God; thus in one as in a summit, I mean the God of the Universe, the Almighty, must the Divine Triad be gathered up and brought together." He continued, "Equally must one censure those who hold the Son to be a work, and consider that the Lord has come into being, as one of the things which really came to be.... For if He came to be Son, once He was not; but He was always, if He be in the Father, as He himself says.... In many passages of the Divine oracles is the Son said to have been generated, but nowhere to have come into being...."

This dispute points up the differing theological vocabulary of East and West. The Greeks, like Dionysius of Alexandria, commonly spoke of three hypostases, not as affirming three Gods but as expressing the real subsistence of Father, Son and Holy Spirit. However, hypostasis and *ousia* were often for practical purposes equivalent, though not strictly identical in meaning. G. L. Prestige comments, "Both hypostasis and *ousia* describe positive, substantial existence, that which is, that which subsists.... But *ousia* tends to regard internal characteristics and relations, or metaphysical reality; while hypostasis regularly emphasizes the externally concrete character of the substance, or empirical reality." But since the Latin *substantia* is the exact equivalent of the Greek hypostasis, when the western theologians heard talk of three hypostases, they immediately understood three substances, therefore three Gods. The Latin West, on the other hand, distinguished substance, by which they designated what is one, from the persons which are three in the Godhead. Until the East too agreed to use *ousia* for what is one and hypostasis exclusively for what are three, there was fertile ground for misunderstanding on all sides.

The western inability to rise beyond materialistic thinking, as is evidenced especially in Tertullian, was not shared by the great eastern theologian Origen. Born at Alexandria of Christian parents (his father was martyred), Origen was well educated and at the early age of eighteen became head of the catechetical school at Alexandria, while attending the classes of Ammonius Saccus, the founder of Neoplatonism. At odds with his bishop, who objected to his ordination to the priesthood by a Palestinian bishop despite his self-mutilation, he continued his teaching and incredibly prolific writing at Caesarea in Palestine until his death in 253 at the age of sixty-nine, his health broken by tortures undergone in the Decian persecutions. Resolutely Origen rejected any account of the generation of the Son according to analogies of human or animal generation and materialistic extrusions from the Godhead. He insisted on transcending any sensible representation of Father and Son. God the Father is strictly immaterial, the source and goal of all existence, transcending mind and being themselves, God in the strictest sense, being ingenerate. Since He is perfect goodness and power, He must always have had objects on which to exercise His perfections. So He brought into being a world of spiritual beings, souls, co-eternal with Himself. He needed, however, a mediator between His own unity and the multiplicty of souls; this is His Son, the very image of the Father. Beyond time, eternally, the Son proceeds from the Father. Father and Son are two hypostases, one coming from the other yet related by mutual understanding and willing. But the Son does not know the Father as the Father knows Himself and the Son's will is only the image of the Father's. Yet the Son, as it were, draws divinity to Himself by perpetually contemplating the Father, following the Father's will, doing all the Father does. The Father is called by Origen *ho theos, the* God, while the Son is simply *theos*, God by participation and sharing in the Father's divinity. The Father is in consequence greater than the Son, for as Christ said, "The Father is greater than I," and the Son is in turn greater than the Holy Spirit. Yet the three are incomparably greater than all else, and though three in hypostasis, they are one in unanimity, harmony and identity of will. The Father's action extends to all reality, the Son's to rational beings, the Spirit's to the sanctified. Although Origen did verbally call the Son a creature, and on this score the Arians would claim him as their own, he did so because he lacked a clear distinction between being begotten and being created, and because of his reliance on Proverbs 8:22: "He made me in the beginning of His ways." Yet Origen held that the Son is eternal, and though not Himself made in the same sense as creatures, was the first born of all that was made, and he denied that the Son had a beginning. Profound though his insights were, Origen, caught up in Platonic essentialism, ended by making the Son and the Holy Spirit divine beings subordinate to the Father.

Now at long last we are in a position to view the overall development of Pre-Nicene trinitarian speculation. Jewish converts could not transcend Old Testament categories of thought and would insist that Jesus was only a teacher, prophet or angel. For the Hellenistic mentality of the Gentile converts, much of the Old Testament was nonsense, and they turned to symbolic speculation in the Gnostic style, separating the supreme God from the Creator, the Christ from Jesus. Thinkers like Irenaeus insisted that the God of the Old Testament, the God of the Gospels and the Supreme Being knowable through reason were identical. The Adoptionists accepted one Supreme God, but saw Jesus only as man. Monarchians too accepted the one Supreme God, but argued that Father, Son and Holy Spirit were one identical being. Many western Fathers would recognize a distinction between the Three while insisting that all were of one substance, often conceived in too material and too subordinationist a fashion. Origen and many Easterners after him would transcend the sensible but, adopting a form of Platonism, would conceive the Three as distinct subsistences, one subordinate to the other, yet one in harmony and concord of intellect and will. With Arius a new stage of development was reached. He ruled out anthropomorphic and metaphorical language, set aside Origen's Platonic categories and posed the question in Scriptural terms of Creator and creature, and argued logically that the Son was a creature. The Church's reaction to this would bring about the Council of Nicaea.

2. Arius and the Beginning of Controversy

Arius, the theologian who brought trinitarian speculation to the crisis stage, was born in Libya, about 256. By 318, the date accepted by most scholars as marking the opening of the controversy (though some would put the date as late as 323), Arius was an elderly priest, tall, austere, ascetically dressed, grim of countenance, urbane in manner. After having joined in the schism of the bishop, Meletius, against the legitimate line of bishops of Alexandria in Egypt, he was reconciled and given by Alexander, the bishop, the care of the fashionable church Baucalis in the port district of the city. Here he was popular, especially with women, and was reputed to have had a following of some seven hundred consecrated virgins. The problem of tracing Arius' intellectual pedigree centers about our ignorance of the teachings of Lucian of Antioch, martyred in 312, under whom Arius had studied. He had been a renowned theologian and exegete and many who later supported Arius were proud of having been Lucian's disciples. Perhaps it was from Lucian that Arius drew certain Antiochene positions: a taste for the literal exegesis of Scripture, a determination to preserve the unicity of God, a tendency to distinguish between the Logos and God. From his Alexandrian milieu Arius was possibly influenced by the apologist Athenagoras (late 2nd century) who insisted that God is one, sole, prior to and separated by an abyss from matter and who avoided the idea of the Son's generation. From Origen (d. 253) he could have drawn the emphasis on the Son's subordination to the Father, and from Dionysius (d. 265) the insistence that Son is distinct from the Father and was made by the Father. The Old Testament concept of a God who is absolutely one and who acts as an artisan in creating all from nothing and not by emanations from Himself seems to have weighed heavily on Arius. Perhaps Arius was influenced by the Jewish exegete Philo of Alexandria (d. 50) in his resolute monotheism, his notion that the contingent universe could not bear the work of the omnipotent hand of the uncreated Creator, and his conception of the Word created from nothing to serve as the intermediary of further creation. Finally, the rigorous use of syllogistic reasoning by Arius points to the influence of Aristotelian dialectic on his thought. At any rate, Arius fashioned all these ideas into a coherent synthesis that would bitterly divide the Church for years to come.

Fundamental to his system is the absolute transcendence and unicity of God who is Himself without source but is the source of all reality. Since the very essence of God is transcendent, unique and indivisible, it cannot be shared. For God to impart His substance to some other being would mean that He is divisible and changeable. There can, of course, be no duality in divine beings for God is unique. Therefore, whatever else exists must come into being not by communication of God's being but by creation from nothing. Since the contingent world could not bear the direct impact of the all-powerful God, He needed an instrument of creation through which to mediate His power. This instrument is the Word, who is a creature, generated or made (these terms, be it noted, are synonyms for Arius), perfect and beyond all other creatures, but a creature nonetheless because he has a source, while God Himself has none. The Word had a beginning; though born outside of time, prior to his generation or creation he did not exist. The Arians would insist that "there was when he was not." The Word can have no communication with nor direct knowledge of God beyond that of other creatures; the titles of Word and Wisdom are his only because he shares in the essential Reason and Wisdom, God Himself. The Word is liable to change and even to sin, though this last affirmation was modified to say that, though he could sin, God foresaw his virtuous steadfastness and bestowed grace upon him in advance. Finally, wrote Arius, "Even if He is called God, He is not God truly, but by participation in grace.... He is God in name only." What then is the nature of Jesus Christ? In Christ the created Word, distinct from the Logos, reason immanent in God, united himself to a human body lacking a rational soul, the Word himself taking the place of the rational element within the human composite.

As Arius' views began to spread among his circle and within the highly independent body of Alexandrian clergy, Alexander the bishop called a meeting of his priests and deacons. An open discussion ensued in which Alexander insisted on the unity of the Godhead. Arius labeled his bishop's position Sabellian and insisted that if the Father had begotten a Son, then the Son began to exist; and therefore there was a period in which He did not exist. Though called upon to recant, Arius refused and continued to spread his teachings in the city. By 320 Alexander called a synod of the bishops of Egypt and Libya. Of the hundred bishops gathered at Alexandria eighty voted for the condemnation and exile of Arius. Two bishops continued to support him without qualification, Secundus of Ptolemais and Theonas of Marmarica in today's Libya, along with some seventeen Alexandrian priests and deacons. With Alexandria rapidly growing too hot to hold him, Arius fled to Caesarea in Palestine where he was welcomed by the eloquent and erudite father of ecclesiastical history, Eusebius, bishop of Caesarea, who was strongly influenced by Origenist theology with its insistence on three distinct hypostases within the Godhead. Some of the bishops of Palestine rallied to Arius, but most notably the bishops of Antioch and Jerusalem opposed him. Arius continued on to Nicomedia in northwestern Asia Minor where the emperors were frequently in residence and where a second Eusebius, bishop of the city and Arius' fellow disciple of Lucian of Antioch, became his staunchest and most influential supporter. From Nicomedia Arius enlisted the allegiance of an increasing number of bishops, many of whom were disciples of Lucian, including those of neighboring Chalcedon and Nicaea.

Meanwhile from Alexandria, Alexander sent out the customary synodal letter to at least seventy bishops informing them of the condemnation of Arius and soliciting in return letters of communion, thus effectively excommunicating Arius. This Alexander followed up with letters refuting Arius' views. Though accused by Arius of Sabellianism, Alexander conceived of the Word as a person or nature distinguishable from the Father. In Origenist fashion, the Word mediates between the Father and creation, but the Word is not a creature Himself, being derived from the Father's being. The Word is co-eternal with the Father, for the Father must always have been Father. The sonship of the Word is, for Alexander, natural, not adoptive. The Word is eternally generated from the Father and is the Father's express image and likeness, not subject to change.

The party supporting Arius held their own synod at Nicomedia, proclaiming Arius' orthodoxy and condemning Alexander. While soliciting episcopal support at Nicomedia, Arius wrote up his teaching in popular poetic form called the Banquet (Thalia). This was sent back to Alexandria by way of sailors sympathetic to Arius to keep his views before the crowds of the great metropolis. The whole situation became even more confused as the emperor of the East, Licinius, launched the final persecution of the Christian Church before going down in defeat before the Christian-sympathizing emperor of the West, Constantine, in 324.

With his victory over Licinius, Constantine became sole ruler of the Roman world. Much to his distress he found religious division within his politically unified realm. Thereupon he dispatched his chief ecclesiastical advisor, Ossius, bishop of Cordoba in Spain, who at sixty-seven was a veteran in Church politics, to Alexandria armed with personal letters to Alexander and Arius, who had returned to the city amid the political turmoil. As his letters show, Constantine was far from understanding the significance of the controversy. He reproached both Alexander and Arius for raising such questions at all. They were mere debating points arising from misused leisure, results of intellectual exercises which should have been kept to oneself and not unadvisedly entrusted to the ears of the crowds. For, he asked, who can comprehend or explain subjects so sublime and abstruse in their nature? Counseling mutual forgiveness, he advised the two that they were not really divided by any major doctrines or involved in any heretical opinions but were actually of one and the same judgment and so should join in communion and fellowship. He ended by warning them: "For as long as you continue to contend about these small and very insignificant questions, I believe it indeed to be not merely unbecoming, but positively evil, that so large a portion of God's people which belongs to your jurisdiction should be thus divided." Needless to say, Ossius' attempts at reconciliation failed.

On his way back to Nicomedia, Ossius stopped at Antioch to order affairs there. Early in 325 he presided over a Council of Antioch attended by fifty-nine bishops of the civil diocese of the Orient, forty-six of whom will later be at the Council of Nicaea. Under Ossius' direction, the bishops introduced an innovation in ecclesiastical practice: they issued a creedal statement. Hitherto, creeds were for catechumens, this one was designed for bishops. Rather tortuously, the Council declared its belief in ". . . one Lord Jesus Christ, only begotten Son, begotten not from that which is not but from the Father, not as made but as properly an offspring, but begotten in an ineffable, indescribable manner . . . who exists everlastingly and did not at one time not exist. . . but the Scriptures described Him as validly and truly begotten as Son so that we believe Him to be immutable and unchangeable, and that He was not begotten and did not come to be by volition or by adoption. . . . For He is the image, not of the will or of anything else, but of His Father's very substance." The bishops continued, "And we anathematize those who say or think or preach that the Son of God is a creature or has come into being or has been made and is not truly begotten, or that there was when He was not. . . Furthermore, we anathematize those who suppose that He is immutable by His own act of will, just as those who derive His birth from that which is not, and deny that He is immutable in the way the Father is." Eusebius of Caesarea and the bishops of Neronias and Laodicea were provisionally excommunicated until the forthcoming general council for not confessing the otherwise unanimous teaching of the council. In addition, Eustathius, who will later be one of the principal leaders of the Nicene party, was elected to the vacant bishopric of Antioch.

But all this was just preliminary to the main bout. In 324 Constantine had called a council of all the bishops to meet at Ancyra; he now changed its venue to Nicaea, today the insignificant village of Isnik in Turkey. Nicaea, he said, was more accessible for the bishops of Italy and Europe and had a more congenial climate. The city was also more accessible for the emperor only thirty miles away at Nicomedia. "Wherefore," said the emperor, "I signify to you, my beloved brethren, that all of you promptly assemble at the said city."

3. The Events of the Council of Nicaea

The battle was now well and truly joined. But before continuing the narrative of the events of the council, it might be well to reflect for a moment on the fact that it was the emperor who summoned the bishops to the council. Only in the seventh and eighth centuries did the legend arise that Sylvester, bishop of Rome, was responsible, although there may have been extensive discussions between the emperor and the principal bishops over the matter. Francis Dvornik argues that Constantine thought he had the right to call a council because ". . . in the spirit of the definition of Hellenistic royal competence, he regarded himself as legally entitled to interfere in religious affairs. He represented the Divinity on earth and was given by God supreme power in things material and spiritual. He thought that it was his foremost duty to lead men to God." After the council Constantine wrote to the bishops: "As I discovered from the prosperous state of the Republic how great the divine power has been, I thought it my primary duty to bring it about that the saintly multitudes of the Catholic Church shall preserve one faith, a sincere charity and a profound reverence for the Almighty."

Even though his political outlook was colored by Hellenistic conceptions, as we have seen, Constantine was no longer simply pagan in belief by the time of the Council of

Nicaea, nor a cynical manipulator of the Christians for his own purposes. Also, as we have seen, he found in the organization of the ecclesiastical synods a procedure akin to the workings of the Roman Senate itself. In Dvornik's view this customary procedure helped shape church-state relations in the Constantinian period. One important element of procedure saved the relative autonomy of the bishops in doctrinal matters: the emperor though present never had the right to vote in the Senate. Constantine took an active part in its debates, but there is no evidence of his voting at the Council of Nicaea; he only confirmed the decisions of the bishops and made them binding under Roman law. Conciliar procedure thus modeled on that of the Senate enabled the Church to safeguard a certain independence in all matters of doctrine by encouraging the emperor to work through assemblies of bishops to achieve unity of belief. As Constantine would write later to the bishops on the subject of Easter: "Whatever is decided in the holy councils of the bishops must be attributed to the divine will." In addition, this procedure provided a privileged position for the Bishop of Rome. His representatives gave their opinion and signed the acts before the other bishops as did the Princeps Senatus, the senior member of the House. That Ossius alone signed before the papal legates at Nicaea was due to his special position as imperial counsel as well as the fact that he was a bishop, the legates being only priests. As Dvornik admits, it cannot be proved conclusively that Senatorial procedure was followed point by point at Nicaea, but it was followed by local councils before Nicaea and at the subsequent six general councils.

Firmly invited by the emperor and conveniently provided with transport by state agencies, bishops headed toward Nicaea. How many came? There exist lists of the bishops who signed the final creed and canons, but none seems to be complete or in full agreement with another. Eusebius of Caesarea, an eyewitness, said there were 250; Athanasius, a 25 year old deacon and secretary of Alexander of Alexandria present at Nicaea, said 300. Some modern scholars analyzing the extant lists estimate as few as 220. Soon after,

however, the symbolic number 318 was assigned to the
Council, the number of Abraham's armed servants in Genesis 14:14, a number which in Greek read TIH, symbol of the
Cross and Jesus. These 318 of Nicaea will be appealed to in
the six subsequent general councils.

The major sees of the Eastern Empire were well represented: on the anti-Arian side were Alexander of Alexandria, Eustathius of Antioch, Marcellus of Ancyra (modern
Turkish Ankara) and Macarius of Jerusalem. On the Arian
side were Eusebius of Palestinian Caesarea, Arius' fellow
Lucianists Eusebius of Nicomedia, Theognis of Nicaea,
Maris of Chalcedon and the diehard Libyans Secundus and
Theonas. Some western bishops were present as well: Caecilian of Carthage (near modern Tunis), Domnus of Pannonia
(roughly modern Austria), Nicasius of Gaul, Mark of Calabria and Ossius of Cordoba, who was present as an imperial
counselor and not as papal legate, as was once thought. The
papal legates were the priests Vito and Vincent, Sylvester of
Rome having asked to be excused on the score of old age
and infirmity. Two bishops came from beyond the confines
of the Empire—John of Persia and Theophilus of Scythia,
the ill-defined area north of the Black Sea. As confessors of
the faith, some of the bishops bore the signs of the recent
persecution on their persons: Paul of Neo-Caesarea had lost
the use of his hands because of torture, the half blind and
hamstrung Paphnutius of Egypt was kissed by Constantine
himself in a touching diplomatic gesture. Another bishop,
Nicholas of Myra, noted for his charity, would live long in
human memory as Santa Claus.

Yet, as one of the curial cardinals said before Vatican II, a
council is not a Boy Scouts' meeting; Nicaea was to prove no
exception. Before the opening of proceedings, Constantine
was deluged with denunciations submitted by the bishops
against one another. It is said that in a statesmanlike gesture
the emperor publicly burned these unopened. On about May
20, 325, as nearly as we can judge, the Council was formally
opened in the airy precincts of the imperial summer palace.
The bishops, ranged down each side of a large hall, stood
expectantly silent as the emperor in purple and gold entered

with three members of the imperial family and a few senior
advisors. He was, said Eusebius, "distinguished by piety and
godly fear…indicated by his downcast eyes, the blush on
his face, and his gait." Proceeding to a low golden chair, he
refused to sit until all the bishops had seated themselves. An
unknown bishop on the emperor's right, perhaps Eustathius
of Antioch, senior bishop of the East since the bishop of
Alexandria's case was under review by the Council, gave a
speech of welcome. Constantine himself addressed the
bishops in Latin, perhaps because of his imperfect Greek or
more likely because Latin was the language prescribed even
in the East for official state functions.

Unfortunately, if there were any official minutes of the
sessions, they have not survived. It seems that Eusebius of
Nicomedia was first off the mark and offered a creedal
statement favorable to Arian views. This the Council indignantly rejected. Eusebius of Caesarea seems next to have
offered the baptismal creed of Palestinian Caesarea. This
was accepted by the bishops and the emperor and served the
purpose of rehabilitating Eusebius personally under provisional excommunication decreed by the earlier Council of
Antioch. However, it seems not to have been, as was often
claimed, the basis of the Council's new creed. Then apparently various attempts were made to fashion a creed using
only scriptural terms, but it proved impossible to word such
a creed so as to exclude the Arian position in the strictest
fashion possible. Arian-sympathizing bishops could be seen,
it is said, winking and nodding, confident that they could
twist a scripturally worded creed to their advantage.
Throughout this prolonged discussion, according to Eusebius, the emperor himself took an active and kindly part in
debate. Finally, it seems, a Syro-Palestinian creed was used
as the basis for a new creedal statement designed to bar the
way to Arian interpretation. The deacon Hermogenes, later
bishop of Cappadocian Caesarea, was the secretary in
charge of the work. The finished creed has been preserved in
the writings of Athanasius, of the historian Socrates and of
Basil of Caesarea and in the acts of the Council of Chalcedon of 451.

We believe in one God the Father Almighty, Maker of all things visible and invisible; and in one Lord Jesus Christ, the Son of God, begotten of the Father, only-begotten, that is, from the substance of the Father, God from God, Light from Light, True God from True God, Begotten, not made, of one substance with the Father, through Whom all things were made.

Who for us men and for our salvation came down and became incarnate, and was made man, suffered and rose on the third day, And ascended into heaven, And is coming with glory to judge living and dead, And in the Holy Spirit.

But those who say, There was when the Son of God was not, and before he was begotten he was not, and that he came into being from things that are not, or that he is of a different hypostasis or substance, or that he is mutable or alterable —the Catholic and Apostolic Church anathematizes.

It is clear that the Arians could easily accept the phrases "begotten from the Father" and "only begotten," for they could understand begotten as the equivalent of made from nothing by the creative fiat of the Father. But the phrase "from the substance of the Father" excluded their interpretation and emphasized that so far from being produced like creatures from nothing, the Son is generated from the Father's very substance or being. "True God from true God" was added to rebut the Arian contention that even though the Son is God, He is not true God but is God only by grace and is called God in name only. However, when pressed, the Arians would even call the Son true God in the sense that He is God by grace and is a really existent being. So the phrase is not fully effective against the Arian position. "Begotten not made" was a more direct attack against the Arian view that the Son is a creature, though the most perfect of all, who came forth from nothing at the will of the Father. In the view of the anti-Arians, it is of the very nature of the Father to beget the Son; the Father was never other than Father; therefore, Son and Father must have existed from all eternity, the Father eternally begetting the Son. The vitally important phrase in the orthodox reply to Arianism was "of one substance (*homoousios*) with the Father." This phrase asserts that the Son shares the same being as the Father, and is therefore fully divine.

However, *homoousios* was at the time a notoriously slippery word and could have three principal meanings. First, it could be generic; of one substance could be said of two individual men, both of whom share human nature while remaining individuals. Secondly, it could signify numerical identity, that is, that the Father and the Son are identical in concrete being. Finally, it could refer to material things, as two pots are of the same substance because both are made of the same clay. Constantine himself explained that "*homoousios* was not used in the sense of bodily affections, for the Son did not derive His existence from the Father by means of division or severance, since an immaterial, intellectual and incorporeal nature could not be subject to any bodily affection. These things must be understood as bearing a divine and ineffable signification." The point was that the third meaning of *homoousios*, with its connotations of materiality was not the meaning used in the creed. That left the two previous meanings. It seems that the Council, intent on stressing the equality of the Son with the Father, had the first meaning explicitly in mind. Father and Son are *homoousioi* in that they are equally divine. But implicit in their statement was numerical identity, that Father and Son are of a single divine substance, an aspect brought out by Athanasius in the course of the long struggle following the Council.

The word *homoousios* had a long history as we have previously indicated, and, even though accepted in the creed, it was objectionable to the majority of the bishops for at least four reasons. First, the term, despite Constantine's statement, had strong materialist overtones which would connote that Father and Son are parts or separable portions of the same "stuff." Secondly, if Father and Son were of one numerically identical substance, then the doctrine of the creed could well be Sabellian, Father and Son being identical and indistinguishable. Thirdly, the term was associated with heresies since it had been coined by the Gnostics and had, in fact, been condemned at the Council of Antioch in 268 as used by the Adoptionist Paul of Samosata. Fourthly and importantly for many of the more conservative bishops, the term was not scriptural.

Despite the misgivings of perhaps the majority of the attending bishops the term was added to the creed. It seems clear that the authority of Constantine was the main motivating force. Yet behind Constantine was his long-time chief ecclesiastical advisor, Ossius of Cordoba, a bishop immersed in the theology of the western church. Though the Latin equivalent of *homoousios*, consubstantial, was not yet a fully accepted term in the western theological vocabulary, it was suited to describe the type of Trinitarian theology fashionable in the West with its strong insistence on the divine monarchy. It is likely that in pre-conciliar discussions Ossius had gained the support of Alexander of Alexandria and the cooperation of Constantine to urge the term on the assembled bishops. The very ambiguity of the word would possibly have appealed to the politician Constantine was. Within limits the bishops could read their own meaning into the term which still had the merit of scotching the Arian view. So *homoousios*, coined by Gnostic heretics, proposed by an unbaptized emperor, jeopardized by naive defenders, but eventually vindicated by the orthodox, was added to the Creed of Nicaea to become a sign of contradiction for the next half-century.

The final anathemas of the Creed directly attack the Arian positions. The phrase, "there was when He was not," and its near equivalent, "before being born He was not," summed up the Arian denial of the Son's co-eternity with the Father. These two phrases are singled out for the Council's specific condemnation. The phrase, "He came into existence out of nothing," had already been excluded in the Creed by its statement that the Son was begotten not made and was from the substance of the Father; now it too is specifically condemned. More important is the anathema against the phrase, "the Son of God is of a different hypostasis or substance." The idea had already been dealt with positively in the Creed with the statement that the Son is of the same substance as the Father. The phrase also points up the terminological difficulty which continued to bedevil Eastern theology and to confuse the West about the East's position — substance (*ousia*) and hypostasis were regarded as synonymous. Athanasius himself would say at a far later date: "Hypostasis is ousia, and means nothing else than being." Only gradually, as we have indicated earlier, would hypostasis come to mean theologically what the West would call person, while *ousia* remained equivalent to the Latin substance. The final anathema strikes against Arius' doctrine that the Son, as a creature, was morally changeable and remained steadfast in virtue only by an exercise of will. The Council affirms rather that the Son is of the substance of the Father; immutable, therefore, as He is.

When the Creed was finished, perhaps by June 19, eighteen bishops still opposed it. Constantine then intervened to threaten with exile anyone who would not sign it. Eusebius of Nicomedia, Theognis of Nicaea and Maris of Chalcedon then consented to sign the Creed itself but not the anathemas. In the end, only Arius and his die-hard supporters, the Libyans Secundus and Theonas, refused to sign anything. Secundus and Theonas were deposed as bishops and with Arius sent into exile. It is said that as Secundus left the chamber, he called to Eusebius of Nicomedia, "You signed only to avoid exile; I prophesy that you will be in exile within the year." and so indeed did Eusebius of Nicomedia, Theognis of Nicaea and Maris of Chalcedon go into exile before the year was out.

Finally, the bishops turned to matters of church discipline and drew up twenty canons dealing with actual problems affecting the orderly administration of ecclesiastical affairs. The canons are in no particular order but they do fall into five main categories — church structures, the dignity of the clergy, the reconciliation of the lapsed, the readmission to the Church of heretics and schismatics, and liturgical practice.

The fourth canon prescribed ordination of a bishop by all the bishops of a province or at least by three in cases of emergency accompanied by a written approval by the absent bishops. In a novel addition to this canon, the Council reserved confirmation of episcopal elections to the metropolitan of the civil province, thus increasing his jurisdiction. In the fifth canon, bishops were forbidden to receive into communion laymen or clerics excommunicated by another bishop, though they could inquire into the justice and legality of the excommunication. Bishops were told to assemble in provincial synods twice a year, preferably before Lent and in the autumn, to resolve cases of excommunication. The much discussed sixth canon foreshadowed the rise of the super-metropolitans, the great patriarchs of later centuries. It specified that the ancient customs of Egypt, Libya and the Pentapolis should hold good whereby the bishop of Alexandria had authority over these areas. The reason for insisting on this was, apparently, to submit Libya and the Pentapolis where Arianism was especially strong to the firm discipline of the Nicene bishop of Alexandria. Vague referral was made to the customs of the bishop of Rome by which he had supra-provincial authority over the bishops of central and southern Italy, Sicily and Sardinia, and of the bishop of Antioch who supervised an unspecified area in Syria. Again the bishops insisted in this canon that the metropolitans have the right to confirm the choice of bishops in their areas. The seventh canon gave the bishop of Aelia, the name the Romans had imposed on conquered Jerusalem, a position of honor, while still subjected to the metropolitan of Caesarea. The canon perhaps reflected the successful lobbying of Macarius of Jerusalem with the emperor who, like his mother Helena, had a mystical devotion to the holy places. The fifteenth canon forbade bishops, priests and deacons to transfer from place to place and ordered them to remain attached to the church for which they were ordained. In canon sixteen clerics were enjoined to return to the churches in which they were enrolled under pain of excommunication and bishops forbidden to ordain persons from another church without permission of their own bishops, otherwise such ordinations were void. In these canons the organizational structure of the Church was beginning to emerge:

priests and deacons were attached to local churches which were presided over by local bishops tied for life to their charge, forbidden to poach clergy from other bishops or receive those excommunicated by them; above these bishops were the metropolitans residing in the chief cities of the civil provinces who could approve the election of local bishops and preside at the semi-annual provincial synods; above all were the super-bishops of Rome, Alexandria and Antioch whose territory and supervisory powers were as yet specified only by custom.

Six other canons dealt with the dignity of the clergy. The first canon forbade those who had castrated themselves to continue to minister as clerics or to be promoted to the clergy in the future. Those who were so mutilated for reasons of health or by violence were excepted. Eunuchs, quite numerous in those times especially as servants within the women's quarters of the imperial palaces, had a bad reputation for immorality and political intrigue; this caste was now barred from the clerical ranks. The second canon prohibited the hasty promotion of the newly baptized to the rank of priest and bishop. Such persons, if found unworthy, were to be deposed from the clergy. Still, this practice continued and not always with evil results, as in the promotion of St. Ambrose from catechumen to bishop of Milan some fifty years later. The third canon forbade any of the clergy to have a woman dwelling with him except mother, sister, aunt or someone above suspicion. The canon referred only to that section of clergy who were celibate, for the Church allowed a married clergy. It is said that the bishops considered a canon enjoining celibacy on deacons, priests and bishops as did the western council of Elvira, c. 306, but were dissuaded from such a course by Paphnutius, the famous celibate bishop and confessor from Upper Egypt. The ninth canon forbade the ordination of notorious sinners even after they had reformed their lives, for, said the bishops, "the Church vindicates only those of irreproachable life." Canon 10 enjoined the deposition from clerical ranks of anyone who had denied his faith, whether he had been ordained in ignorance of this fact or not, and canon 17 forbade clerics to engage in usury even if they charged only the 12% interest allowed by Roman law.

Four other canons dealt with the reconciliation of those who had lapsed from the faith during the recent persecutions and with their public penance. Canon 11 provided that those who fell away from the faith without having been threatened must repent and then spend two years among those who could only hear, not participate in the liturgy, seven years among those required to kneel before their fellow Christians on Sundays to beg forgiveness — two classes which with the catechumens were compelled to leave the liturgy before the beginning of the Canon — and for an additional two years continue to remain during the whole liturgy but without receiving the Eucharist. In canon 12, those who left the eastern emperor Licinius' army because of the measures he took to expel Christian soldiers and then by bribery returned to the colors to fight under Licinius against Constantine were ordered to spend three years among the hearers at the liturgy. After that time those who were clearly repentant could be allowed by the bishop to participate in the entire liturgy; those not obviously repentant were condemned to an additional ten years among the kneelers. According to canon 13, the lapsed who were dying were allowed to receive the Eucharist, but if they recovered, they were to attend the liturgy only. In canon 14, catechumens who had lapsed were ordered to remain among the hearers of the liturgy for three years and then take their places as catechumens once again. Severe as these measures were, they were more moderate than any previous synodal decrees, especially in providing that the lapsed when dying could receive the Eucharist.

Two canons dealt with the more difficult problem of the readmission to the Church of schismatics and heretics. Since the Novatianists, who broke with the Church over the question of penance from 251 on, differed only in discipline and not in doctrine, they were treated with great moderation. After having received the imposition of hands and professed in writing that they would follow the decrees of the Church and in particular that they would communicate with the twice married and the reconciled lapsed (two classes of sinners which as Novatianists they shunned), they might be restored to the clergy at the rank they held as Novatianists. However, in places where there was a Catholic bishop, the reconciled Novatianist bishop was to be made only a chorepiscopus, a rural auxiliary bishop, so that no city would have two bishops. Another group, the Paulianists, followers of Paul of Samosata, condemned in 268, were involved in his Adoptionist heresy. The bishops thought that their heresy concerning the divinity of the Son rendered their baptismal formula invalid. Thus all Paulianists were to be rebaptized, and since their original baptism was invalid, their subsequent ordinations as clerics were invalid as well. Consequently, all clerics and even deaconesses were to be reordained. One should not forget that the Donatist controversy, centering on the question of rebaptism, was raging at this time in North Africa, and the Catholic bishop Caecilian of Carthage, the storm center of the controversy, was at the Council. Since no Trinitarian or Christological question was at stake in the case of the Donatists, Catholics denied the necessity of their rebaptism. But because the heresy of the Paulianists so centered on Christ's nature, it was regarded by the bishops as invalidating baptism and orders conferred among them.

Finally, two liturgical matters were dealt with in canons 18 and 20. Deacons were to stay properly subordinated to bishops and priests, and were not to administer the Eucharist to them nor receive it before them. Nor were deacons to be seated among the priests at the liturgy. Failure to comply with these regulations would result in expulsion from the diaconate. Lastly, the Council prescribed standing at prayer during the liturgy even on the Lord's Day and during Pentecost when some were accustomed to kneel. As is obvious, the Canons of Nicaea are by no means a systematic code of canon law but rather a collection of *ad hoc* measures characterized by cautious moderation. However, they became important and respected additions to the growing corpus of church law.

In a separate declaration, the Council dealt with the Meletian schism in Egypt which grew out of the attempt of the priest Meletius to exercise episcopal functions while the bishop Peter of Alexandria was imprisoned during the persecution of Diocletian. Since Meletius too had been imprisoned in the quarries of Egypt, he used his prestige as a confessor of the faith to put himself at the head of the Church of Martyrs, a group of fanatical confessors, who thought that their privileges as sufferers for the faith were not sufficiently recognized by the Church. By 325 Meletius' church numbered some twenty-eight bishops. Overriding Alexander of Alexandria's apprehensions, the Council promised the Meletians that their ordinations would be recognized when they returned to the Church, on condition that their bishops cease exercising their functions in favor of those consecrated by Alexander. Meletius himself was ordered to withdraw to Lycopolis, content himself with his title of bishop and discontinue further ordinations.

In a second declaration, the bishops ruled that Easter should be celebrated at the same time throughout the empire. Those churches which observed Easter on the Sunday after the Passover reckoned according to Jewish calculations were ordered to observe the custom of Alexandria and Rome where a different and non-Jewish cycle of calculation was employed. Unfortunately for the peace of the church, the bishops did not realize that Alexandria and Rome themselves differed in their methods of calculation.

The council finished its work perhaps on August 25, and its closing coincided with Constantine's vicennalia, the twentieth anniversary of his elevation by the legions to imperial rank in succession to his father in far-off York in Britain. The bishops were invited to an imperial banquet held in the innermost parts of the palace. Eusebius assures us quite humanly that none of the bishops missed the event. As they passed into the palace between the ranks of the palatine guardsmen with drawn swords, it seemed to them, says Eusebius, "that a picture of Christ's kingdom was thus shadowed forth, a dream rather than a reality." Gifts were given by the emperor to all according to rank, and the Council was ended. Later Constantine wrote to all the churches enjoining obedience to the Council's decrees:

That which has commended itself to the judgement of three hundred bishops cannot be other than the judgement of God; seeing that the Holy Spirit dwelling in the minds of persons of such character and dignity has effectually enlightened them respecting the Divine will. Wherefore let no one vacillate or linger, but let all with alacrity return to the undoubted path of truth; that when I shall arrive among you, which will be as soon as possible, I may with you return due thanks to God, the inspector of all things, for having revealed the pure faith, and restored to you that love for which we have prayed.

4. *The Significance of the Council of Nicaea*

Four additions to an older baptismal creed, two inefficacious decisions concerning the date of Easter and the Meletian schism at Alexandria, and a hodgepodge of twenty disciplinary canons — verbally this is the sum total of the work of the Council. Much ado about very little, or so it seems. But what is the real significance of what was done at Nicaea? Bernard Lonergan appears to me to have best described the real meaning and importance of the Council. He argues that within the dialectic of the pre-Nicaean speculation about the Trinity there was operative a twofold movement which reached its goal at Nicaea. Trinitarian and Christological doctrines were evolving explicitly, but implicitly the very notion of dogma was evolving as well. Three aspects of this twofold evolution need consideration: objective, subjective and evaluative.

Objectively, the Gospels and the apostolic writings teach the truth about Christ but in a way that appeals to all human powers; as Lonergan says, "they penetrate the sensibility, fire the imagination, engage the affections, touch the heart, open the eyes, attract and impel the will of the reader." However, the creedal statements of Nicaea declare the truth but bypass senses, feelings and will to appeal only to the intellect. Two kinds of transition occur in this objective doctrinal development. The first is from the Scriptures addressed to the whole person to conciliar statements appealing only to the intellect. The second is from the scriptural statement of a multitude of truths to conciliar decrees which emphasize a single truth which is the foundation of the multitude of truths in Scripture.

Corresponding to this objective transition is a subjective one. What Lonergan calls undifferentiated consciousness is the response of the whole person operating with all powers of sense, imagination, emotion, will and intellect. Differentiated consciousness, however, subordinates or checks all other levels of consciousness to concentrate on the intellect. The Gospels appeal to all levels of human operation; dogmas focus attention on the truth grasped by a judgment of the intellect. To appreciate the significance of dogma requires personal intellectual effort proportionate to the intellectual effort of the framers of dogma.

There is as well an evaluative aspect to this Trinitarian and Christological evolution. Some would judge that the Gospels are clear; dogmatic statements obscure. But one has only to consult the vast literature dealing with the Bible so full of conflicting opinions to realize that the Gospels are not limpidly clear. Nor when one is trained to the exercise of intellect are dogmas so very obscure. Others would judge that the Gospels with their appeal to all human powers are more properly religious, whereas dogmas with their single appeal to intellect are not. But surely, argues Lonergan, the intellect should not be regarded as outside the orbit of religious values. For the intellect passes judgment on religious matters and can affect the whole tenor and direction of religious life. To appeal to it alone, without denying the further appeal to the other levels of human consciousness, cannot be simply irreligious. Dogma is thus a religious appeal to the intellect inviting it to assent to the word of God as true, as stating objective reality, prescinding for the time being from all its other riches.

The Judaeo-Christians did not take this step, being content to apply Old Testament images to illustrate the New. The Gnostics saw truth as a matter of things emerging from concealment to reveal themselves. The Adoptionists denied that objectively the Son is God; the Sabellians affirmed that He is the same person as the Father; the Arians proclaimed Him a creature made by God as are all other creatures. These views forced the Church to search the Scriptures to see if these assertions really correspond to the truth enunciated there. Tertullian and others could not rise above sense perception and imagined the Son as a portion of "stuff" of the Father. Origen, moving up to a purely spiritual realm, could conceive the Son only as the subordinate image of the Father, an essence sharing in essence. But what the Council of Nicaea was doing through its creedal statements with its use of the term *homoousios* was enunciating a judgment about reality as revealed in the Scriptures: what is said of the Father is also said of the Son, except that the Son is Son and not Father; therefore, the Son is of the same substance as the Father but not the same person as the Father. What the Council of Nicaea did in its creedal statement was simply to attend to what the Scripture asserts as true about the Word of God, reduce that multitude of true statements to the one judgment which is the foundation of all the rest and appeal to the intellects of Christians for their assent to this judgment as the foundation of further religious belief and experience.

Explicitly the Council moved from one kind of clarity about the Son of God contained in Scripture appealing to undifferentiated human consciousness to another kind of clarity contained in dogmatic statements directed to differentiated, intellectual consciousness. But, implicitly, without their fully adverting to what they were about, they paved the way for the development of dogma. This first defined dogma in the history of the Church is what the old Latin liturgy expressed succinctly in its Preface of the Holy Trinity: "What from your revelation we believe about your glory, that without difference or distinction we hold about your Son...."

That this judgment of the truth about the Son is truly fundamental and affects other aspects of belief and practice is well illustrated in G. H. Williams' analysis of the differing views of Church and State among Nicenes and Arians. The Nicenes were loyal to what they regarded as the truth of revelation, even though rationally it was difficult to reconcile monotheism with the subsistence of two equally divine persons, Father and Son. The Arians, more rationally, reduced the Son to the most perfect of creatures or to a subordinate deity and could thus reconcile belief in the Trinity with monotheism more easily. The Arians too conceived the Son primarily as a mediator between God and the universe in a cosmological sense; subordinate to the Father, he orders the universe, human society and human personality. The Incarnate Son had the rather modest role of proclaiming the oneness of God and reminding humans of their natural immortality. But for the Nicenes the Son is the Savior, a mediator between the just and eternal God and sinful, mortal humans in an economy of historical redemption. Christ is the divine mediator with the Father, and through His life, death and resurrection reconciles us to the Father that we too may become divine. For the Nicenes scriptural law and tradition center on Jesus Christ and His law may run counter to imperial dictates. The Nicenes held tenaciously to the historic Christ who by His divine self-sacrifice secured the salvation of humankind and established the law to which even the Christian sovereign is subject. In contrast, the Arians with their low Christology could see in the emperor an instrument used by God for the ordering of society. Law centered upon the historical Christ could not take precedence over the living law, the emperor himself, ordained as such by God.

These differing views affected four crucial sectors of religious life in the fourth century: the authority of the emperor in respect to creed and canons; the Eucharist; the office of bishop; the headship and kingship of Christ.

Given his markedly subordinationist view of the Logos, Eusebius of Caesarea saw both Christ and Constantine as instruments of the Logos, one to proclaim the coming of God's kingdom; the other to establish monotheism. Constantine was for Eusebius a kind of second savior: Christ as the universal Savior opens the gates of his Father's kingdom;

the emperor purging his earthly realm of error, desires to save all the crew of the vessel of which he is pilot. Also in establishing order and harmony, the emperor does on earth what the Logos does in the cosmos. The emperor, said Eusebius, "directs his gaze above, and frames his earthly government according to the pattern of that divine original, feeling strength in its conformity to the monarchy of God." Christ and the emperor are for Eusebius almost coordinate under God, each leading men to knowledge and worship of God, each bringing order and peace to mankind. The Nicenes, however, feeling the heavy hand of imperial disfavor throughout the struggles after the Council of Nicaea, thought differently. Eustathius of Antioch denounced the Arians as atheists in denying the full divinity of the Son and sycophants in their excessive devotion to the emperor. Athanasius excoriated those at Sirmium in 359 who denied the eternity of the Son but spoke of the eternal emperor. At Sardica the Nicenes would insist that Christ is Son of God by nature; Christians, the emperor implicitly included, became what He is only by grace. Athanasius, Lucifer of Cagliari and Hilary of Poitiers finally went to the length of denouncing the emperor as the forerunner of Antichrist or even Antichrist himself.

Both parties regarded the Eucharist as the center of liturgical life, but Nicenes emphasized the Eucharistic community in which members of the Body were sustained and united, while Arians viewed the Eucharist as the unbloody, reasonable sacrifice, the substitute for the pagan sacrifices. The Nicenes refused to recognize the Arian Eucharist as valid and went to great lengths to demonstrate this, even throwing the bread consecrated by Arians to the dogs. Nor would the Nicenes admit the sacrilegious Arians to their own Eucharist, confident they were participating together in the body of Christ and drawing therefrom energy to oppose the foes of Christ' full divinity. On the other hand, Arians for the most part strove for intercommunion. The union of believers within the body of the empire was for them more important than union in the Body of Christ. Thus the liturgical counterpart of the Nicenes' belief in the full divinity of Christ was their exclusion of Arians from communion.

The Nicene bishops attempted to preserve their bonds with their local churches and trace their lineage to the earthly Christ through the Apostles. The Arians, seeing the emperor as the instrument of the Eternal God, were more inclined to accept imperial appointment and imperial approval as validation of their episcopal authority and willingly accepted transfer from see to see. Lucifer of Cagliari scorned the Arian bishops as pseudo-bishops because where two or three of them were together, Christ, fully God, was not among them; nor could they be channels of the Holy Spirit whose full divinity they denied. Ambrose of Milan developed the concept of bishop as priest deriving by apostolic succession authority from the earthly Christ and as prophet endowed with authority stemming from the eternal Christ. As prophets the bishops had the duty to rebuke even emperors, as Ambrose did Theodosius I and Valentinian II. Their experience with imperially convened councils developed a distaste for them in the minds of the Nicenes. Athanasius, comments Williams, "moved all the way from the original acceptance of the Christian emperor's right to call an ecumenical council, to judge on matters of faith and discipline, and to interfere in local affairs of the Church — through an intermediate 'theory' of a free Church protected by the State — to an insistence...upon the complete independence of a council from the emperor...the only function remaining to him being to summon the council." Perhaps the growing insistence of Nicenes on the consubstantiality of the Holy Spirit was partly motivated by the desire of the bishops to enhance their collective authority over that of the emperor as conduits of the divine Spirit.

For the Nicenes, the Son, their head, consubstantial with God, true God from true God, was King of Kings and protector of the Church. They saw the Church as the reflection of the heavenly kingdom. In the Church the bishops, tracing their credentials to the historic Christ, could exhort, even rebuke Christian rulers on the basis of apostolic tradition and biblical law. The Arians, denying the consubstantiality of the Son, were more inclined to emphasize the fact that while Christ is head of man, God is head of Christ and that thus the God-enthroned ruler is superior to the bishops instituted by Christ. For the Arians, the Christian empire was the earthly image of the heavenly kingdom. At the beginning of the century, Eusebius hailed Constantine as the instrument of the Supreme God, raised above men, the earthly counterpart of the cosmic Logos. By the end of the century, Ambrose could successfully rebuke an emperor and assert confidently that Theodosius I was a subject of Christ. Concludes Williams, "The sense of disparateness between the Christ-founded Church and the God-ordained Empire, recovered in the course of the Arian controversy under Constantius, became a permanent feature of Western Christianity even after the reestablishment of Nicene orthodoxy to imperial favor under Theodosius, as the resounding words of Ambrose testify: 'The Emperor is in the Church, not above it.'"

5. Aftermath

By 327 Constantine was having second thoughts about the work of the Council. In this he was perhaps influenced by Eusebius, bishop of the imperial capital, Nicomedia, who was related by blood to the imperial family and was the spiritual confidant of Constantine's half-sister. As a disciple of the martyred theologian Lucian of Antioch, he would have been acceptable to the Empress Mother Helena who had a special devotion to that saint. An amnesty was granted to the Arian leaders, and Eusebius himself together with Theognis of Nicaea and Maris of Chalcedon returned to their sees by 328. Alexander of Alexandria died that year and his successor Athanasius, under pain of deposition and exile, was ordered to grant free admission to all who wished to return to the Church. Ruthlessly, Eusebius of Nicomedia now led the effort to undermine the Nicene bishops. Eustathius of Antioch was the first to go. Accused of inciting tumults at Antioch, he apparently made the mistake of speaking disparagingly of the Empress Mother Helena, calling her a *stabularia*, a chamber-maid, a term which, says Duchesne, given the standards of hospitality of the age, implied a good deal. He was deposed from Antioch, to die in exile in 330. Eusebius of Caesarea, sensing trouble, declined to accept transfer to Antioch. Eustathius' supporters refused to accept his imperially appointed successor and a prolonged schism opened at Antioch, crippling that great metropolis' influence in ecclesiastical affairs for the next sixty years. Marcellus of Ancyra was next. He was perhaps the staunchest supporter of the *homoousios* of Nicaea since it seemed to support his basically Sabellian views. For Marcellus, Son and Spirit emerged from the Godhead as distinct persons only for the purposes of creation and redemption. At the end of the world, both would be resumed into the divine unity. These statements of Marcellus convinced many that the Creed of Nicaea was suspect of Sabellianism, and he would long be an albatross about the necks of the orthodox Nicenes. Marcellus made the mistake of sending a book embodying his views to Constantine. For his pains he was deposed in 336, surviving through many vicissitudes until his death at the age of ninety in 374.

Finally it was the turn of Athanasius who in 328 had embarked upon his troubled forty-five year episcopate at Alexandria. He was accused, among many charges, of immoral conduct, illegally taxing the Egyptians, supporting rebels against the throne, tyrannizing dissident bishops, breaking the chalice of a rebellious priest and murdering a bishop, keeping his severed hand for magical rites. Athanasius successfully refuted the charges, even bringing the man supposedly murdered into the courtroom and dramatically revealing his intact two hands. But he was again called to stand charges in 335 before the Synod of Tyre, stacked with his enemies, fresh from the dedication of Constantine's great new Church of the Holy Sepulchre in Jerusalem. Athanasius was condemned by the Synod, but fled to the newly founded Constantinople where he confronted the emperor unexpectedly on a road leading into the city and obtained exoneration in a personal interview with him. Still his enemies persisted in accusing him before the emperor of interfering with the grain supply from Egypt to the growing new capital. Since Constantinople was dependent on the export through Alexandria of the 80,000 bushels of grain a day it was soon to need, Constantine could brook no tampering with the food supply by an Egyptian bishop. The emperor exiled Athanasius in 336 to Trier in Rhineland Germany. The reaction in Alexandria was tumultuous; even the great hermit Antony, reputed founder of monasticism, wrote a protest to the emperor. But since the three leaders of the Nicene party were now out of action, Arius was to be rehabilitated. Because Alexandria was still too hot to hold him, he went to Constantinople for his formal readmission to the Church. However, on the day before the ceremony in 336, he suffered an intestinal hemorrhage in a public bathroom and was found dead.

In 337, the first Christian emperor, Constantine himself passed from the scene. After putting aside the imperial purple, he was clothed in the white garment of the new-born Christian and baptized by Eusebius of Nicomedia before his death. He was buried by his son Constantius in his new Church of the Holy Apostles in Constantinople surrounded by the cenotaphs of the Twelve. A coin was issued showing him seated on a horse-drawn chariot, a hand reaching from heaven to welcome him. With his passing the first round in the battle after the Council of Nicaea was ended.

6.   Chronology

c. 96	Clement of Rome.
145-155	Shepherd of Hermas completed.
c. 160	Marcion died.
c. 165	Justin martyred.
189-199	Pope Victor.
175-200	Councils against Montanism.
c.130-c.200	Irenaeus of Lyons

c. 220	Tertullian died.
217-222	Pope Callistus.
235	Hippolytus died.
251-253	Pope Cornelius.
c. 254	Origen died.
278/9	Novatian martyred.
c. 264	Dionysius of Alexandria died.
259-268	Dionysius, bishop of Rome.
268	Paul of Samosata deposed by Council of Antioch.
284	Accession of Emperor Diocletian.
306	Constantine proclaimed Caesar Augustus at York in Britain.
312	Constantine completed conquest of the Western Empire.
313	'Edict of Milan' proclaimed universal religious toleration.
314	Council of Arles against Donatists.
c. 319	Beginning of the Arian Controversy.
324	Constantine defeated Licinius to become sole emperor.
325	Council of Antioch under Ossius condemned Arius.
325	COUNCIL OF NICAEA.
326	Exile of Arius.
328	Athanasius became bishop of Alexandria.
334	Arius returned to Constantinople from exile.
335	Council of Tyre; first exile of Athanasius to Trier.

336	Marcellus of Ancyra exiled.
336	Arius died in Constantinople.
337	Constantine died, succeeded by sons Constantine, Constantius, Constans.
339	Eusebius of Caesarea died.

7. Select Bibliography

The events of Church history in this period are well covered by the Protestant Hans Lietzmann, *A History of the Early Church*, vol. 2 (London, 1961) and the Catholic Louis Duchesne, *Early History of the Christian Church*, vol. 2 (London, 1912). Many of the pertinent documents dealing with all questions are to be found in J. Stevenson, *A New Eusebius: Documents Illustrative of the History of the Church to A.D. 337* (London, 1957). Brief sketches of the lives, works and theology of the various Fathers of the Church are in J. Quasten, *Patrology*, vols. 1 and 2 (Utrecht-Antwerp, 1965). Perhaps the best history of early theology is J. N. D. Kelly, *Early Christian Doctrines* (New York, 1958); more synthetic is Jaroslav Pelikan, *The Emergence of the Catholic Tradition*, vol. 1 of *The Christian Tradition: A History of the Development of Doctrine* (Chicago, 1971). A splendid book which clarifies early theological vocabulary is G. L. Prestige, *God in Patristic Thought* (London, 1936). The best brief history of the councils is H. Jedin, *Short History of the Councils* (New York, 1964); useful too are the essays in H. J. Margull, ed., *Councils of the Church* (Philadelphia, 1966). Most recent is Colm Liubheld, *The Council of Nicaea* (Galway, 1982). This chapter draws heavily on the interpretation of the work of the Council of Nicaea in Bernard Lonergan *The Way to Nicaea: The Dialectical Development of Trinitarian Theology* (London, 1976). The creed issued by the Council is carefully analyzed in J. N. D. Kelly, *Early Christian Creeds* (London, 1972). Useful discussions of Arianism are T. E. Pollard, "The Origins of Arianism," *Journal of Theological Studies*, 9 (1958), 103-111; H.

A. Wolfson, "Philosophical Implications of Arianism and Apollinarianism," *Dumbarton Oaks Papers*, 12 (1958), 5-28; L. W. Bernard, "The Antecedents of Arius," *Vigiliae Christianae*, 24 (1970), 172-188. For a revisionist view that Arius was not really concerned about the Trinity but about soteriology, see now R. Gregg and D. Groh, *Early Arianism: A View of Salvation* (Philadelphia, 1981). Other factors relating to the Council are discussed in Henry Chadwick, "Ossius of Cordoba and the Presidency of the Council of Antioch, 325," *Journal of Theological Studies*, 9 (1958), 292-304, and his "Faith and Order at the Council of Nicaea: A Note on the Background of the Sixth Canon," *Harvard Theological Review*, 53 (1960), 171-195, and especially G. H. Williams, "Christology and Church-State Relations in the Fourth Century," *Church History*, 20-III (1951), 3-33; 20-IV (1951), 3-26. A useful survey of recent scholarship is F. M. Young, *From Nicaea to Chalcedon* (Philadelphia, 1983). The principal texts of the Councils of Nicaea, Ephesus and Chalcedon may be found in T.H. Bindley and F.W. Green, *Oecumenical Documents of the Faith* (London, 1950).

3

Council of Constantinople I, 381

1. Esusebians vs. Nicenes to the Death
of Emperor Constans

Upon Constantine the Great's death in 337, there occurred an act of violence more befitting the Turkish Seraglio than a Christian court. With at least the knowledge of Constantius, the only son in Constantinople at the time, Constantine the Great's two half-brothers and six young princes of the blood were massacred by the Army. Only two young cousins survived: Gallus and the future emperor Julian. With this bloodletting the will of Constantine was set aside but the unity of the Constantinian dynasty secured. His three sons parceled out the Empire among themselves. Constantine II, aged 21, received Gaul, Britain and Spain; Constantius II, 20, Asia Minor, Syria and Egypt; Constans, only 14, Italy, Africa and the Danubian provinces. Three years later, war broke out between Constantine II and Constans, who managed to defeat and execute his elder brother and occupy his provinces. As a result, Constans ruled the West; Constantius, the East from 340 on.

With the old emperor gone and a new order dawning, Athanasius returned to Alexandria from Rhineland Trier by way of Constantinople and Palestine where he attempted to rally the bishops anew to the creed of Nicaea. In the face of opposition from the Arian-sympathizing Eusebian party who vainly protested to Pope Julius at Rome against the return of Athanasius, deposed from his see at the Council of Tyre in 335, the bishops of Egypt in council at Alexandria declared their support for their metropolitan. The Eusebians, however, consecrated a certain Gregory as bishop of Alexandria. Provided with an armed guard, Gregory so terrorized the people that he could install himself in Athanasius' place in 339. At Pope Julius' invitation, Athanasius fled to Rome where he joined the other Nicene exiles, including Marcellus of Ancyra. Whereupon, in 340 Julius called a synod at Rome in the Church of Vito, the former legate at Nicaea, in which he accepted a profession of faith from Marcellus and pronounced Athanasius the legitimate bishop of Alexandria. To the East Julius addressed a dignified letter which revealed the Pope's consciousness of his authority. He asked why, contrary to custom, he had not been informed of what was occurring at Alexandria, notifying the eastern bishops that if any suspicion rested on the bishop there, notice ought to have been sent to the bishop of Rome. The easterners failed to reply. The Church historian Socrates (380-450) describes the failure of mutual understanding: "The situation was like a battle by night, for both parties seemed to be in the dark about the grounds on which they were hurling abuse at each other. Those who objected to the term *homoousios* imagined that its adherents were bringing in the doctrine of Sabellius and Montanists. So they called them blasphemers on the ground that they were undermining the personal subsistence of the Son of God. On the other hand, the protagonists of *homoousios* concluded that their opponents were introducing polytheism, and steered clear of them as importers of paganism.... Thus, while both affirmed the personality and subsistence of the Son of God, and confessed that there was one God in three hypostases, they were somehow incapable of reaching agreement, and for this reason could not bear to lay down arms."

In 341 the dedication of the great new Golden Church at Antioch gave the Eusebians the opportunity to consolidate their position by holding a council. At Antioch in the presence of Constantius II, ninety-seven eastern bishops proceeded to draw up a profession of faith. They announced that as bishops they were not followers of Arius, a mere priest, but that as his judges they admitted him posthumously to communion. In the so-called Second Creed of Antioch, the only one of four creeds associated with this council which was fully ratified by the assembled bishops, they relied apparently on a formulary drawn up by the long-dead Lucian of Antioch which was probably edited by the Arian sophist Asterius. In this creed, in Origenist and anti-Sabellian fashion, the bishops proclaimed their faith in a "Father who is truly Father, and a Son who is truly Son, and in the Holy Spirit who is truly Holy Spirit, the names not being given without meaning or effect, but denoting accurately the peculiar subsistence (hypostasis) rank and glory of each named, so that there are three in subsistence, and in agreement one." They continued, "if any teaches contrary to the sound and right faith of the Scripture, that time or season or age either is or has been before the generation of the Son — or if any says that the Son is a creature or one of the creatures — let him be anathema." As is obvious, this Second Creed of the Dedication Council of Antioch is far from being Arian, yet it lays great stress, as did Origen, on the subsistence of three united by agreement of wills and makes no mention of the Nicene *homoousios*. The creed exemplifies the abiding concern of the East to safeguard the distinction of the Three as opposed to the West's insistence on the divine unity.

At this point Constans, ruler of the West, asked his eastern brother Constantius II for information about the teaching of the East. This request resulted in a deputation of eastern bishops to Trier where Constans was in residence. To Constans they presented what is called the Fourth Creed of Antioch, which though not drawn up by the Dedication Council was destined to be reissued repeatedly by councils of eastern bishops. It will be presented to the East at Sardica (343), as the basis of the Long-Lined Creed (345), as the first Creed of Sirmium (351), in the dated Creed (359), and at the

Council of Seleucia (359). In an attempt to head off any desire of Constans to call another council, the bishops professed belief in the Father's "only-begotten Son, Our Lord Jesus Christ, who was begotten from the Father before all ages, God from God, Light from Light, through whom all things came into being in heaven and on earth, visible and invisible, being Word and Wisdom and Power and true Light...whose reign is unceasing and abides for endless ages." They added that "those who say that the Son is from nothing, or is from another hypostasis and is not from God, and that there was time when he was not, the Catholic Church regards as alien." It is clear that these eastern bishops rejected outright Arianism, and they heaped epithets of divinity on the Son, all the while avoiding the term *homoousios.* By the clause about the reign of Christ, they registered their hostility to the views of Marcellus of Ancyra who regarded the Son as only a temporary projection of the Father for purposes of creation and redemption. Approval of Marcellus by Athanasius of Alexandria and Julius of Rome fed the suspicions of the East that the Nicene formulation was Sabellian.

This declaration of the eastern bishops encouraged Julius and others to ask the Emperor Constans to call a council to discuss further the issues dividing East and West. The western emperor acceded and called the bishops of East and West to Sardica (modern Sophia in Bulgaria), a city lying on the easternmost province of his jurisdiction. In the autumn of 342, or more probably 343, the council opened with about ninety western bishops headed by Ossius of Cordoba and about eighty easterners, including the principal sees — Antioch, Ephesus, Caesarea in Palestine, Caesarea in Cappadocia, and Heraclea, metropolitan see of the region around Constantinople. The easterners were joined by the Balkan Arian bishops, Valens of Mursa and Ursacius of Belgrade. Julius, bishop of Rome, was represented by two priests and a deacon. The easterners promptly challenged the right of Athanasius, Marcellus of Ancyra and Asclepeas of Gaza in Palestine to sit in the council since they had been deposed, and their cases would be under review by the council. When their challenge was rejected, the easterners left by night on the excuse that they had to go East to celebrate Constantius II's victory over the Persians. From Philippopolis just over the Susa Pass from Sardica in the jurisdiction of the emperor of the East, they issued an encyclical letter to the whole Church, explaining their case against Marcellus and Athanasius and condemning among others Julius of Rome and Ossius of Cordoba. To this they affixed their profession of faith, the so-called Fourth Creed of the Dedication Council of Antioch.

Meanwhile, the western bishops continued their deliberations at Sardica, unreservedly supporting Athanasius and Asclepeas of Gaza. The case of Marcellus of Ancyra was more difficult, but after a public reading of his book, the westerners, somewhat at sea in the complexities of Greek theology, professed to find him orthodox. Ossius then wanted to issue a new creedal statement, but when Athanasius convinced the bishops that any defection from the pronouncements of Nicaea would be fatal to their cause, they contented themselves with the re-issue of the Nicene Creed. To it they attached explanations drawn up by Ossius and Protogenes of Sardica. Opposing Ursacius and Valens, "two vipers born from the Arian asp," who are said to maintain that the "Father, Son and Holy Spirit are of diverse and distinct hypostases," the bishops taught that "Father, Son and Holy Spirit have one hypostasis, which is termed substance." They continued, "If it were asked, 'What is the hypostasis of the Son?' we confess that it is the same as the sole hypostasis of the Father; the Father has never been without the Son, nor the Son without the Father, nor is it possible that what is Word is Holy Spirit. We do not say that the Father is the Son nor that Son is the Father. We confess that there is but one God, and that the Divinity of the Father and of the Son is one. No one can deny that the Father is greater than the Son; this superiority does not arise from any difference in hypostasis...but simply from the name of the Father being greater than that of the Son. The following words uttered by Our Lord, 'I and the Father are one' (John 10:30), are by some persons explained as referring to the concord and harmony which prevail between the Father and the Son, but this is a blasphemous and perverse interpretation. But we believe and maintain and think that these holy words, 'I and the Father are one,' point to the oneness of the hypostasis which is one both of the Father and of the Son." J. N. D. Kelly remarks that "the doctrine which is anathematized was scarcely that of Arius himself but included any teaching which admitted three hypostases in the Godhead and ascribed to the Logos or Son of God an independent personal existence side-by-side with the Father. Herein lies its great importance, for such an official declaration of war on the Origenist theology was unprecedented." The bishops declared that the substance of Father and Son is identical, making fully explicit something only implicit in the Nicene Creed. Although stressing against the Origenists the unity of the Godhead in uncompromising fashion, their explanation failed to state the way in which Father, Son and Holy Spirit are separate in any comprehensible sense. The bishops also reinstated the deposed Marcellus of Ancyra, but they were careful to separate themselves from some aspects of his teaching. They added to their explanation of the Creed: "We also believe that the Son reigns with the Father, that His reign has neither beginning nor end, for what has always existed can never have commenced and can never terminate." Thus the insistence of the Origenist-inclined bishops of the East on three hypostases in the Second Creed of Antioch and the Nicene bishops' avowal at Sardica of the identical substance of Father and Son put East and West on a collision course which the compromise statement of the Fourth Creed of Antioch could not alter.

In a series of canons, the bishops at Sardica tried to bring order to the troubled Church by ruling against the transference of bishops from one see to another, interference of bishops in one another's sees, the poaching of clerics from another's see, and the hasty ordination of bishops without their having passed through the lower clerical orders. They also deprecated bishops' absence from their sees and their uninvited visits to the imperial court. Most importantly, in Canon 3, they ruled that a bishop judged by his peers could appeal to the bishop of Rome, who could either refuse to review the case, thereby letting the previous judgment stand, or appoint judges to try the case afresh, sending if he wished one of his priests to sit with the bishop-judges. In Rome, Julius apparently had the canons recorded immediately after the Canons of Nicaea, a fact which created confusion later on. Unfortunately these canons would long be in abeyance, and the restatement of creeds by East and West left the Church badly divided.

The effects of this division were soon felt. Emperor Constantius began in the East, especially in Egypt, the deposition and exile of bishops and priests who supported Nicene views. The West attempted to heal the breach in 344 by sending Vincent of Capua, the former papal legate at Nicaea, and Euphrates of Cologne to visit Constantius at Antioch. There the bishop of Antioch, Stephen, attempted to compromise Euphrates by sending a young prostitute to his room. Though the attempt failed and Stephen was promptly deposed, the incident shows the growing bitterness between the factions. However, the mission of Vincent and Euphrates at least persuaded Constantius to call off the persecution of Athanasius' followers in Egypt. In 345 the East responded with a delegation of its own, four bishops who brought to the western emperor, Constans, at Milan a new creed, the so-called Long-lined (Macrostich) Creed based on the Fourth Creed of Antioch. The creed rejected the two principal opinions of Arius that the Son is from nothing and that there was when He was not. The bishops explained that in confessing three realities and three persons we do not therefore "make three gods since we acknowledge the self-complete and unbegotten and the unbegun and invisible God to be only one, the God and Father of the Only-begotten, who alone was being from Himself, and alone, as an act of grace, confers this on all others bountifully." We acknowledge, continued the bishops, that Our Lord Jesus Christ, "though He be subordinate to His Father and God, yet, being before the ages begotten from God, He is God according to nature and true God." We believe him "to be perfect from the first and like in all things to the Father." Knowing God the Father is absolute and sovereign, the bishops added "that He generated the Son voluntarily and freely." Father and Son "are united with each other without mediation or interval, and they exist inseparably; all the Father embosoming the Son, and all the Son hanging and adhering to the Father and alone resting on the Father's breast continually." In addition, the bishops rejected the opinion of Marcellus of Ancyra and his disciple Photinus (man of light), whom they called Scotinus (man of darkness), soon to be bishop of Sirmium, that Christ's kingdom had a beginning with His incarnation and would end with the final judgment. The whole creed, though conciliatory toward western sensibilities and avoiding the confusing terms "ousia" and "hypostasis," still had a decided subordinationist and Origenist tone about it. Besides, the bishops substituted the term *homoios* (like) in all things for the Nicene *homoousios* (consubstantial). Since Photinus went even beyond Marcellus of Ancyra in diminishing the divine element in Jesus, regarding Him as only a man whose eminent virtue merited the favor of special intimacy with God, the western bishops agreed to condemn him. But they demanded that the easterners in turn sign a renunciation of the doctrine of three hypostases. Refusing, the easterners returned home. Two years later, again at Milan, the western bishops declared Photinus deposed from his see of Sirmium, but, since his people refused to part with him, the sentence remained without effect. Nevertheless, Athanasius now realized that Marcellus and Photinus were compromising the faith of Nicaea and broke off relations with them, though, loyal to an old comrade in arms, he never condemned Marcellus personally.

In 345 with the death of the intruder Gregory, the see of Alexandria fell vacant, and Emperor Constantius asked Athanasius to return. In fact, he had to make the request three times before Athanasius finally agreed. Even then he traveled through Gaul to interview Emperor Constans, stopped at Rome to confer with Pope Julius and met Constantius himself at Antioch. Only in the fall of 346 did he enter Egypt to be met one hundred miles out in the desert by the civil officials of the province. Then as he neared his city, his people flowed about him like the Nile, and he entered Alexandria in triumph. Four hundred bishops from all parts of the Empire proclaimed communion with him. In the West the Balkan Arians Valens and Ursacius submitted to the bishop of Rome, signed a statement condemning Arius and declared communion with Athanasius. The breach between East and West over the faith of Nicaea seemed healed at long last. But in 350, the western emperor Constans, supporter of the Nicene party, died. A rebellion followed in which Count Magnentius was declared emperor by the legions at Autun in France.

With Athanasius triumphant for the moment, let us consider briefly, without tracing his intellectual development, the doctrine which he will defend in season and out for the next twenty-five years. Unlike the Arians who were concerned primarily with the Son's place in creation, Athanasius begins with the firm conviction that the Word became flesh to redeem the human race, to make men godlike. But the Word could never divinize mankind if He were merely divine by participation in the Father's nature and not Himself the essential Godhead, the very image of the Father. God, argues Athanasius, can never be without His Word, as light can never cease to shine. Just as the Father is always good by nature, so He is by nature always generative. "The Father's being," he continued, "was never incomplete, needing an essential feature added to it; nor is the Son's generation like a man's from his parent, involving His coming into existence after the Father. Rather, He is God's offspring, and since God is eternal and He belongs to God as Son, He exists from all eternity.... His nature is always perfect." Though the Son derives from and shares the Father's nature, He is not a portion of substance separated out of the Father, for God is wholly immaterial and without parts. Nor does the Son come forth eternally from the Father by an act of the Father's will. Certainly the generation of the Word is according to the Father's will, but it comes about by an eternal process inherent in the Father's very nature. As the Father's offspring, the Word is really distinct from the Father, and distinction is eternal just as is generation. Nor did the Word come from the Father just for the sake of the economy of creation and redemption. Moreover, the Word is other in kind and nature from mere creatures. He belongs to the Father's very substance and is of His nature: he who sees Christ sees the Father.

At first Athanasius did not much use the Nicene *homoousios*, but gradually he saw its full implication and became its most resolute defender. The likeness and unity of Father and Word cannot consist in just harmony and concord of mind and will, but must be in respect of essence. The divinity of the Father is identical to the divinity of the Word. The Word is other than the Father because He came forth from the Father, but as God, the Word and the Father are one and the same. What is said of the Father is said of the Son, except the Son is not called Father. Humans can be said to be *homoousioi* because they share human nature, but they cannot possess one and the same identical substance. The divine nature, however, is indivisible; possessed equally by Father and Word. God is thus the unique, indivisible monad; there is only one monarchy and supreme principle. But though Father and Word are one identical substance, "two they are because Father is Father and not Son; the Son is not the Father." G. L. Prestige brings out very clearly how Athanasius went even beyond Nicaea. "Though Father and Son are not one but two objects as seen in relation to each other — the names denote distinct presentations of the divine being —yet their 'substance' is identical; if you analyze the meaning connoted by the word God, in whatever connection, you arrive in every case at exactly the same result, whether you are thinking of the Father or of the Son or of the Spirit. That is the point at which the creed was directed: the word God connotes precisely the same truth when you speak of God the Father as it does when you speak of God the Son. It connotes the same truth. So much the Council affirmed. But Athanasius went further. It must imply, he perceived, not only the same truth about God, but the same actual God, the same being. If you contemplate the Father, who is one distinct presentation of the deity, you obtain a mental view of the one true God. If you contemplate the Son or the Spirit, you obtain a view of the same God; though the presentation is different, the reality is identical." Still, Athanasius has no word to express the subsistence as persons of Father and Son. For him even in 369 hypostasis which designates the three is the same as ousia which designates the one, and both signify being itself. This lingering imprecision in terminology will continue to bedevil theological discourse.

2. *Athanasius vs. Constantius*

With the death of his brother Constans in 350 and the suicide of the defeated Magnentius in 353, Constantius embarked securely upon his reign as sole emperor without the religious constraints put upon him by Constans' pro-Nicene sympathies. Constantius soon assured Athanasius of his respect and support. Nevertheless, toward the end of 351 at Sirmium, a group of eastern bishops, of whom the moderate Basil of Ancyra was the chief spokesman, re-opened the case of Photinus, condemned him anew and with the emperor's cooperation replaced him with Germinius of Cyzicus. Once again the bishops proclaimed the Fourth Creed of Antioch as the expression of their faith. In 352, Julius, bishop of Rome, died, to be succeeded by the far less able but much loved deacon Liberius. Immediately, the eastern bishops reopened their campaign against Athanasius by sending a delegation to the new pope, presenting him with a protest against Athanasius signed by eighty bishops. At the same time, an imperial envoy arrived at Alexandria requesting Athanasius to appear at the imperial court. This Athanasius refused to do without a direct order from Constantius himself. For twenty-six months Athanasius waited for the order which never came while preparing a series of speeches to be given in his defense before the court. Meanwhile, the western bishops approached Constantius naively asking him to call another council to discuss outstanding problems with the East. Readily acceding to their request, Constantius convoked a council at his imperial residence in Arles in southern France. There the emperor pressured the assembled western bishops, among whom was Vincent of Capua, papal legate at Nicaea, into signing a condemnation of Athanasius; the sole dissenting bishop was exiled. Next Pope Liberius was subjected to allegations by the emperor of pride and ambition. In defending himself the pope asked the emperor to assemble yet another coucil. To this council held at Milan in 355 Liberius sent as legate the stormy petrel of the Nicene party, Lucifer, bishop of Cagliari in Sardinia. At the council, Eusebius of Vercelli, a staunch Nicene, presented the Creed of Nicaea for the bishops' signatures. When the unsuspecting bishop of Milan, Dionysius, prepared to sign, the Arian bishop, Valens of Mursa, struck pen and paper from his hand, shouting, "Certainly not that." Whereupon Valens and Ursacius, at imperial orders, threatened the bishops with exile if they did not sign a condemnation of Athanasius. Episcopal resistance was cowed; all signed but Lucifer of Cagliari, Eusebius of Vercelli and Dionysius of Milan. To the see of Milan the staunch Arian Auxentius was elected to make the city a center of Arian resistance to the Nicene Creed until 373, when the senatorial aristocrat Ambrose was acclaimed bishop. From exile Lucifer assailed the emperor in fiery pamphlets like "Apostate Kings" and "Let Us Die for the Son of God." Hilary, the newly elected bishop of Poitiers, who had only recently become aware of the existence of the Nicene Creed, now became the soul of resistance to imperial dictation at the Council of Beziers, but he was quickly exiled to the East for his pains in 356.

When Pope Liberius wrote a letter of encouragement to the three bishops exiled at the Council of Milan of 355, his messengers were condemned to exile, and he was ordered to appear before the emperor at Milan. Supported by his congregation, Liberius refused to go and threw the offering left by the imperial envoy at St. Peter's basilica into the street. Shortly afterward, in the secrecy of night, Liberius was forcibly taken to the emperor at Milan. Despite a dignified defense and refusal to condemn Athanasius, Liberius was exiled to Thrace where the Arian bishop Demophilus served as his jailer. The archdeacon Felix was appointed to the see of Rome in his place. Next it was the turn of the aged Ossius of Cordoba to bear the brunt of imperial disfavor at his refusal to forsake the definition of Nicaea. In 356 the old bishop told the emperor: "I was a confessor at the first, when persecution arose in the time of your grandfather Maximian (303); and if you persecute me, I am ready now too to endure anything rather than shed innocent blood and betray the truth.... Do not intrude into ecclesiastical matters, and do not give commands to us concerning them; but learn from us. God has put into your hands the kingdom; to us he has entrusted the affairs of the Church; and as he who would steal the Empire from you would resist the ordinance of God, so likewise fear on your part lest, by taking upon yourself the government of the Church, you become guilty of a great offense." Ossius, for his resistance, was put under arrest at Sirmium.

With the Church in both East and West cowed into submission, Constantius attacked Athanasius. The Dux Syrianus was ordered to assemble the legions of Egypt and Syria and remove the bishop from Alexandria. On the night of February 8, 356, imperial troops broke into the Church of Theonas, where Athanasius, surrounded by his clergy and consecrated virgins, was conducting a vigil service. As the arrows flew and the dead and wounded fell, his clergy hurried the reluctant bishop from his throne and Athanasius dropped completely from sight. In the next year George of Cappadocia ceremoniously entered the sullen city to be enthroned as the new bishop. He soon unleashed a reign of terror against Athanasius' supporters while on the side organizing profitable monopolies in pork, salt, papyrus and funeral arrangements. In the desert, moving from one hiding place to another, welcomed by the monks, never once betrayed by his people, Athanasius remained the religious leader of Egypt, pouring out a steady flood of well-informed books and pamphlets defending the Nicene faith. From the security of the desert he wrote about Constantius: "who that beheld him as chorus leader of his pretended bishops, and presiding in ecclesiastical causes, would not justly exclaim that this was the abomination of desolation spoken of by Daniel?" But now in very truth it was Athanasius against the world.

The Arian faction seemed supreme, but new developments would soon open divisions within their ranks. Instigator of these developments was Aetius, a Christian dialectian in Antioch of dubious antecedents, who owed his reputation to overwhelming skill in debate. His specialty was to reduce Arian doctrine to a chain of syllogisms. Associated with him was Eunomius, later bishop of Cyzicus in Asia Minor. Their position theologically was that God is unique and uncomposed, totally ungenerated essence. The Son, however, is generated and, therefore, must be of a different essence from the Father. The Son is unlike (*anomoios*) the Father. Yet the Father communicates a divine energy to the Son, confers divinity on him, with the result that the Son shares the Father's activity and creative power. With supreme confidence in reason, they declared the Father perfectly comprehensible because perfectly simple. Since the key word in their position was that the Son was unlike (*anomoios*) the Father, they were called Anomeans. Aetius' Arian and arid dialectic made him unpopular in Antioch where he had been ordained deacon, and he took refuge with George, Athanasius' supplanter at Alexandria. In addition, he gained the support of Germinius of Sirmium and of the indefatigable Balkan Arians Valens and Ursacius.

In the summer of 357, this group contrived a new creedal statement at the Second Council of Sirmium. Here the bishops agreed that "since some of many persons were disturbed by questions concerning substance, called in Greek *ousia*...of *homoousion*, or what is called *homoiou-*

sion, there ought to be no mention at all." After outlawing *homoousion*, the rallying cry of the Nicenes, and the *homoiousion* of the conservative middle, they proceeded to give their own view of the matter. "No one can doubt that the Father is greater than the Son in honor, dignity, splendor, majesty, and in the very great name of Father, the Son Himself testifying, 'He that sent me is greater than I.' And no one is ignorant that it is Catholic doctrine that there are two Persons of Father and Son; that the Father is greater, and that the Son is subordinated, together with all things which the Father has subordinated to him; that the Father has no beginning and is invisible, immortal, and impassible, but that the Son has been begotten of the Father, God from God, Light from Light, and that the generation of this Son, as has already been said, no one knows but his Father." In effect, the Nicene Creed toward which all had hitherto paid respect, though not full allegiance, was condemned, and vague terminology gave a free hand to the Arians. Hilary of Poitiers responded to this Creed of the Second Council of Sirmium labeling it "The Blasphemy."

As outrage mounted on all sides, the new Creed's protagonists proceeded in 357 to force Ossius, who had sat in councils since that of Elvira in 306, to sign it. One hundred years old and befuddled by theological argument, he at last gave way, but even then refused to condemn his old comrade in arms, Athanasius. Pope Liberius in his Thracian exile was pressured by his ecclesiastical jailer, Demophilus, until he too gave way and condemned Athanasius, signing a mildly Arian creed, probably the old standby, Fourth Creed of Antioch. The Gallish and African bishops, horrified at the new creed, promptly registered their protests against it. But the new bishop of Antioch, the Arian Eudoxius, just as promptly accepted it. But the moderates of the East were now thoroughly aroused. Led by Basil of Ancyra, successor to the Nicene but Sabellian-inclined Marcellus, they met at Ancyra in 358. The moderates now began to realize that Marcellus and Sabellius were not the only dangers to the Catholic faith but that the radically

Arian Aetius and his friends were equally threatening. The moderate bishops were agreed that the proper teaching about the Son was that He is like in substance (*homoiousios*) to the Father. They denied in the nineteenth anathema appended to their creed that the Son is consubstantial with the Father or is the same substance as the Father.

The results of their deliberations were conveyed to the emperor by Basil of Ancyra, and Constantius was convinced that a new creed must be drawn up in order to provide a formula of imperial orthodoxy. This new formula was to avoid the ambiguity of the Nicene *homoousios* and the denial of the Son's full divinity by the radical Arians now unmasked by the Blasphemy of Sirmium. With imperial orthodoxy about to be defined, Pope Liberius signified agreement with the mildly Homoeousian statement and was allowed to return to Rome where his popularity soon made it prudent for the intruder Felix to leave the city. From exile Hilary of Poitiers wrote to the bishops of Gaul and Britain exhorting them to stand loyal to *homoousios* yet not reject the Homoeousians who had at least broken with the radical Anomoeans. From hiding in Egypt Athanasius wrote to his followers in the same vein. The Nicenes, rid of the incubus of the Sabellian-leaning Marcellus of Ancyra, and the moderates, set against the radical Arians, were beginning at last to look to the truth of each other's position and to pull together.

Victorious, the Homoeousian Basil of Ancyra now wished to cap his triumph with a new ecumenical council. It was finally decided to call it in two sections: for the West at Rimini in eastern Italy, for the East at Seleucia in southern Asia Minor. To prepare for the double council, a committee of bishops assembled at Sirmium in 359 where Mark, bishop of Arethusa, drew up the Dated Creed, so called from the precise dating of its preamble, a peculiarity later ridiculed for its presuming to date the Word of God. The new creed registered faith in "one only-begotten Son of God, who, before all ages, and before all beginning, and before all conceivable time and before all conceivable essence was begotten impassibly from God; through whom the ages were disposed and all things were made; and Him begotten as the only-begotten, only from the only Father, God from God, like unto the Father who begat Him . . . ." They added the ominous paragraph: "But whereas the term essence (*ousia*) has been adopted by the Fathers in simplicity, and gives offense as being unknown to the people, because it is not contained in the Scriptures, it has seemed good to remove it, that essence be never in any case used of God again, because the divine Scriptures nowhere refer to the essence of Father and Son. But we say that the Son is like (*homoios*) the Father in all things. . . ." The new watchword of imperial orthodoxy was not to be *homoiousios* as Basil of Ancyra so confidently expected, but the far weaker *homoios*, like in all things. Valens of Mursa had wanted to weaken the creed still further by striking out "in all things," but Constantius had the words restored. To keep the forthcoming double council firmly in hand it was agreed that deputations of ten bishops from each meeting would carry the results to the emperor and work out a final accord.

The council called to Rimini opened first in the summer of 359 with some four hundred bishops in attendance. Strangely enough, the bishop of Rome was never even represented. By far the majority were orthodox Nicenes, but a group of eighty led by Ursacius, Valens and Germinius of Sirmium formed a pro-Arian faction. The majority rejected the newly drawn Dated Creed, proclaimed that of Nicaea and excommunicated Ursacius, Valens and Germinius. The bishop of Carthage was elected as leader of the delegation to carry the results to the emperor busy in the East with the war against Persia. Ursacius and Valens managed to get to the emperor first, and the delegation from Rimini was told to await the emperor's pleasure at Nike in Thrace. There Ursacius and Valens forced the reluctant delegates to sign the Dated Creed with the words "in all things" deleted after "like" (*homoios*). The bishops in Rimini were held in session by a pretorian prefect, and at the return of the delegation from Nike were forced in their turn to sign the Dated Creed. Only fifteen held out, but finally, after condemning Arius, they too signed. The rout of the western bishops was complete.

By the autumn of 359, about 150 eastern bishops gathered at Seleucia, among them the Nicene Hilary of Poitiers, dragooned by the imperial police. Basil of Ancyra and Silvanus of Tarsus led the party favorable to a creed based on *homoiousios*; George of Alexandria and Eudoxius of Antioch led the Anomeans; Acacius of Palestinian Caesarea, the erudite and eloquent pupil of the long-dead Eusebius and heir to his library, favored a unifying and therefore equivocal formula. Basil of Ancyra, because of his absence on the opening day of the Council and later accusations leveled against him, lost influence on the proceedings. At first 105 bishops, under the leadership of Silvanus of Tarsus, agreed to sign the old Fourth Creed of Antioch. Indignantly, the Acacians walked out of the assembly, and meeting separately, agreed on a declaration repudiating *homoousios*, *homoiousios* and *anomoios* and proposing simply *homoios* as the key to understanding the Trinity. But the majority refused to accept their position as well as the *homoiousios* of Basil of Ancyra and the phrase — like in all things — of the Dated Creed of Mark of Arethusa. The Council remained so divided that the imperial commissioner withdrew, telling the bishops: "Now, go quarrel with each other." Various matters dealing with persons were dispatched and the ten delegates requested by the emperor were elected, but no decisive vote could be taken on a creedal statement. Acacius beat the delegation from Seleucia to Constantinople and gained the emperor's ear. In the end both delegations were prevailed upon to join in with the wishes of the Homoean Acacius and support his equivocal formula — the Son is like the Father —the holdouts being browbeaten by the emperor personally far into the night of December 31, 359. The next day Constantius inaugurated his tenth consulate by proclaiming the newly-established unity of the Church. To sanction this enforced unity there were assembled at Constantinople on January 20 the twenty delegates from Rimini and

Seleucia together with the neighboring bishops of Bithynia and Thrace, among them the Gothic bishop Ulfilas who would spread the doctrines of this council among the Germanic tribes beyond the borders of the Empire.

At Constantinople in 360 the assembled bishops confessed belief in "the only begotten Son of God, who was begotten from God before all ages and before all beginning, through Whom all things came into existence, visible and invisible, begotten only-begotten, alone from the Father alone, God from God, like the Father who begot Him. . . ." And they added that because the word essence or substance offends the people, neither it nor the word hypostasis should be used of Father, Son and Holy Spirit. "We say the Son is like the Father," they conclude. From Bethlehem St. Jerome lamented: "Down with the faith of Nicaea was the cry. The whole world groaned, astonished to find itself Arian." However, as Kelly remarks, "Arianism, it will be appreciated, is really a misnomer, for the creed asserts none of the articles of the old heresy and explicitly condemns Anomoeanism. Its deliberate vagueness, however, made it capable of being recited by Christians with very different sets of ideas." So this statement was better suited to Constantius' purpose than terms drawn from more elaborate speculative theologies.

Now began the search for episcopal signatures to enforce compliance with the new creed. In the West so many had already accepted the creed at Rimini that not much remained to be done. In the East, the task was more difficult. From hiding Athanasius exhorted the bishops of Egypt and Libya to refuse to sign. Egypt, except for George at Alexandria, remained firm in its opposition, and the imperial commissioners backed down. Elsewhere, many like old Dianius of Cappadocian Caesarea signed any imperial document set before them. Only a few held out. The Homoean leaders were rewarded: Eunomius, a radical Arian, got the bishopric of Cyzicus; Eudoxius was transferred from Antioch and made bishop of Constantinople. There in his first sermon he jested that the Father is impious, the Son, pious. When the crowd murmured in surprise, he added that his proposition was true because the Son reveres the Father while the Father has no one to revere. Such was the new race of imperial bishops. At Antioch, Meletius, former bishop of Sebaste in Armenia, was installed in the chair just vacated by Eudoxius. But his surprising Nicene stance resulted in his banishment a month later. Euzoius, one of Arius' original disciples was consecrated in his place. Homoeans or outright Arians had replaced Nicenes or moderate Homoeousians in every major eastern see. The creed of Nicaea seemed to have gone down to defeat.

Constantius, however, had little time to savor his triumph. The Persian War was going badly, and when he ordered the crack legions of Gaul to the eastern front, they revolted and proclaimed as emperor the Caesar Julian, survivor of the family massacre of 337 and the last member of the Constantinian dynasty. As Julian moved east against his cousin Constantius, the Danubian garrisons rallied to his side. Ill with fever, Constantius was baptized by the old Arian Euzoius of Antioch. As death came, he named Julian his heir. Thus in the late fall of 361 Julian entered on his reign as sole emperor.

3. Time Out: Pagan Revival under Julian

Quite unexpectedly all the squabbling Christian factions suffered a rude shock. The new emperor soon revealed himself as a pagan intent on restoring the old ways. He had no deep loyalty to the religion of a family who had killed his father, uncle, cousins and brother. As a child he was confided to a series of Christian tutors, all Arian: Eusebius of Nicomedia, George the usurper of Alexandria and the radical sophist Aetius. Yet he was duly baptized and even entered Christian orders as a lector. Increasingly, however, his real passion became not the aridities of Arianism but the glories of Hellenistic antiquity. In his active mind the myths and cults of ancient Greece mingled with the exotic magical love of the later Neoplatonists. As Caesar and able general in Gaul, he kept up the pose as a Christian. But with the death of Constantius, he threw off the Christian mask and showed himself an austere, studious prince piously devoted to all the ancient pagan lore.

Toleration was granted to all religious sects, but imperial favor fell especially on those who restored the pagan temples and cults. With the tacit approval of the emperor, any Christians who attacked the restored idols were left to the savage treatment of the pagans. Cities which did not cultivate the old gods were denied military protection. Julian attempted as well to reform the pagan priesthoods, preaching them sermons on austerity, kindness to the unfortunate, fraternity and devotion to the instruction of the people. Pagan priests were enjoined to stay out of taverns and avoid jobs base and unworthy of their calling. Money from the imperial treasury was distributed to the pagan priests for the establishment of charitable institutions in imitation of the Christians. But as the emperor, shabbily dressed and wearing the wispy beard and long hair of the philosopher, sacrificed beasts and sprinkled incense, the masses remained indifferent or mocked his dogged seriousness.

Exiled bishops were allowed to return to sees occupied by others, for, said the pagan historian Ammianus, the emperor knew that no wild beasts were so hostile to men as were the Christians to one another. In Alexandria a pagan mob promptly lynched the usurper George, and Athanasius returned after fifteen years in exile. But Christian bishops, priests and monks lost their immunities from civil services and taxation. Episcopal courts lost civil jurisdiction. Since Christian teachers of the classics could not practice what they taught, they were told to embrace paganism or resign their posts. At least two of the most famous teachers in the Empire promptly resigned their posts. The bishop of Palestinian Laodicea, Apollinaris, soon to be accused of heresy, and his school-teacher father set to work to give the Christian Scriptures classic form by turning the Book of Genesis into an epic, the Psalms into hexameters and the Gospels into Platonic dialogues. Churches and martyria were removed from the premises of pagan temples. Christian funeral processions were forbidden by day. When these measures failed to weaken the Church, bishops were forced into exile once again. As Athanasius boarded his barge for exile, he told his people,

> "Let us retire for a brief while, my friends;
> 'Tis but a little cloud and soon will pass.".

As the imperial police raced up the Nile to arrest him, Athanasius had his oarsmen reverse their course. As the police passed shouting had they seen Athanasius, he replied, yes, he is quite close. The police sailed upstream as Athanasius returned to hiding in Alexandria itself. But this state of affairs proved to be of short duration, for in a disastrous retreat from Persia, Julian was wounded and died in 363 after reigning only twenty months as emperor.

Amid the disturbances of Julian's rule, the doctrinal differences within the Church continued. In 361 the radical Arians met at Antioch under the leadership of Euzoius and declared their belief in a Son unlike the Father. In 362 Athanasius, before his exile, called a peace conference at Alexandria consisting of representatives from Egypt, Palestine and Italy along with delegates sent by the fanatical Nicene Lucifer of Cagliari, Apollinaris of Laodicea and the priest Paulinus, chief of the Nicene community at Antioch. Athanasius' main concern was to reconcile the moderates and the Nicenes by getting behind party catchwords to the deeper meaning of each position. He recommended asking those who held three hypostases if they meant three in the sense of three subsistent beings, alien in nature like gold, silver and brass, as did the radical Arians. If they answered no, he asked if they meant by three hypostasis a Trinity, truly existing with truly substantial Father, Son and Holy Spirit, and if they acknowledged one Godhead. If they said yes, he allowed them into communion. Then he turned to those who spoke of one hypostasis and asked if they meant this in the sense of Sabellius, as if the Son were not substantial and the Holy Spirit impersonal. If they said no, he asked them if they meant by one hypostasis one substance or ousia because the Son is of the substance of the Father. If their answer was yes, he accepted them into communion. Finally, in a statesmanlike fashion Athanasius brought out the truth each side was fighting for and showed that between the moderates and the Nicenes there was really no ground for disagreement. The results of these deliberations were sent off to Antioch divided into three factions: the Arians led by Euzoius, the imperially recognized bishop, the Homoeousians led by the exiled Meletius and the old Nicenes led by the priest Paulinus, loyal to the long-dead Eustathius. The way seemed open for peace.

But the way was to prove long and rough. For while Athanasius was laying the groundwork for reconciliation at Alexandria, Lucifer of Cagliari had gone to Antioch and made things worse. Instead of attempting to reconcile the moderate bishop Meletius who had already declared for the Nicene faith, Lucifer consecrated the Old Nicene Paulinus as bishop. The two parties which Athanasius had been attempting to reconcile were now separated by rival bishops, while the old Arian Euzoius held the churches of the city. This schism at Antioch would impede reconciliation between moderates and Nicenes for years to come as Athanasius and the bishops of Rome came to support Paulinus, while the rising leader of the East, Basil of Caesarea, remained loyal to Meletius.

4. *Two New Battles*

As the Trinitarian controversy continued on its weary way the Church was being buffeted by two new dangers — errors in the theology of Christ and of the Holy Spirit. A new chapter in Christology was being written by Apollinaris of Laodicea (the modern Latakia) in Syria. Born about 310 the son of an Alexandrian priest and grammarian, he had been a student at Athens with the young future emperor Julian. When Julian banned Christian schoolmasters from teaching literature, it was Apollinaris and his father who attempted to rewrite Scripture in classical forms. Bishop of Laodicea from

361 to 390, he also taught at Antioch where Jerome attended his lectures. By 362 Apollinaris' views on Christology were being noticed, and by 375 he had broken with the orthodox Church, consecrating Vitalis, a disciple, as the fourth bishop in strife-torn Antioch. Basil of Caesarea denounced him to Damasus of Rome, and in 377 a Roman council condemned him. Condemned once more at Antioch in 379, attacked by Gregory of Nazianzus and Gregory of Nyssa, Apollinaris would be condemned yet again by the Council of Constantinople I.

Apollinaris had firmly grasped Athanasius' central Trinitarian insight that Father and Son are a single identical divine substance, but the problem arose when he turned to Christology. Athanasius had developed a Word-Flesh Christology in which the place of the rational mind in Christ was not brought out with sufficient clarity. Arius held that the soul of the Son replaced the soul of the man Jesus, and used this assertion as proof of the changeability and creatureliness of the Son. Eustathius, deposed as bishop of Antioch in 330 for his defense of Nicaea, and other Antiochenes like Diodorus of Tarsus (d. 390) had insisted on a Logos-Man Christology, stressing the full reality of the man Jesus but fell into difficulties in explaining the unity of the God-man. Apollinaris now addressed himself to this problem with great intellectual acumen.

He believed firmly that only in Christ is mankind redeemed and restored. New life comes from a single source, the one mediator between God and us. Christ himself must then be a unity. If the divine were merely conjoined with man, then there would be two, one Son of God by nature, the other by adoption. The flesh of the Savior, therefore, is not something superadded to the Godhead, rather it constitutes one nature with the Godhead. "The flesh," continued Apollinaris, "being dependent for its motions on some other principle of movement and action, is not in itself a complete living entity, but in order to become one it enters into fusion with something else. So it is united with the heavenly governing principle and is fused with it. . . . Thus out of the moved and the mover was compounded a single living entity."

From the first instant of the Incarnation a sentient material body was fused with the unchanging Logos. The Word himself has become flesh without having assumed a human mind, a mind changeable and enslaved to filthy thoughts. "The divine energy fulfills the role of animating spirit and of the human mind," in the God-man. The Logos is thus the sole life of the God-man infusing vital energy into Him even at purely physical and biological levels. In the God-man there is one center of self-determination and will. He is a single, living being in whom the soul directs and the body is directed. There is in Him no conflict of wills, no confusion of separate identities. Rather, the one Son of God is not of two natures but is "one incarnate nature of the divine Word." Apollinaris argued that, "the body is not of itself a nature, because it is neither vivifying in itself nor capable of being singled out from what vivifies it. Nor is the Word, on the other hand, to be distinguished as a separate nature apart from His incarnate state, since it was in the flesh, and not apart from the flesh, that the Lord dwelt on earth." In the Incarnation there takes place an emptying on the part of the Word so as to take flesh to Himself. In us mind is corrupted by subservience to the flesh, but the mind of the Redeemer is never so corrupted. God incarnate in human flesh is Mind that cannot be overcome by the passions of soul and flesh, but rather maintains the flesh and its affections in a Godlike manner and without sin. Yet the flesh of the Savior has not come down from heaven, nor is His flesh consubstantial with God, but the flesh is God insofar as it is united with the Godhead so as to form one person.

There is in all this a strange crossing of the positions of Arius and Apollinaris. For Arius, since the Son is the soul of Christ, the Son is not divine because open to change. But Apollinaris denied a rational soul, a human mind, in Christ precisely so that the Son would not be reduced to the state of a creature, open to change. The consequences which flow from Apollinaris' positions are as follows. Christ's flesh is glorified because it is the flesh of God Himself. Christ's flesh is the proper object of worship because there is in Him one incarnate nature of the Word, to be worshipped with His flesh in one worship. The Word while remaining God shares the predicates and properties of flesh; the flesh while remaining flesh even in the union, shares the predicates and properties of God. Finally, the divine nature is communicated to the faithful when they consume the Lord's flesh at the Eucharist. In sum, Apollinaris has saved the unity of Word and flesh in the Redeemer, the sole source of our redemption, and vindicated His divinity. But has he safeguarded the full humanity of the Redeemer?

St. Gregory Nazianzus would single out the difficulties in Apollinaris' position. Gregory's central principle was: what is not assumed by the Redeemer is not redeemed. If the whole of Adam fell, then the Redeemer must be united to the whole nature of Adam in order to save it wholly. If Christ has a soul and yet is without a mind, how is he really man, for man is not a mindless animal. If the Godhead took the place of the human intellect, how does God touch the rest of mankind, for soul and flesh alone without intellect, the most essential part of man, do not constitute man. For Apollinaris it is inconceivable that the one God-man contain two natures. Gregory grants that on the purely physical level this is true; one bushel measure cannot contain two bushels. But on the mental and corporeal level "I in my one personality can contain soul and reason and mind and the Holy Spirit." Finally, if Apollinaris denies a human mind to the God-man because it is prone to sin and subject to damnation, then he offers an excuse for those who sin with the mind alone, for it is shown impossible even for God to heal the human mind.

With Apollinaris, a new chapter in Christology was opened; at the same time, Trinitarian theology was extended to include the Holy Spirit in its speculations. For Arius the Spirit's essence is utterly unlike the Son's just as the Son's is unlike the Father's. For Origenist-leaning theologians like Eusebius of Caesarea the Holy Spirit is an hypostasis of third rank, one of the entities which have come into being through the Son. For the later Arians like Aetius and Eunomius, the Spirit is the noblest of creatures produced by the Son at the Father's bidding. By 359-60, Athanasius had his attention called to the teaching of some Egyptians who recognized the Son's deity but disparaged the Holy Spirit. Athanasius called them Tropici because they resorted to a figurative analysis of Scripture. For them the Holy Spirit is an angel, superior to other angels in rank, but a ministering spirit, other in substance from Father and Son. This group seems to have been local and unrelated to a larger body called Macedonians, after the Homoeousian bishop of Constantinople deposed by the Arians in 360, who apparently had little to do with their doctrine. They were also called Pneumatomachians, fighters against the Spirit, and were especially strong in Constantinople, Thrace, Bithynia and along the Hellespont. Some of these accepted the consubstantiality of Father and Son; some were more radically Homoeousian preferring to say the Son is like the Father in substance or in all things. But they agreed that the Holy Spirit is neither God nor a mere creature. They argued that the Scripture seems to indicate the inferiority of the Spirit to Father and Son and says nothing explicit of His divinity. Further, there is no other relationship possible in the Godhead but that of Father and Son. Therefore, the Spirit is not God.

In the face of these denials of the Spirit's divinity, Athanasius was compelled to elaborate his own theology of the Spirit. He argued that in the Scripture, the Spirit is said to come from God, to bestow sanctification and life, to be unchangeable, omnipresent and unique; therefore, He is more than a creature. The Spirit makes us partakers of God; if the Spirit thus makes humans divine, His nature must be that of God. The Trinity itself is eternal, homogeneous and indivisible; if the Spirit is a member of it, He is consubstantial with the Father and the Son. The Son and the Spirit are closely related for the Son bestows the Spirit, and Son and Spirit are joined in the work of creation, sanctification and inspiration. Therefore, the Spirit belongs to the essence of the Son as the Son belongs to the essence of the Father. Yet, according to the custom of the time, Athanasius did not call the Spirit God.

By 380, Gregory of Nazianzus provided a spectrum of the views held of the Holy Spirit. Some consider the Spirit a force, some a creature, some God. Others refuse to commit themselves. Among those who say the Spirit is God, some hold the belief as private opinion, some proclaim it publicly, some distinguish degrees of divinity within the Trinity, the Spirit being ranked inferior to Father and Son. As we shall see, the Council of Constantinople will deal with both the Apollinarists and the Pneumatomachians.

5. Basil Versus Valens

With the death of Julian in the summer of 363, the empire received a new ruler, Jovian, a young military commander acclaimed by the legions on the Persian frontier. Christian and Nicene, he began his reign auspiciously, inviting Athanasius to visit him at Antioch. Meletius, leader of the Homoeousians of Antioch, assembled bishops from Syria and Asia Minor who wrote to the new emperor assuring him of their acceptance of the faith of Nicaea, even of the word *homoousios*. Reunion seemed at hand. But when Athanasius visited Antioch in 363, he asked Meletius to enter into communion with him; when Meletius hesitated, Athanasius recognized the newly consecrated Paulinus as legitimate bishop of Antioch. Schism continued at Antioch to poison the relations between Nicenes and Homoeousians in the Church at large.

By February of 364, Jovian, dead of natural causes, was replaced by an officer of his guard, Valentinian I, who promptly assumed rule of the West and associated his brother Valens with himself as emperor of the East. Valentinian was himself attached to the faith of Nicaea, but, as he told the bishops, a layman should not meddle in ecclesiastical affairs. His official policy was to allow the bishops of Gaul, Italy, Spain and Illyria to support the Nicene faith, but he would not interfere with the leaders of the western Arians. When Hilary of Poitiers attempted to incite the people of Milan against their Arian bishop Auxentius, he was firmly ordered out of the city. Except for Milan and sections of Illyria, the battle for Nicaea was largely won in the West.

But in the East it was a different matter. In 364 the Homoeousians gathered at Lampsacus in Asia Minor where they declared null and void the results of the Councils of Rimini-Seleucia-Constantinople which had made *homoios* the centerpiece of imperial orthodoxy. They embraced instead the Origenist Second Creed of Antioch (341), but insisted on the necessity of preserving the term *homoiousios* to guarantee the distinctions within the Trinity. Further, all Anomean bishops were to be deposed and all legitimate bishops returned to their sees. When delegates from Lampsacus carried these decisions to the new emperor Valens, he responded coldly and in the end ordered their exile. In the West. Valentinian could deal with a body of bishops almost unanimously Nicene, but in the East *homoousios* was not a rallying cry to union, and resistance to Athanasius was strong. Consequently, Valens determined to follow the example of Constantius and force the bishops to agree to the minimalist statement of Rimini-Seleucia-Constantinople. The emperor ordered all the bishops who had been deposed by Constantius but allowed to return to their sees by Julian to be expelled once again. Athanasius was saved from exile because he had been expelled by Julian, and so, after a legal battle, the old warrior was allowed to remain at Alexandria.

Dissatisfied with Valens' policy in the East, the Homoeousians decided to appeal to the western emperor, but were unable to contact him at the western front in Gaul. Liberius of Rome, however, received them cordially, but as the price of reunion demanded that they profess the Nicene Creed and reject that of Rimini-Seleucia-Constantinople. The eastern delegates agreed in the name of sixty-four of their confreres, who were now reconciled with Rome. Further reconciliation with the bishops of Sicily followed on their way home. These actions were ratified by a meeting of bishops at Tyana in central Asia Minor. There preparations were laid for a larger council to be held in the spring of 365 at Tarsus where union with the western Nicenes could be discussed. But preparations came to nought, for Valens forbade the convocation of the council.

After 365 with his religious policy in place, Valens had little time to give to the ecclesiastical troubles of the East. In 365/66 he had to put down an attempt on his throne by the usurper Procopius in Constantinople. From 367 to 369 he was occupied with the campaign against the Goths on the Danube frontier. During this campaign he was baptized by the Homoean bishop of Constantinople, Eudoxius, and remained firmly attached to his views. Even some of those Homoeousians reconciled with the West had a falling out with Liberius of Rome and some thirty bishops of Asia rejected *homoousios* expressly and returned to the Second Creed of Antioch.

By 369 Valens was at liberty to attend to Church affairs. His first act was to support the election of the unworthy Thracian Demophilus, former jailer of Pope Liberius, to the see of Constantinople vacated by the death of Eudoxius. When eighty ecclesiastics protested to Valens against this election, he had them abandoned aboard a burning ship. Persecution of his opposition then widened. Clerics were presented with the Creed of Rimini-Seleucia-Constantinople; those who failed to adhere to it were threatened with financial exactions, prison, exile, even death. All over the East, the life of the Church was disrupted by the deposition and exile of recalcitrant clergy. To crown the troubles, in 373 Athanasius died after forty-five stormy years as bishop of Alexandria. The Nicenes immediately elected his brother Peter in his place, but the government refused to ratify the election. Instead, an Arian, Lucius, was ordered installed by force. The major church of Alexandria was invaded by the police and a mob from the gutters. Terrible scenes followed. A young man dressed as a woman danced obscenely on the altar; another, naked, sat in Athanasius' episcopal throne preaching filthy homilies. Finally, the imperially appointed Lucius was enthroned in the desecrated Church, attended by the aged Euzoius of Antioch, one of Arius' original disciples fifty years before, now wreaking vengeance on the dead Athanasius. Amid the reign of terror which now fell on the Nicenes of Egypt, with twelve bishops and over 100 priests and monks in exile, Peter fled to the protection of the bishop of Rome as his brother had done thirty years before.

Leadership of the orthodox East now passed from the dead Athanasius to the new metropolitan of Cappadocian Caesarea, Basil. The family into which Basil was born in 329 was deeply Christian. His grandmother had suffered in the persecution of Diocletian; his mother, whose uncle was a bishop, was the daughter of a martyr; his sister Macrina was a noted ascetic; two of his brothers would become bishops — Gregory of Nyssa and Peter of Sebaste. His father, a wealthy and renowned advocate, had him expensively educated in Caesarea, Constantinople and Athens where he met his later colleague, Gregory of Nazianzus. Attracted to the ascetic life by the eccentric bishop Eustathius of Sebaste, Basil traveled widely through the monasteries of the East and lived for a time as a monk in his native Cappadocia. He would later be the author of two influential rules for monks. By 364 he was ordained a priest to become the mainstay of his bishop, whom he succeeded in 370. As bishop he maintained, partly from his own large fortune, a great institution dedicated to works of charity.

In Basil, Athanasius found a worthy successor. When an imperial commissioner threatened him with confiscation of his property or exile if he refused to conform to the decrees of Rimini-Seleucia-Constantinople, he responded with such vigor that the commissioner remarked indignantly: "No one has ever spoken to me in such a manner and with such liberty of speech." Basil answered, "Perhaps you have never met a bishop before." Suffering cruelly from indigestion brought on by the austerity of his life, Basil welcomed torture, he said, as a possible cure for his liver. When Valens himself came to Caesarea he was so impressed by the bishop's dignity at the liturgy and the force of his personality that on leaving he made a contribution to Basil's charities. While not touching Basil personally, the emperor ordered the division of the civil province, thus cutting Basil's ecclesiastical jurisdiction in half. Whereupon Basil determined to increase the number of sees subject to him as metropolitan by installing his brother Gregory as bishop of Nyssa and his friend Gregory of Nazianzus at the remote relay station of Sasima, from which he soon fled to assist his aging father who was bishop of Nazianzus.

An ecclesiastical statesman of first rank, Basil is more important as a theologian who helped bring the thinking of the East more into line with the faith of Nicaea. At long last he insisted upon the distinction between *ousia* and hypostasis. The only acceptable formula, he argued, is one *ousia*, three hypostases. *Ousia* meant for him the existence or essence or substantial entity of God; whereas hypostasis signified the essence in a particular mode, the manner of being of each of the three persons. His choice of analogies is unfortunate, for he said, *ousia* and hypostasis are differentiated as the universal and the particular. "Every one of us," he wrote, "both shares in existence by the common term *ousia* and is such and such by his own properties." Each of the divine hypostases is the *ousia* or essence of the Godhead determined by its appropriate particularizing characteristics: what is proper to the Father is paternity, to the Son sonship, to the Spirit sanctification. Basil insisted that the term *homoiousios* safeguarded the particularities of each divine hypostasis better than the Nicene *homoousios*. Yet for him each hypostasis shares in the single, simple and indivisible concrete divine nature. G. L. Prestige aptly summarizes Basil's position: "The whole unvaried substance, being incomposite, is identical with the whole unvaried being of each person;. . .the individuality is only the manner in which the identical substance is objectively presented in each several Persons." The one Godhead thus exists in three modes of being, three hypostases. "Everything," said Basil, "that the Father is is seen in the Son, and everything that the Son is belongs to the Father. The Son in His entirety abides in the Father, and in return possesses the Father in entirety in Himself.Thus the hypostasis of the Son is, so to speak, the form and presentation by which the

Father is known, and the Father's hypostasis is recognized in the form of the Son."

Yet Basil refrained in his early days as bishop from public statements about the divinity of the Holy Spirit. But after his break with his old mentor, the Pneumatomachian Eustathius of Sebaste, he became more explicit. The Spirit, in Basil's view, must be accorded the same glory, honor and worship as the Father and the Son. He must be reckoned with and not below them, for "the natural goodness and the inherent holiness and the royal dignity are extended from the Father through the Only-Begotten to the Spirit." He never called the Holy Spirit God however, though he said, "we must glorify the Spirit with the Father and the Son because we believe He is not alien to the divine nature."

Basil's younger brother, Gregory of Nyssa, was of even greater depth of mind though far less able an ecclesiastical statesman. As bishop of Nyssa, he was a sore trial to his masterful brother because of his poor diocesan administration, so much so that his alleged mismanagement of funds served as a pretext for his deposition by the Arians in 376. He returned to his see in 378 and would play a prominent part in the Council of Constantinople, returning to the capital in later years to preach at the funerals of members of the imperial family. To explain the Trinity, Gregory used the somewhat misleading analogy of three individuals sharing in one human nature. Yet he added that whereas individual men share in generic human nature, the three divine hypostases share in one concrete, identical divine substance. For God is one; we can never speak of three gods as we speak of three men. "If we observe," he said, "a single activity of Father, Son and Holy Spirit in no respect different in the case of any, we are obliged to infer unity of nature from the unity of activity." While confessing the unity of nature, he insisted that the difference among the hypostases rises out of their mutual relationships. The Father is Cause, the Son is of the Cause directly, the Holy Spirit of the Cause mediately. The Father has no origin;

the Son is generated from the Father; the Holy Spirit proceeds from the Father through the Son. Yet, he wrote, "...when we say that one is caused and that another is without cause, we do not divide the nature by the word cause, but only indicate the fact that the Son does not exist without generation, nor the Father by generation; but we must needs in the first place believe that something exists and then scrutinize the manner of existence of the object of belief: thus the question of existence is one and that of the mode of existence is another." *Ousia*, nature, which is one should not be confounded with hypostasis, the mode of expression of that nature, which is three. Moreover, every operation extending from God to creation has its origin from the Father, proceeds through the Son and is perfected in the Holy Spirit.

Whereas Athanasius first grasped the absolute identity of the substance shared by Father, Son and Holy Spirit, Basil and Gregory laid stress on the distinction within that unity, the former sharply distinguishing the one *ousia* (substance or existence) and the three hypostases (modes of existence) while firmly grasping the idea of the coinherence of the hypostasis one within the other and clearly labeling the properties of the three hypostases Fatherhood, Sonship and Sanctification. The latter explained the relations of distinction within the divine existence and the operations of the Godhead extending from the Father, through the Son and in the Holy Spirit.

While Gregory was content to write quietly at Nyssa, Basil was tireless in his efforts to bring unity to the Church. In Athanasius' last years he wrote to him proposing that they appeal to the bishop of Rome for legates to help clear up the doctrinal disorder in the East. Unfortunately he mentioned communion with the Homoeousian Meletius of Antioch, who had ordained Basil deacon, as a condition for the ultimate solution. Since Athanasius was in communion with Meletius' rival, the Nicene Paulinus, the suggestion was coolly received. Yet when Athanasius received a letter from Damasus of Rome informing him of the death of the Arian bishop of Milan, he sent the messenger on to

Basil as a gesture of good will. Whereupon, Basil sent letters to Rome describing the lamentable conditions in the East. However, the death of Athanasius in 373 and the flight of his brother and successor Peter to Rome complicated negotiations. Like his brother, Peter refused communion with Meletius and turned Damasus' mind against him. Thus Basil's further correspondence with Rome fell on deaf ears. The Emperor Valens' pressure on the Homoeousians left Basil increasingly isolated, and despite his pleadings for support from Rome, Damasus at last formally recognized the Nicene Paulinus as the legitimate bishop of Antioch. Peter of Alexandria, convinced that Meletius of Antioch was an Arian, thus complicated the relations between Damasus of Rome and Basil of Caesarea, though they remained on cordial personal terms.

6. Nicaea Triumphs

Developments beyond the borders of the Roman Empire now contributed to the breakdown of barriers within the Church. The fierce, horse-riding Huns, cousins to the Mongols, dashed out of the Asiatic steppes and fell on the Germanic Goths lined up against Rome's Danubian frontier. In a panic, Fritigern, the Visigothic chieftain, asked permission from the Roman authorities to cross into the Empire for protection. With imperial authorization, his people streamed over the Danube only to be mistreated and mulcted by the Romans. Thereupon the Visigoths revolted. Without waiting for reinforcements from the West, Emperor Valens impetuously led his legions against the Germans. In 378 at Adrianople he died in the field, and his body was lost amid the defeat and carnage of his armies. With an aroused and alien people loose within the Danube line, the northeastern provinces were in greatest disorder. From Milan the Emperor Gratian, successor in the West to his father Valentinian I since 375, sent the Spanish general Theodosius as emperor to the East to restore the situation. During his successful campaign to restore order, Theodosius fell ill at Thessalonika where he was baptized, professing the faith of Nicaea, by the papal vicar Acholius. Once recovered, Theodosius ratified Valens' permission, given as he went into battle with the Goths, for all exiled bishops to return to their sees. With a Nicene emperor in the East, the tide was once again turning. On the eve of the great change in 379, Basil of Caesarea died, worn out though not fifty years of age.

In the West, the faith of Nicaea was already consolidated. In 373, Ambrose, a Christian catechumen and civil governor of the province of Liguria-Emilia, scion of a great senatorial family and son of a pretorian prefect, was elected bishop of Milan. At Milan and in Illyria, last strongholds of Arianism, he led the fight for the Nicene creed. At the Council of Sirmium in 378, Ambrose, supported by the young Emperor Gratian, deposed six Arian bishops. In a series of laws in 379/80, Gratian, under Ambrose's tutelage, proscribed Arianism in the West.

In 377 a Roman Council presided over by Damasus of Rome addressed the growing problems of Apollinarianism and Macedonianism. The Council expressed surprise to find people with a pious understanding of the Trinity erring in matters pertaining to salvation. Some ventured to say, continued the Council, "that our God and Savior Jesus Christ took from the Virgin Mary human nature incomplete, that is, without a mind. Alas, how nearly they approach the Arians with a mind like that! The latter speak of an incomplete divinity in the Son of God; the former falsely affirm an incomplete humanity in the Son of Man. Now if human nature were taken incomplete, then the gift of God is incomplete, and our salvation is incomplete, because human nature has not been saved in its entirety." Further, the Council observed that it was through the mind that the first sin was committed; therefore, the human mind too needs redemption. The Council added: "We, who know that we have been saved whole and entire according to the profession of the Catholic Church, profess that complete God took complete man." With regard to the Holy Spirit, the Council, holding fast to "the inviable faith of Nicaea," affirmed that they "do not separate the Holy Spirit, but together with the Father and Son . . . offer Him a joint worship as complete in everything, in power, honor, majesty and Godhead. . . . "

Meanwhile in the East, the Nicene Peter of Alexandria returned to his see, and the now Nicene Meletius returned to Antioch where he was forced to contend over the bishopric with the Arian Dorotheus, the Apollinarian Vitalis and the old Nicene Paulinus. Despite the schism, at a council held in Antioch, 153 bishops signed an accord with the Bishop of Rome. At Constantinople itself the old Arian Demophilus kept a firm hold on the churches of the city. Gregory of Nazianzus, episcopal colleague of Basil of Caesarea, was sent by the Nicenes to Constantinople to rally support for the faith of Nicaea. Gregory set up a temporary chapel in a private residence which he called the Anastasia, Resurrection, and in such humble quarters he set about the resurrection of the Nicene faith in the imperial capital. In a series of great sermons he explained to his people the orthodox doctrine of the Trinity.

He preached to his growing flock of one sole God, found three in unity, in every respect equal, in every respect one and the same, each distinct in His personal property, each God because of His consubstantiality. There are, he said, three individualities or hypostases or persons, but they are one in respect of substance or Godhead. There is in the Godhead a complete identity of substance among the persons, but they are distinct because each differs in relation to origin. The distinction of the Father is founded on His personal property of being unoriginate; the Son is originate from the Father; the Holy Spirit proceeds or goes forth from the Father in a manner different from that of the Son, but Gregory confessed his inability to explain this difference. He drew an analogy for this from Adam, Eve and Seth (their eldest son): Eve comes from Adam by being fashioned from his rib; Seth comes from Adam and Eve as a product of both. However, he is careful to point out that the analogy is inexact because Father, Son and Holy Spirit all share in an absolutely simple and indivisible substance.

Gregory argued that there has been an order of development in the revelation of the truth about the Trinity: "The Old Testament proclaimed the Father clearly, but the Son more darkly; the New Testament plainly revealed the Son, but only indicated the deity of the Spirit. Now the Holy Spirit lives among us and makes the manifestation of Himself more certain to us; for it was not safe, so long as the divinity of the Father was still unrecognized, to proclaim openly that of the Son; and so long as this was still not accepted, to impose the burden of the Spirit, if so bold a phrase may be allowed." Gregory clearly referred to the Holy Spirit as God. He asked, "Is the Spirit God? Most certainly. Well, then, is He consubstantial? Yes, if He is God." This uncompromising statement of the Nicene faith magnificently presented with great oratorical force, drew the people to Gregory's humble chapel.

But the Arians rioted against him, and once almost killed him at the altar. When Gregory, a timid man, wanted to flee, his people pleaded with him to stay and not to take the Trinity way from them. He had to face other enemies as well. His congregation was joined by a long-haired philosopher, Maximus the Cynic, who so impressed Gregory that he preached a homily praising the man's virtues. Sometime later as the people opened the chapel for the morning's Mass, they surprised a group of Egyptian bishops busily consecrating Maximus bishop of Constantinople. In confusion the bishops retired to finish their work elsewhere, incidentally discovering that Maximus' long locks were as false as the man himself. It turned out that he had been insinuated into Gregory's congregation by Peter of Alexandria, anxious to ensure a sound Nicene and loyal cohort in the see of the capital. Failing to get Emperor Theodosius' approval of his consecration, Maximus fled to Peter at Alexandria. From Rome, Damasus condemned the attempted usurpation. Peter, mightily embarrassed by the whole affair, died soon after to be replaced at Alexandria by Timothy.

In 380 shortly before Peter's death, Theodosius condemned the Arians and enjoined upon the East the faith which "the Apostle Peter had taught in days of old to the Romans, and which was now followed by the pope Damasus and by Peter, bishop of Alexandria, a man of apostolic sanctity." All who failed to adhere to this faith were branded heretics, denied the name Catholic, and had all their assemblies forbidden. The churches of Constantinople were taken from the Arians, and their bishop Demophilus was deposed. Theodosius was himself present at the installation of Gregory Nazianzus, hailed as bishop by the people as the sun triumphantly lit the darkened basilica.

7. Unecumenical Council of Constantinople

With the Nicene faith victorious, Theodosius proceeded to convoke a regional council of eastern bishops to ratify the new order. In May, 381, 150 eastern bishops assembled in the imperial palace at Constantinople, among them, Gregory of Nazianzus, Basil's brothers Gregory of Nyssa and Peter of Sebaste, Meletius of Antioch, and Cyril of Jerusalem. At the emperor's wish, Meletius of Antioch presided. Thirty-six Macedonian or Pneumatomachian bishops attended the early sessions. The Council formally approved Gregory of Nazianzus as bishop of Constantinople. Then tragedy struck; the president Meletius of Antioch died. The bishops adjourned to celebrate his funeral with the emperor himself attending and Gregory of Nyssa preaching. When the Council reassembled, Gregory of Nazianzus was elected president. In statesmanlike fashion he pleaded with the bishops to elect Paulinus of the Old Nicene party to the vacant see of Antioch, finally ending the schism there. But the bishops could not overcome their aversion to Paulinus and agreed to leave the see vacant. It is probable that during Gregory's presidency the Council discussed the doctrine of the Holy Spirit and attempted to conciliate the Macedonian faction on the basis of a creed embodying the faith of Nicaea. In this the bishops failed, and Eleusius of Cyzicus led the thirty-six Macedonian bishops out of the Council.

At this point, Timothy, the new bishop of Alexandria

arrived, shortly followed by Acholius of Thessalonika. Acholius, as papal vicar, had received instructions from Damasus of Rome to put a stop to the translation of bishops from see to see. In accordance with his instructions and seconded by Timothy, Acholius challenged Gregory's legitimacy as bishop because in contravention of the fifteenth canon of Nicaea he had accepted the see of Constantinople though he had originally been ordained bishop of Sasima by Basil of Caesarea. Gregory's supporters pointed out that this canon had long been in abeyance in the East and that Gregory had never formally taken possession of the see at Sasima. Disheartened by all this controversy, Gregory resigned his see and the presidency of the Council. In an emotional sermon, he bade farewell to his people: "Farewell, mighty Christ-loving city.... Farewell, O Trinity, my meditation and my glory. May you be preserved by those who are here...for you are mine even if I have my place assigned elsewhere, and may I learn that You are ever extolled and glorified in word and deed." In his place, Theodosius recommended to the bishops Nectarius, an elderly civil official from the imperial legal department. Though only a catechumen, he was hurried through baptism and ordained a bishop in his baptismal robes, two bishops being assigned to instruct him in his episcopal duties. The new bishop of Constantinople became the third president of the Council and probably saw to the drawing up of the Council's canons and the now lost Tome, an explanation of the doctrine of the Holy Spirit and condemnation of views opposed to it. By July 9, 381, the Council ended its work, and on July 30 Theodosius ruled the orthodox faith was found in agreement with the bishops of Constantinople, Alexandria, Iconium, Antioch in Pisidia, Caesarea, Melitene, Nyssa, Sythia, Tarsus and Marcianopolis. Antioch in Syria was not mentioned because the see was still vacant after the death of Meletius. These bishops were singled out because of their undoubted orthodoxy and not because of the importance of their sees; Nyssa, for example, was only a hamlet.

Since the official acts of the Council are no longer extant, it is difficult to determine exactly what the fathers really did.

The most important missing document is the so-called Tome, a detailed dissertation on orthodox Trinitarian doctrine and condemnation of heretical opinions, said by a council held at Constantinople in 382 to have been issued by the Council of 381. Apparently, this lost Tome was distinct from the Creed and Canons which have come down under the Council's name. Many scholars think that even the so-called Constantinopolitan Creed is not the work of this Council. Their reasons for so thinking are: (1) there is no mention of a Constantinopolitan Creed from 381 to 451, not even by the Council of Constantinople of 382 nor by the Council of Ephesus of 431; (2) the ancient historians of the period seem to indicate only ratification of the Nicene Creed at the Council of 381; (3) Epiphanius of Salamis as early as 374 used a creed almost identical in form with the Constantinopolitan Creed. However, these authors vary on the question of how an older creed came to be connected with the Council of Constantinople. Some say it was a creed presented by Cyril of Jerusalem to clear himself of charges of Arianism and they attempt to reconstruct the creed from Cyril's writings. Others, like the editors of the recent edition of conciliar documents, say it became associated with the Council of Constantinople because it was the creed used at the baptism and consecration of Nectarius.

J. N. D. Kelly, the most recent English authority on creedal statements, does not agree. His argument is long and intricate, but his main conclusion may be summarized as follows. He maintains that silence about the Creed of Constantinople is not so absolute as supposed but that there are hints of it in the writings of Gregory of Nazianzus, Pseudo-Athanasius and Theodore of Mopsuestia. Moreover, until the Council of Chalcedon in 451, the Council was not regarded as ecumenical and, therefore, not of the stature of Nicaea. Some may have downplayed its activities to lessen the prestige of the bishops of Constantinople. As for Epiphanius' use of an identical creed as early as 374, Kelly argues that the creed as it now stands in his writings is a later scribal interpolation for the Nicene Creed which originally stood there. He sees no reason to think that, by the time of the Council, Cyril of Jerusalem had any reason to clear himself of long-buried charges of Arianism. Besides, the Creed of Cyril is a scholarly reconstruction and differs from the Creed of Constantinople.

The present text of the Creed of Constantinople made its first appearance as an official formulary at the second session of the Council of Chalcedon in 451. It was produced from the episcopal archives of Constantinople and read out to the assembly by the archdeacon of Constantinople. It was regarded with initial suspicion by the fathers of Chalcedon, many of whom had never heard of it before. However, it was apparently proved to be authentic to their satisfaction, and they ratified it as such. It was again ratified by the Council of Constantinople III, the sixth ecumenical council in 680. So, concludes Kelly, the text as we now have it in the acts of the Council of Chalcedon is the original and authentic shape of the Creed:

> We believe in one God the Father Almighty, Maker of heaven and earth and of all things visible and invisible; And in one Lord Jesus Christ, the only-begotten Son of God, begotten from the Father before all ages, Light from Light, true God from true God, begotten, not made, of one substance with the Father, through Whom all things were made, Who for us men and for our salvation came down from heaven, and became incarnate from the Holy Spirit and the Virgin Mary, and was made man, And was crucified for us under Pontius Pilate, and suffered, and was buried, And rose the third day according to the Scriptures, And ascended into heaven and sits on the right hand of the Father, And is coming again with glory to judge both living and dead, Whose kingdom shall have no end; And in the Holy Spirit, the Lord and Giver of life, Who proceeds from the Father, Who with the Father and the Son is jointly worshipped and jointly glorified, Who spoke through the prophets; In one holy Catholic and Apostolic Church; We acknowledge one baptism for the remission of sins, We look for the resurrection of the dead, And the life of the world to come, Amen.

At the Council of Chalcedon this Creed was regarded as merely an expansion of the original Nicene Creed. During the Monophysite crisis and down through the Council of Constantinople II in 553, it continued to be so regarded. In the Middle Ages the Creed of Constantinople came to be known simply as the Nicene Creed. F. J. A. Hart and A. Harnack, however, have shown that the two creeds are in fact two entirely different documents. Following the Hart-Harnack thesis, Kelly points out that the Creed of Constantinople obviously omits some phrases of the Nicene Creed: "from the substance of the Father," "God from God," "things in heaven and things on earth" and the anathemas against Arius. There are ten additions to the Constantinopolitan Creed, most of them slight. Only two— "from the Holy Spirit and the Virgin Mary" following "was incarnate," and "sits at the right hand of the Father" after "ascended into heaven" — have doctrinal significance, as will be shown later. Moreover, there are some five changes in word order and sentence construction. Finally, of the some 178 words in the Creed of Constantinople only thirty-three are derived from the Nicene Creed. So, concludes Kelly, the Creed of Constantinople is not just the Nicene Creed with a few additions but a wholly different document.

Yet he admits that the Council very probably did not draw up a completely new creed but used as a framework for its labors a previously existing baptismal creed drawn up in the 370's in Jerusalem or Antioch which embodied the faith of Nicaea. In the minds of the fathers of Constantinople, they were not thereby replacing the old sacrosanct Nicene Creed but rather ratifying the Nicene faith in the shape of the Creed of Constantinople. Kelly conjectures that the Creed, which he labels C, was drawn up under the brief presidency of Gregory of Nazianzus to explain the faith of Nicaea in a conciliatory way to the Macedonian bishops at the instigation of Emperor Theodosius who wanted to heal the schism between them and the orthodox. Says Kelly:

It seems clear that the council's primary object was to restore and promote the Nicene faith in terms which would take account of the further development of doctrine, especially with regard to the Holy Spirit, which had taken place since Nicaea. This it did in its first canon and also, more circumstantially and without any attempt at eirenical compromise (there was no need for that now), in the dogmatic *tomos* which, according to the synodal letter of 382, it published. Nevertheless, at a critical juncture in its proceedings it had adopted C and used it as a negotiating instrument. In consequence C could with some justification claim to be the creed of the 150 fathers, and all the more so as they had promulgated no other.

In large part, then, the Council of Constantinople simply restated the basic tenets of the Nicene faith, but it added new provisions to deal with problems not yet envisioned at Nicaea. It has been suggested that the phrase, "from the Holy Spirit and the Virgin Mary" was added to refute a position of Apollinaris. According to some, comments Kelly, "the Apollinarians were thought to teach that the body born of Mary was consubstantial with the divinity of the Word, that the Word was transformed into flesh, that the Savior had a body in appearance and not by nature, that His divinity itself underwent human experiences, that Jesus did not assume a passible body from the Blessed Virgin but formed one out of His own substance, that His body was co-eternal with His divine nature. . . ." But this was not Apollinaris' view at all but a misunderstanding of his view, for he affirmed the birth of Christ from the Virgin. That this phrase was added to rebut Apollinaris seems to be an opinion that gained currency only in the great Christological discussions leading to the Council of Chalcedon. The phrase, "of His kingdom there shall be no end," was directed against the old enemy of the Anti-Nicenes, Marcellus of Ancyra (d. 374) and his even more radical disciple Photinus who taught that the Word is a transitory projection of an energy of the Father for the purpose of redemption and would be absorbed again into the Father after the final judgment.

The main force of the Creed falls upon the Macedonians or Pneumatomachians who are called in the Council's first canon Semi-Arians. They attempted to find a middle ground for the Holy Spirit between the divine and the creature. Basil of Caesarea's old ascetic mentor Eustathius of Sebaste perhaps best represents their views. "For my part," he said, "I neither choose to name the Holy Spirit God, nor should I presume to call him a creature." The clauses of the Creed dealing with the Holy Spirit are cautious and conciliatory. They do not contain references to *homoousios* as applied to the Holy Spirit, nor do they in so many words call the Holy Spirit God. At the instigation of Emperor Theodosius, the Council wanted to effect a reconciliation with the Macedonians, so softer, biblical phrases were employed. There were besides many orthodox bishops who, in deference to custom, did not yet refer to the Holy Spirit as God in public teaching before their congregations. Sensitive to these parties, the Council declared its faith in the Holy Spirit in phrases drawn from the Bible. In II Cor. 3:17 the Holy Spirit is clearly called "Lord"; in Rom. 8:2 the Spirit is associated with life; in II Cor. 3:6 and Jn 6:63, the Spirit is referred to as "Life-giver." In Jn 15:26 the Fathers found a verb, to "come forth," to express the Spirit's origin from the Father. In II Pet. 1:21 the Spirit is associated with prophetic utterance. The phrase, "together worshipped and glorified" reflects the view of Basil of Caesarea who spoke of "that sound doctrine according to which the Son is confessed as *homoousios* with the Father, and the Holy Spirit is numbered together with them with identical honor." For Basil conglorification and identification of honor were the equivalent of *homoousios* because their applicability to the Holy Spirit was based on the identity of being of Father, Son and Holy Spirit. In softening their language to win over the Macedonians, the bishops were following the example of Athanasius who deliberately exercised restraint in his language about the Spirit and of Basil who, says Kelly, "in particular, practiced a diplomatic caution which was sometimes harshly judged in more uncompromising circles." In the end, all the Council's efforts at reconciliation were in vain, for thirty-six Macedonian bishops led by Eleusius of Cyzicus left the Council and continued in schism. But the Council had clearly attributed to the Holy Spirit (1) a divine title, "Lord," (2) divine functions of giving life which He possesses by nature and of inspiring the prophets, (3) an origin from the Father not by creation but by procession, (4) supreme worship equal to that rendered to Father and to Son.

At the end of its deliberations the Council issued four canons; the fifth and sixth canons sometimes attributed to Constantinople I are in fact from the local Council of Constantinople of 382, and a so-called seventh canon is a still later document describing the practice to be used in receiving converts from heretical sects. The first canon provides that "the faith of the 318 fathers who assembled at Nicaea in Bithynia is not to be made void, but shall continue to be established." The rest of the canon lists the heresies to be anathematized beginning with the Eunomians or Anomeans. Eunomius, later bishop of Cyzicus, and the logician Aetius were the intellectual leaders of those bishops who promulgated the "Blasphemy" of Sirmium of 357; they held that Son and Holy Spirit as creatures are unlike the divine Father. Next condemned were the Arians or Eudoxians. Eudoxius, bishop of Constantinople from 360 to 370, was one of the leaders of the Arian-leaning Homoeans who supported the equivocal formula of Rimini-Seleucia in 359 and Constantinople in 360, affirming weakly that the Son is like the Father. The Semiarians or Pneumatomachians rank next in the anathemas. They, of course, refused to apply the Nicene *homoousios* to the Holy Spirit, yet refused to call the Spirit a mere creature. Heresies of the other extreme, Sabellianism and Marcellians, follow. Sabellius so stressed the unity of God that he denied any distinct subsistence to Son and Holy Spirit, while Marcellus of Ancyra viewed the Word and Spirit as transient projections of the Father who are ultimately drawn back into His being. Condemned too are the Photinians, followers of Photinus, bishop of Sirmium, disciple of Marcellus, but teacher of a more radical Christology, reducing Jesus to a man adopted by the Father as Son. Finally, it is the turn of the Apollinarians, followers of Apollinaris of Laodicea, who affirmed that the Word fulfilled in the sentient flesh of Jesus the function of the rational soul.

In the second canon the fathers renewed Nicaea's instructions that bishops were to confine their activities to their own churches and not leave the boundaries of their own local jurisdictions to ordain or exercise ecclesiastical functions unless invited. Behind the prescriptions of the fathers about the jurisdiction of the bishops of Alexandria and Antioch lies what the orthodox churches of the East will later call the principle of accommodation, that the importance of an episcopal see depends on its prominence in civil matters. The ninth canon of the Council of Antioch of 341 had already specified this principle: "It behooves the bishops in every province to acknowledge the bishop who presides in the metropolis, and who has to take thought for the whole province; because all men of business come together from every quarter to the metropolis. Wherefore, it is decreed that he have precedence in rank...." Thus, according to the bishops at Constantinople, the bishop of Alexandria had precedence in rank in Egypt but he was to confine his attentions to Egypt alone. In the minds of the conciliar fathers there should be no more attempted intrusion of bishops into another's eparchy like that perpetrated by Peter of Alexandria in the case of Maximus the Cynic. The bishop of Antioch was granted precedence in the civil diocese of the Orient.* Bishops of Asia, Pontus and Thrace were warned to confine their activities to their respective regions. Though the Council did not allude to the fact, these regions were looking increasingly to metropolitans of their own: Asia (eastern Asia Minor) to the bishop of Ephesus, Pontus (central Asia Minor) to Caesarea in Cappadocia, Thrace (roughly modern Bulgaria) to Heraclea. The Council also specified that the churches of the barbarians were to be administered according to custom. In practice this meant

*From now on we shall call Orientals those bishops whose sees were located in the diocese of the Orient; Easterners will refer to bishops in the Eastern half of the Empire.

that the Scythians north of the Black Sea depended on Heraclea, the Persians on Antioch, the Abyssinians on Alexandria.

Continuing the principle of accommodation, the fathers proclaimed: "The Bishop of Constantinople shall have primacy of honor after the Bishop of Rome because Constantinople is the new Rome." Nothing was said of Constantinople at the Council of Nicaea because the Emperor Constantine had not yet begun to turn the old Greek town of Byzantium into the great new eastern capital of the Empire. Now this metropolis, only fifty years old, was placed ahead of Alexandria and Antioch, just behind Old Rome. Future bishops of Alexandria would labor to keep the upstart capital in its place to the great detriment of the eastern Church. Though the canon was not directed against Rome, no notice was taken of the claim of its bishop to a primacy among bishops based on his succession from Peter, head of the Apostles. This short canon will be the cause of turmoil in the Church for centuries to come.

In the fourth and final canon, perhaps drawn up under the presidency of Meletius when the see of Constantinople was under discussion, the Council quashed the ordination of Maximus the Cynic as bishop of Constantinople and invalidated all his ordinations and official acts. He was a remarkable man who "by sheer impudence, clever flattery, and adroit management of opportunities, contrived to gain the confidence successively of no less men than Peter of Alexandria, Gregory of Nazianzus and Ambrose [of Milan], and to intrude himself in one of the first sees of the Church, from which he was with difficulty dislodged by the decree of an ecumenical council."

The work of the Council of Constantinople was completed. Theologically, it had carried on the logic of the Council of Nicaea and cautiously applied that Council's reasoning about the Son's relation to the Father to the Holy Spirit, though confining its statement to biblical terminology. Administratively, the Council continued the eastern practice of accommodating the ecclesiastical organization to the civil organization of the Empire, sowing the seeds of discord among the four great sees of East and West by raising the ecclesiastical status of Constantinople to correspond to its civil position as New Rome. All in all, it proved to be a remarkable Council. It was never intended to be an ecumenical Council: the Bishop of Rome was not invited; only 150 Eastern bishops were present; only one by accident from the West. Only at the Council of Chalcedon of 451 did it begin to rank in the East with the Council of Nicaea as more than a local council. Because of the schism at Antioch, its first president, Meletius, was not in communion with Rome and Alexandria. Its second president, Gregory of Nazianzus, was not in western eyes the legitimate bishop of Constantinople. Strong doubts were later expressed about the authenticity of its creed. Its canons were rejected in the West for nine hundred years.

8. Aftermath

After the closure of the Council of Constantinople, Ambrose of Milan in September, 381, presided over a council of thirty-five western bishops at Aquileia. Here Arianism was again condemned and two more Arian bishops deposed. The council complained of the uncanonical ordination of Nectarius as bishop of Constantinople and registered its support for Maximus the Cynic as the legitimate bishop. The council also continued its communion with Paulinus at Antioch and appealed for resolution of the schism there. Only in 382 did Ambrose realize the character of Maximus and withdraw his support of that clever schemer. Despite protests from the West, Flavian was elected bishop at Antioch in 382 and entered into communion with the bishops of the East. But by 388, with the death of the embattled Paulinus, Flavian was recognized by the West, and the lamentable schism at Antioch finally ended.

In 382 Damasus called a council at Rome from which issued a document, later called erroneously the Decretum Gelasianum. The Council declared "...the holy Roman church has been set before the rest by no conciliar decrees, but has obtained the primacy by the voice of our Lord and Savior in the gospel: 'Thou art Peter and upon this rock I will build My Church.' There is added also the society of the most blessed apostle Paul, 'a chosen vessel,' who was crowned on one and the same day, suffering a glorious death, with Peter in the city of Rome, under Caesar Nero; and they alike consecrated the above-named Roman church to Christ the Lord, and set it above all others in the whole world by their presence and venerable triumph." Damasus' response to the eastern principle of accommodation was clear; the Bishop of Rome owed his primacy to succession from Peter and Paul. The hierarchy of sees was based on Peter: Rome is the first see of Peter; Alexandria is the second see because consecrated by Peter's disciple Mark; Antioch is the third see because there Peter lived before going to Rome. Already in 376 the western Emperor Gratian had recognized in civil law the right of the bishop of Rome to hear appeals in the first instance from metropolitans in Gaul and Italy and appeals from defendants who had not received justice from their metropoltans. In 380 Emperor Theodosius had singled out Damasus of Rome and Peter of Alexandria as guardians of orthodoxy. Damasus customarily referred to his see as apostolic, adopted the imperial "we" and began to address his fellow bishops not as brothers but as sons. Clearly East and West differed on the basic principles of ecclesiastical organization.

In the West Pope Felix III, who died in 492, recognized only three ecumenical councils — Nicaea, Ephesus and Chalcedon. Pope Hormisdas (d. 523) finally recognized Constantinople as on a par with the other three, while Pope Gregory I (d. 604) compared the first four general councils with the Four Gospels. Gregory, though not accepting the canons of Constantinople, addressed the notification of his election first to the bishop of Constantinople. It was only at the Second Council of Lyons in 1274 that the canons of Constantinople were accepted in the West.

9. Chronology

335   Condemnation of Athanasius at Tyre.
Return of Arius from exile.

336   First exile of Athanasius.
Death of Arius.

337   Death of Constantine the Great.
Constantine II, Constantius II, Constans
co-emperors.
Julius of Rome (337-352).

340   Constans rules West; Constantius, East.

341   Council of Dedication at Antioch; Antioch
Creed 2 (Eusebian).

343   Councils of Sardica (Nicene) and Philippopolis (Eusebian).

345   Synod of Milan condemned Photinus.
Long-lined Creed presented to West (Eusebian).

350   Death of Constans; Constantius sole emperor.

351   First Council of Sirmium (Eusebian).

352   Liberius succeeded Julius at Rome (352-66).

353   Council of Arles (Eusebian).

355   Council of Milan (Eusebian).
Exile of Ossius and Liberius of Rome.

356   Exile to East of Hilary of Poitiers.

357   Second Council of Sirmium: "The Blasphemy." (Anomean).

358   Council of Ancyra (Homoeousian).
Return of Liberius to Rome.

359   Dated Creed or Fourth Creed of Sirmium
(Homoean).
Council of Rimini-Seleucia (Homoean).

360   Council of Constantinople (Homoean).

361   Julian succeeded Constantius as sole emperor.

362   Conference of Alexandria led by Athanasius.

363   Jovian succeeded Julian as sole emperor.

364   Death of Jovian; Valentinian I emperor in West; Valens in East.

366   Final return of Athanasius from exile.
       Damasus replaced Liberius at Rome (366-384).

370   Basil became bishop of Caesarea in Cappadocia.

373   Ambrose elected bishop of Milan.

375   Death of Valentinian I; accession of Gratian in West.

377   Council of Rome condemned Apollinaris.

378   Battle of Adrianople: death of Valens.

379   Accession of Theodosius the Great in the East.
       Death of Basil of Caesarea.

380   Theodosius outlawed Arians.

381   COUNCIL OF CONSTANTINOPLE I.

382   Council of Rome refused to accept third Canon.

384   Death of Damasus of Rome.

10. Select Bibliography

The history of the period is worked out in great detail by L. Duchesne, *Early History of the Christian Church*, vol. 2 (London, 1912); more generally in H. Leitzmann, *A History of the Early Church*, vols. 3 and 4 (London, 1961). A mine of documentary material with useful notes is J. Stevenson, *Creeds, Councils and Controversies* (London, 1966). The various creedal statements are translated and carefully analyzed in J.N.D. Kelly, *Early Christian Creeds* (London, 1973). The best book in English on the history and variations of Arianism, though now somewhat dated, is H. M. Gwatkin, *Studies of Arianism* (Cambridge, 1900). The most recent study is R.C. Gregg, ed., *Arianism: Historical and Theological Reassessments* (Philadelphia, 1985). One of the few monographs in English on Athanasius is F. L. Cross, *The Study of Athanasius* (Oxford, 1945). The history of Trinitarian doctrine in Athanasius and the Cappadocians is briefly but well treated in J. N. D. Kelly, *Early Christian Doctrines* (New York, 1959); useful too are H. von Campenhausen, *Fathers of the Greek Church* (New York, 1959) and B. Otis, "Cappadocian Thought as a Coherent System," *Dumbarton Oaks Papers*, 12(1958), 95-124. A good treatment of Apollinaris is C. E. Raven, *Apollinarianism: An Essay on the Christology of the Early Church* (Cambridge, 1923). A book full of deep insights into the theologies of Athanasius and Apollinaris is G. L. Prestige, *Fathers and Heretics* (London, 1940). For the story of two other Nicenes, see R. V. Sellars, *Eustathius of Antioch* (Cambridge, 1928) and J. T. Lienhard, "Marcellus of Ancyra in Modern Research," *Theological Studies*, 43 (1982), 486-503. Useful short sketches of the fathers with bibliographies of publications before 1958 are in J. Quasten, *Patrology*, vol. 3 (Utrecht/Antwerp, 1966). For an explanation of the principle of accommodation, see F. Dvornik, *Byzantium and the Roman Primacy* (New York, 1966).

4

The Council of Ephesus, 431

1. The Late Empire

Between the closure of the Council of Constantinople in
381 and the assembly of the Council of Ephesus in 431, the
Roman Empire was a state under siege, a situation which in
the long run would have grave effects on the unity of the
Christian Church. Upon the death of Theodosius the Great
in 395, who proved to be the last sole ruler of the Empire, his
young sons succeeded: Arcadius in the East, Honorius in the
West. Like their father, the new emperors were orthodox
Christians increasingly intolerant of the lingering remains of
paganism. They continued their father's policy of prohibit-
ing pagan sacrifices and suppressing public pagan worship,
even going beyond him to bar all pagans from service at the
imperial court and from military and civil office and to order
destruction of rural temples.

Theirs was a time of crisis, for the vast Germanic folk
migrations disrupted the East and swept from the Empire
large areas of the more sparsely populated and economically
weaker West. In the depths of the winter of 406/7, the Vandals, Alans and Sueves crossed the frozen Rhine near Mainz
in force. For three years they wandered through Gaul before

occupying the Iberian peninsula; Roman administration was precariously confined to the northeastern corner of Spain. The Visigoths who had defeated the Roman emperor and his legions at Adrianople in 378 now ravaged Thrace, Greece, Illyria and northern Italy before putting Rome itself to a three-day sack in 410 under their great chieftain Alaric. A shudder of horror ran through the Empire while in Africa Augustine soon began his masterwork, *The City of God*, to answer the pagan taunts that their gods had never permitted such a disaster to befall the city. Searching for land and food, the Visigoths marched the length of Italy before filtering into southern Gaul to found a kingdom based at Toulouse. The emperor Honorius' own sister Galla Placidia, a captive of the Goths, was married to the new king Ataulf who presented her with part of the spoils of Rome as a wedding present. The Burgundians forced their way across the Rhine and began settlement on the middle Main River and in Savoy. The Alamanni pressed into the Upper Rhine. The Franks, still pagan, began their century long drive south across Gaul from the Lower Rhine. Ephemeral usurpers to the imperial throne rose and fell as Honorius, "pale flower of the women's quarter," cowered behind the swamps of northern Italy at Ravenna. For twenty-three years effective command of the legions was in the hands of the Vandal Stilicho who himself married the emperor's niece and induced the emperor to marry successively two of his daughters. In 423 Honorius was succeeded by the equally inept Valentinian III, son of Galla Placidia, whose general Aetius struggled to defend the dwindling western Empire confined to Italy, central Gaul, northeastern Spain and Africa with an army composed largely of the fierce, horse-riding Huns from out of Central Asia. In 429 the restive Vandals left Spain to cross the strait into Africa where in ten years they founded a kingdom with its capital at Carthage. From the coasts of the Mahgreb they infested the islands of the western Mediterranean, disrupting the commerce of what had been a peaceful Roman lake.

By the time of the Council of Ephesus, throughout much of the West the Germans were raising new kingdoms, replacing the majestic Roman law with primitive barbarian custom, worshipping according to their Arian Christian faith. The old Romanized aristocracy fled the decaying cities to fortified country villas where they were forced to share usually one third of the arable and one half of the woods with their German "guests." Carrying on as best they could Roman customs and culture, they consoled themselves with the fiction that the Germans, given honorific Roman titles, were allies in the military defense of the Empire. Orthodox Christian bishops stayed on in the old Roman cities to become their "defenders" and the mediators between the German conquerors and their Roman subjects.

The eastern arc of the Empire, ruled from the impregnable bastions of Constantinople, held firm against the marauding Goths and the ferocious assaults of the Huns on the Danube frontier. Though here too foreigners stiffened the feeble administration of Arcadius and the legions, they never gained sole command of the military. In 408 Arcadius died "without having ever really lived," to be replaced by his seven-year-old son Theodosius II. Under the influence first of his regent-sister Pulcheria and then of his philosopher-wife Eudoxia, he presided over the erection of a great new circuit of walls around Constantinople and the codification of Roman law that bears his name. It was Theodosius II who like his grandfather Theodosius the Great would call another general council, this time to Ephesus in 431.

2. Ecclesiastical Rivalries

Against this background of a tottering Empire, the bishops of the East became embroiled in bitter rivalries. In 397 Nectarius, who had replaced Gregory of Nazianzus as bishop of Constantinople during the Council itself, died quietly after a peaceful episcopate. Yet his rule began the evolution of the see of Constantinople, granted a primacy of honor over the other eastern sees by the third canon of the Council of 381, into the real primatial see of the East much to the disgust of the other sees of Alexandria and Antioch.

Theophilus of Alexandria intrigued to put one of his supporters into the see now vacated by Nectarius. But the emperor himself had the unsuspecting priest, John of Antioch, known from the seventh century as Chrysostom, the golden tongued, kidnapped to Constantinople and consecrated its new bishop by the unsuccessful Theophilus. Simple in his personal life though devoted to lavish public festivals, John preached eloquently, imposing austerity on his clergy, confining the monks to their monasteries and railing at the vanities of rich Christian women. Factions of all these groups gradually turned against him. At a synod of Asian bishops at Ephesus, John exercised his primacy by reducing six bishops convicted of simony to the lay state, thus stirring up resentment among the bishops of western Asia Minor.

In 401 he received hospitably fifty monks of Egypt led by the four Tall Brothers exiled because of their Origenist sympathies by Theophilus of Alexandria. John cautiously admitted the monks to church services but not to full communion. When the monks appealed to the Empress Eudoxia, she ordered Theophilus to Constantinople to explain his expulsion of the monks. Protesting this indignity, Theophilus came to the capital accompanied by twenty-nine Egyptian bishops and his nephew Cyril. He promptly allied himself with John's enemies. The opposition party was soon joined by the empress, whom John had the imprudence to liken to Jezebel. Money spent in the right places enabled Theophilus to gain the upper hand against the politically inept John. Theophilus gained control of the synod called at the village of the Oak near Chalcedon across the Bosporus and, supported by the emperor, summoned John to judgment for a long list of charges trumped up by his enemies. When John refused to appear before his accusers, he was declared deposed from his see and ordered into exile, all the while demanding a fair trial. When the people of the capital heard of the proceedings, they rioted in John's support, making it prudent for Theophilus and his friends to withdraw from Constantinople. After an earthquake shook the city, the superstitious empress veered around to John's side, and he returned triumphant, telling his people in an allusion to the Book of Genesis: "My Church has remained faithful to me; our modern Pharaoh has desired to take it from me as he of old had taken Sara, but once more Sara has remained pure; the adulterers are put to confusion."

The Pharaoh Theophilus hastily patched up his quarrel with his monks and returned to Alexandria amid the mockery of his people. But at Constantinople John could not hold his golden tongue. When a silver statue of the empress was erected in front of his cathedral amid riotous festivities, he said of Eudoxia, "Again Herodias dances, again she desires to receive John's head on a platter." This of course again exasperated the empress. Since John demanded a new trial in order to be fully exonerated, a group of bishops assembled and trumped up a new charge: John by continuing to exercise his office after being deposed by a synod had violated the canons and had ipso facto incurred permanent deposition. On Holy Saturday, 404, imperial troops drove his congregation from the baptismal font, mingling their blood with the newly blessed water. For the peace of the city, John agreed to exile. As he left Constantinople, a fire broke out in his cathedral, spread to the Senate House and leveled a whole adjacent quarter full of irreplaceable works of art. His enemies quickly fastened the blame on John. A new bishop was elected in his place; his episcopal supporters were hounded from their sees; bishops whom he had deposed returned. Vainly Innocent I of Rome quashed the sentences against John and broke off communion with his persecutors. For three years John was harried from prison to prison until finally on the far side of the mountains of Pontus he died saying, "Glory to God in all things." Alexandria had won its first victory over upstart Constantinople.

By 414 the recently installed bishop of Antioch replaced John's name on the diptychs containing the names of those to be remembered in the liturgy, thus posthumously restoring communion with him. Atticus, bishop of Constantinople, was soon persuaded to do the same. Only Alexandria held out. There Cyril, who had been present at the Synod of the Oak, had succeeded his uncle Theophilus as bishop in

412. To restore John to communion, said the obstinate Cyril, would be like replacing Judas among the Apostles. Nevertheless, he renewed communion with Constantinople and Antioch. Cyril was man of great learning and purity of private life, but, like his uncle, bold and hard. When one of his followers was disciplined by the civil prefect after a riot with the Jews, Cyril encouraged his Christian congregation to disperse and plunder the numerous Jews of Alexandria. A monk fanatically loyal to Cyril was arrested for assaulting the prefect and died under torture. He was promptly canonized by Cyril. Even more notorious was the murder by Christians of Hypatia, uniquely famous among women in those times as a pagan scholar and leader of a Neoplatonist school. It was this new pharaoh, Cyril of Alexandria, a saint of the Church, "not all of whose actions were saintly," who figured largely in the next conflict between Constantinople and Alexandria.

In 425, Atticus, the conciliatory patriarch of Constantinople, died. The clergy, badly divided over his successor, fixed finally on an old and pious priest who died two years after his election. Again the clergy was so divided that the imperial court went outside the city to choose Nestorius, the eloquent and austere superior of a monastery in Antioch. At his installation in 428, he launched an attack on all heretics. Nestorius promised Emperor Theodosius II: "With me, Sire, overthrow the heretics; with you I will overthrow the Persians." Five days later, as Nestorius attempted to evict the Arians from their church, a fire broke out, leveling a large area of the city. Nothing daunted, he began successfully to harry the Quartodecimans who refused to accept the Council of Nicaea's ruling on the calculation of Easter and the Macedonians who denied the Council of Constantinople's doctrine on the Holy Spirit. The morally rigorous Novatians saved themselves only by an appeal to the imperial court. Ironically, however, this hammer of heretics was himself about to be accused of heresy.

3. Theological Controversy

By the end of 428, one of the Antiochene clergy whom Nestorius had brought with him to the capital began to preach against the Theotokos, the title Mother of God as applied to Mary: "Let no one call Mary Theotokos, for Mary was only a human being and it is impossible that God should be born of a human being." The title was, however, an ancient one, to be found in the oldest Greek prayer to Mary, dating from the third century. It had been used by Origen, Athanasius, Eusebius of Caesarea, Cyril of Jerusalem, Gregory of Nazianzus, to mention only a few. Since it was a part of the traditional faith of the church of Constantinople, the common people protested attacks against it. Supporting his priest, Nestorius began to attack the title at every opportunity; he seemed, says one account, scared of the term, as though it were a terrible phantom. Others in the city took up Mary's defense, even interrupting Nestorius' sermons to shout that Mary is the Mother of God. A placard was stuck on the wall of the cathedral accusing Nestorius of following Paul of Samosata by denying that Jesus is God. This accusation was leveled against Nestorius especially by the firebrand layman, Eusebius, later bishop of Dorylaeum. The charge, as we shall see, was unfair. When the monks of Constantinople deeply devoted to Mary protested before the patriarch, they were imprisoned and scourged. Nestorius himself extended the controversy by publishing his sermons far and wide. He even sent them to Celestine, bishop of Rome, but made the bad mistake of asking the pope at the same time what was wrong with the teaching of Julian of Eclanum and Celestius, the two leaders of the Pelagian party who had fled to Constantinople. The bishops of Rome and Africa, especially the great Augustine of Hippo, had been engaged for years in rooting this heresy out of the West. Since his immediate predecessors had cooperated in this effort in the East, Nestorius should have been in a position to know that any leniency toward Pelagianism would arouse a storm of protest from the West. Relations between Celestine of Rome and Nestorius of Constantinople were off to a bad start.

The West too had been recently disturbed by Christological controversy. Liporius, a monk of Trier, had put forward the view that the Divine Word was one person, Jesus the man another. By his virtues Jesus had merited closer and closer union with the Divinity and had ultimately become God. Condemned by the bishops of Gaul and the famous Cassian, abbot of Marseilles, Liporius had taken his difficulties to Aurelius of Carthage and Augustine of Hippo who led him to change his mind, induced him to sign a public retraction and enrolled him among the priests of Hippo. Peace in the West was maintained through open-minded discussion. It was to be different in the East.

Celestine of Rome put Nestorius' letters into the hands of the deacon Leo, the later pope, who sent them on to Cassian of Marseilles who had lived in the East and presumably knew the Greek mind and tongue. Cassian who had already condemned Liporius for his strongly dualist Christology now wrote seven books critical of Nestorius for the Roman authorities. Unfortunately, Cassian was no great theologian. For him, Nestorius was saying that Mary could not be called Theotokos but only Christotokos because Jesus was not fully divine but only a man adopted by the Divine Word. Marius Mercator, a Latin layman living in Constantinople, also kept the pope informed about the situation there. Celestine was forming a very poor impression of Nestorius, an impression complicated by his distance from the scene and his need to rely upon Latin translations of Nestorius' Greek writings.

At Alexandria a more dangerous opponent was following events in the capital — the patriarch Cyril, armed with the aggressive tradition of his see, the wealth of Egypt and the armies of monks who filled its deserts. At Easter of 429 he wrote a letter to the monks of Egypt warning them of Nestorius' errors. The letter immediately found its way to Constantinople as Cyril intended it should. Nestorius promptly preached against Cyril's letter and had one of his clergy draw up a detailed refutation which he sent to Cyril. While this letter was crossing the Mediterranean, Cyril sent his first direct letter to Nestorius. As Prestige remarks, "If all parties had been bent on conciliation, and had, without abating anything of the substance of their own convictions, made a genuine effort to understand one another, the task might well have been accomplished and the Nestorian and Monophysite schisms averted, at least on a serious scale. An Athanasius might have succeeded in consolidating Christian thought and preserving Christian unity. But neither Cyril nor Nestorius was an Athanasius; none of the chief figures combined his strong grasp of truth with his sympathetic penetration of the minds of others and his large-hearted charity; they lacked something essential to that great and exceptional synthesis of character." And so the battle was joined.

Theologically, what was the battle all about? It began, as we have seen, over the title "Mother of God," but support of the title or opposition to it involved differing Christologies. Nestorius represented the Antiochene tradition; Cyril, the Alexandrian. Just as all philosophers are said to be basically either Aristotelian or Platonist, so, roughly speaking, all theologians are in Christology either Antiochene, beginning with the Jesus of the Synoptic Gospels and attempting to explain how this man is also God, or Alexandrian, beginning with the Word of John's Prologue and attempting to understand the implications of the Logos taking flesh. In the last chapter we alluded to the Word-Man Christology of Eustathius of Antioch, deposed in 330 during the Eusebian reaction to the council of Nicaea. His followers at Antioch kept his teaching alive under the leadership of Paulinus, insisting at the Council of Alexandria of 362 against the Apollinarians that the Lord's humanity included an animating principle and a normal human mind.

Related to the Meletian party at Antioch were two other outstanding theologians — Diodorus of Tarsus (d. 394) and Theodore of Mopsuestia (d. 428). Diodorus would later be regarded as heretical, but he was in his own time respected as a pillar of orthodoxy. Against the Apollinarians he had resolutely defended the full divinity and humanity of Christ and had been singled out in Theodosius I's letter ratifying the Council of Constantinople of 381 as an orthodox model for other bishops. In the fragments of his works which remain, Diodorus looks at times to be working in the framework of a Word-Flesh Christology, but the Word-Man framework was apparently his primary model. He distinguished two subjects in Christ's person — God the Word and the man born of Mary, the form of God and the form of a servant. The complete human nature of Christ was the temple in which the Word dwelt. Yet the indwelling of the Word in the man Jesus was different from the indwelling of God in the prophets. In the prophets God dwelt in a transitory fashion, but the Word permanently and completely filled the Son of David with glory and wisdom. Still the conjunction of Word and Man was not of essence but of grace. Grace informed but did not change the nature of the man; it imparted to the Son of Mary power and wisdom but did not change the human subject of attribution. Grace established unity whereby one honor and one worship was addressed to Christ: "the unity of worship," argued Diodorus, "does not imply the blasphemous worship of a man, since the man is worshipped because of his union with the Word. On the other hand, the unity of worship does not imply a union of essence. The human and divine essences remain distinct." Diodorus insisted that we do not say that there are two sons of one Father, but one who is by nature Son of God, God the Word. And we say that one born of Mary is by nature David's son, but by grace the Son of God. By nature there are two; by grace, honor and worship there is one. Diodorus decisively rejected the one nature theory of the Apollinarians. If the Word and His flesh were related to each other as human soul to body such that the Word was in some sense the subject of Christ's human attributes, then the Word would be subject to limitation and change — something unthinkable in relation to God.

More remains of the work of the controversial Theodore of Mopsuestia who against the Arians and Apollinarians stoutly defended the full humanity of Christ. Like Gregory

of Nyssa he insisted that since sin originated in the soul,
Christ must have assumed a human soul in order to redeem
it. Whereas the Apollinarians insisted that the Word fulfilled
the place of the human soul in Jesus as the vital animating
force and rational directive principle, Theodore pointed out
that this theory did away with any sensible weakness, like
hunger, thirst and weariness in the Lord's humanity since the
Godhead would thereby supply any deficiencies in the flesh.
Moreover, he argued, this scheme would allow no room for
Christ's fear and His need for prayer. For Theodore, the
Word took to Himself not just a body but a complete man,
body and soul. The soul of Christ was a real principle of
human life and activity. Theodore took seriously the Lord's
earthly life in which He underwent growth in mind and body
and struggled with temptation. But he seems at times to have
spoken of the Word's adopting an already existent man: "He
who assumed is God and only-begotten Son; he who is
assumed is man." Yet there were not for Theodore two sons.
His favorite description of the relation between the two was
indwelling, the human being a shrine or temple in which
God dwells: "It was our very nature that He assumed,
clothed Himself with and dwelt in...with it He united Himself." The coming together of the Word and man resulted in
a single person or *prosopon*, that is, one individual object of
perception, one subject who could be addressed now as God,
now as man. "When we distinguish the natures," he says, "we
assert the integrity of the nature of God the Word, and the
integrity of its *prosopon*, for a real object (*hypostasis*) without perceptible presentation (*prosopon*) is a contradiction in
terms; we also assert the integrity of the nature of the man,
and its *prosopon* likewise. But when we regard their combination, then we assert a single *prosopon*." He continues, "we
preach that the *prosopon* constituted by both the natures is
single, the manhood receiving through the godhead the
honor rendered by the created world, and the godhead
accomplishing all appropriate action in the manhood."

Theodore could say things that sound close to the Christological formula proclaimed at Chalcedon in 451: "Thus there
results neither any confusion of the natures nor any untena-

ble division of the person; for in our account the natures must remain unconfused, and the person must be recognized as indivisible." And again, "We must display a distinction of natures, but unity of person." Theodore's intent is perfectly clear, but his method, dualistic in approach, would not satisfactorily account for the unity of Christ's person. Kelly pinpoints the defects in Theodore's system. His habitual contrast of Word and Man; God and His shrine; assumer and assumed seem to lay too great a stress on the distinct elements in Christ. Though he insisted on the unity of person, his favorite term for this was conjunction not union. But the greatest difficulty is that the single metaphysical subject in Christ, the "I," was not the person of the Word but the *prosopon*, product of the conjunction of the Word with the man. Cyril would object that Theodore lacked the recognition that in Christ, the Word and the "I" are one subject; the human nature is quite subordinate to this single subject. Theodore put this single "I" as a third element over and above the two natures and resulting from them. Defective in method Theodore's Christology may be, but he emphasized the full mahood of Christ including His soul with its full physical and moral activity. In his view of Christ, the significance of His human acts and spiritual life had a secure place.

Like the other Antiochenes, Nestorius started with diversity to explain Jesus Christ, and then lapsed into difficulty when trying to explain His unity. Against Arius and Apollinaris he attempted to do full justice to the complete humanity of Christ. For Nestorius, to say that Mary is Theotokos smacked either of Arianism, for it seemed to imply that the Son was a mere creature born of a woman, or of Apollinarianism, for it could be understood to mean that the manhood of Jesus was completed by the presence of the Word. Christotokos was for Nestorius a more theologically exact title for Mary, since she bore Christ, a man, who was at the same time a vehicle for divinity. Some, as we have indicated, jumped to the conclusion that Nestorius was an Adoptionist, splitting the God-man into two distinct persons artificially linked together in a moral union by the exercise of mutual good will. Repeatedly he insisted against his detractors that

God the Word and the man in whom He came to be were not numerically two. Rather, Nestorius held that in Christ there are two natures. By nature he meant the concrete character of being. Each of these two natures was a *prosopon*, a term expressing its external aspect as an individual; each was an *hypostasis* or concrete subsistent being. These metaphysical distinctions meant in the end not that each nature was an actually subsistent entity but that each nature was objectively real. These two natures remained unaltered and distinct in the union, the Godhead existing in the man; the man, in the Godhead without mixture or confusion. Divinity and humanity remained objectively real, each retaining its own characteristics and operations. The humanity was not swallowed up in the divinity, for Christ must have lived a genuinely human life if mankind is truly to be redeemed. Yet he said, "Christ is indivisible in His being Christ, but He is twofold in His being God and man. We know not two Christs or two Sons or Only-Begottens or Lords, not one and another Son, not a first and a second Christ, but one and the same, who is perceived in His created and His incarnate natures."

The two natures, then, are not for Nestorius two persons juxtaposed in loose connection but are conjoined in one who combined in Himself two distinct elements, Godhead and manhood, with all the characteristics proper to Word and man, complete and intact, though united. When speaking of the connection between Word and man, Nestorius preferred the term conjunction rather than union in order to avoid any suspicion of confusing or mixing the natures. This conjunction he described as voluntary, by which he meant that the drawing together of natures was not of physical necessity but was brought about by the gracious condescension of the Godhead and the love and obedience of the man. This conjunction resulted in a single *prosopon*, Christ, that is, one object of perception, one external undivided appearance. This is the one *prosopon* of Jesus Christ in whom God is transparent in the manhood and the manhood is glorified in the Godhead. This single *prosopon* resulting from conjunction of natures is one in dignity and honor and worshipped by all creation.

Since each nature is distinct and neither is identical with the *prosopon* of union, human attributes attributed to Christ should be predicated of His human nature, divine attributes of His divinity. But because of the conjunction of natures in Christ, both divine and human attributes can be attributed to the *prosopon* of union. Thus we can say in truth: the Son of God is eternal; the Son of Man died; Christ, though eternal, died. One should not, therefore, say that God was born of the Virgin because this is to attribute a human activity to the divinity. More properly, one should say that Christ, the *prosopon* of union, was born of the Virgin. The Virgin then is more correctly called Christotokos than Theotokos. Since Nestorius shared with all the Fathers the conviction that the divine nature is immutable, the Incarnation could not have involved the Word in change or suffering. The Word could be said to suffer only in the sense that a mortal suffers when his statue is dishonored. Real redemptive life on earth, the suffering, death and resurrection cannot be predicated of the Word Himself but only of Christ, the person resulting from the conjunction of humanity and divinity.

Nestorius' theory is a laudable attempt to preserve intact and complete the two natures, Godhead and manhood, of Christ. To his credit, Christ's humanity remains complete and objectively real. The problem which defeated Nestorius was how to unite these two real natures into a single person, a single metaphysical subject. Nestorius would not recognize the Word as that subject for fear that this would involve the Deity in suffering or imperil the complete reality of the human in Christ. So he had recourse to a third element, the result of the conjunction of natures, the common *prosopon* which could not adequately explain to the satisfaction of the Church the union of the two complete and objectively real natures which he sought so sincerely. "The unorthodoxy of Nestorius," concludes Prestige, "was not a positive fact but a negative impotence; like his master Theodore, he could not bring within the framework of a single, clearly conceived personality the two natures of Christ which he distinguished with so admirable a realism."

As the quarrel heated up, dissident Alexandrian clergy fled the heavy hand of Cyril to Constantinople to stir up troubles for him among the authorities of the capital. When warned that Nestorius might proceed against him, Cyril replied, "Let not this poor creature imagine that I shall allow myself to be tried by him... The roles will be reversed; I shall refuse to recognize his jurisdiction, and I shall know well enough how to compel him to make his own defense." Prophetic words! In February, 430, Cyril wrote his important Second Letter to Nestorius outlining his own position. He strengthened his defenses by writing to Celestine at Rome giving his view of the situation and enclosing a dossier of evidence against Nestorius. With the information he had, Celestine held a synod at Rome in August, 430, which declared Nestorius' teaching unacceptable and ordered him to recant and accept the teaching of Rome, Alexandria and the universal Church within ten days of the receipt of the pope's letter. To carry out this sentence Celestine appointed Cyril, informing him that he was to appropriate the authority of the Roman see and use the bishop of Rome's position so that the papal judgment, or rather, the divine sentence of Christ might be enforced. Clearly, Celestine thought that the bishop of Rome had the authority to excommunicate the bishop of Constantinople, using the bishop of Alexandria as his agent.

Meanwhile, to hedge his bets, Cyril wrote to Emperor Theodosius II, the Empresses Eudoxia and Pulcheria and two imperial princesses. These letters the emperor received coldly, suspecting an attempt to divide the imperial family. Theodosius informed Cyril that he had decided to call a general council, which among other topics would rule on complaints against Cyril himself. Cyril was determined that Nestorius not he would be the defendant. Empowered by the papal commission, Cyril called a synod at Alexandria citing Nestorius and notifying him in a third letter of his deposition unless he recanted. Then Cyril proceeded to exceed Celestine's instruction and appended to his letter a series of Twelve Anathemas which embodied Cyril's theology in a particularly uncompromising fashion which could not fail to horrify the theologians of the Antiochene School. Nestorius was informed that he must accept these Anathemas within ten days of receiving them or face the consequences.

In his Second Letter to Nestorius, Cyril recorded his own teaching as simply continuing the work of the Council of Nicaea. It was the only begotten Son of the Father, true God of true God by whom the Father made all things, who was incarnate, made man, suffered, rose and ascended into heaven. These affirmations must be respected when one considers what is meant when one says that the Word of God was incarnate and made man. "The Word," Cyril said, "having in an ineffable and inconceivable manner personally united to himself flesh animated with living soul, became man and was called Son of Man, yet not of mere will or favor, nor again by simple assumption to himself of a human person, and that while the natures which were brought together into this true unity were diverse there was of both one Christ and Son: not as though the diverseness of the natures were done away with by this union, but rather Godhead and Manhood completed for us one Lord and Christ and Son by their unutterable and unspeakable concurrence into unity."

Inasmuch as the Word, having for us and for our salvation personally united to Himself a human nature, came forth of a woman, He is said to have been born after the flesh. Having been made one with the flesh from the very womb itself, He is said to have submitted to a birth according to the flesh, as appropriating and making His own the birth of His own flesh. We do not say that God the Word suffered in His own divine nature, for the Godhead is impassible. But inasmuch as that which had become His own body suffered, we say that He Himself suffered for us. For the Impassible was in a suffering body. Since His own body by the grace of God, as Paul says, tasted death for every man, once more He Himself is said to have suffered death for us. The resurrection too is His resurrection, for it was His body that was raised. We do not worship man conjointly with the Word; we worship one and the same Lord because the body of the Lord is not alien from the Lord with which body He sits with the Father himself.

If we reject this personal union, continued Cyril, we fall into the error of making two sons. For in that case we must distinguish a man in his own person dignified with the name Son and the Word which is of God in His own person possessing by nature the name Son. Scripture does not say that the Word united himself to the person of man but that He became flesh, that is, He became partaker of flesh and blood like us. So the Virgin is called Theotokos, not as if the nature of the Word or his Godhead had its beginning from the Virgin, but inasmuch as His holy body, endued with a rational soul, was born of her, to which body the Word was personally united.

In his Third Letter to Nestorius, Cyril added that flesh was not converted into the divine nature, nor was the nature of God debased into the nature of flesh. Rather, the Son of God, while visible as a baby, yet filled all creation as God and was seated with the Father. Cyril confessed a personal union of the Word with the flesh not merely with a man who carried God with him. United by a union of natures, the Word brought about an indwelling such as the soul of man has with the body. In the Incarnation a man is not conjoined with God in a unity of dignity and honor; neither conjunction nor juxtaposition is adequate to signify this mode of union. In the Eucharist we receive not ordinary flesh nor the flesh of a man associated with the Word by a unity of dignity or indwelling but the very flesh of the Word Himself. All expressions used in the Gospels must be attributed to the one incarnate person of the Word. We say that the Holy Virgin is Theotokos because she brought forth after the flesh God personally united to the flesh. The Word, coeternal with the Father and Creator of the universe, did not begin to be with the flesh, but, having personally united man's nature to Himself, the Word consented to be born in the flesh from her womb.

To this letter Cyril added twelve propositions to which Nestorius was ordered to subscribe. Mary is Theotokos because she brought forth after the flesh the Word of God. The Word has been personally united to the flesh; the same person is both God and man. The human and divine in the one Christ cannot be divided nor connected merely by common dignity, authority or rule. One cannot attribute the expressions of Scripture now to the man apart from the Word, now exclusively to the Word. Christ is not just man carrying God within him. One cannot say that the Word is God or Master of Christ; rather one must confess Christ to be both God and man alike. Jesus is not just a man actuated by the Word or invested with His glory. Word and man are not worshipped jointly, but are accorded one worship. Jesus exercised His own power when working miracles and not just power received from the Holy Spirit. The Word Himself became our high priest, not the man separate from Him. The flesh of the Lord is life-giving, for it is the flesh of the Word of God. The Word suffered, was crucified, tasted death and rose in the flesh.

For Cyril, loyal to the statement of the Nicene Creed, the Word who existed before the Incarnation was the same person after the Incarnation but now embodied, enfleshed. The Incarnate was the eternal Word in a new state. Unity was presupposed from the very beginning. There was not first an ordinary man on whom the Word descended; rather the Word was made one with animated flesh in Mary's womb. The Word appropriated to Himself the birth of His own flesh; thus Mary is rightly called Theotokos. This union of Word and flesh was real and described by Cyril as a natural or hypostatic union. That is, explains Prestige, a "concurrence of the divine and human forms in one person, so that whether as God or as man or as both Christ constituted a single objective reality (*hypostasis*); just as by his phrase 'physical union' [Cyril] indicated a personal unity in whch the two elements expressed different embodiments of a single '*physis*' or personal existence." Yet there was no confusion or mingling of the divine and the human, for humanity and divinity are different in essence. Union excludes division but does not eliminate difference. Difference, however, involves no separation and can be apprehended only by intellectual analysis. "The deity," comments Prestige, "has its personality and the manhood its personality, but the two personalities are identically one and the same. . . . The reason why the two are identical is because the human personality is simply that of the divine subject under submission to physical conditions." In this union there is no mechanical necessity; it involves a continuous act of the divine will, a condescension of the loving kindness of God.

Thus the Word became flesh to make the human scale His own. The Jesus of history was God Himself living, suffering, dying and rising according to the flesh. Said Cyril: "He makes His own all that belongs, as to His own body, so to the soul, for He had to be shown to be like us through every circumstance both physical and mental, and we consist of rational soul and body: and as there are times when in the Incarnation He permitted His own flesh to experience its own affections, so again He permitted the soul to experience its proper affections, and He observed the scale of the emptying in every respect." So God learned through personal condescension what it is to be a man. Knowing all as God, Christ subjected Himself to the scale of ignorant manhood to make even ignorance His own. "Christ's human life," says Prestige, "was a real addition to His eternal life, yet an addition characterized rather by a new mode of action than a fresh content: what was always within His range as God He now experienced over again as man." The Impassble was in a suffering body, and since His flesh tasted death, the Word is said to have suffered for us. But the Word did not suffer in His impassible nature but as incarnate in respect of His human nature. Suffering and ignorance thus became the actual experience of God in human embodiment. All expressions found in the Scriptures are predicated of the Word, for the Word is the single metaphysical subject, the single 'I' in Jesus Christ. Further, in the Eucharist we partake not of ordinary flesh nor that of a man sanctified in whom God dwells but of the life-giving flesh of the Word Himself.

Still Cyril rejected the formula "in two natures," for this, he thought, involved separation. Nature was for him the equivalent of *hypostasis*, a concrete, objective existence. He preferred to talk of two natural properties or qualities. The nature of the Word, the concrete personality of the Word, is God the Word Himself, the personal subject of all His actions and experiences. Cyril made his own the Apollinarian formula — one incarnate nature of the divine Word —found in pseudepigraphical books, thinking that it came from Athanasius. He insisted that this is the correct formulation, though once he realized that talk of two natures did not always involve separation, he was willing to compromise.

In December of 430, the Alexandrian citation commissioned by Celestine of Rome was duly delivered to Nestorius. However, in November the emperor, not regarding the papal condemnation as definitive, had already convoked a general council to Ephesus on Pentecost Sunday, June 7, 431. Like his predecessors, Theodosius claimed the right to intervene in ecclesiastical affairs because in his mind the Empire depended on the true worship of God. No one in East or West questioned the emperor's decision to call a council. In the interval before the council, John of Antioch, an old friend of Nestorius, wrote to him counseling moderation and acceptance of the term Theotokos. Nestorius answered by accepting the term, leaving to the coming council the task of explaining its exact meaning. John wrote as well to the respected theologians Theodoret of Cyrus and Andrew of Samosata, requesting from them a formal refutation of Cyril's Twelve Anathemas. Acacius of Beroea (Aleppo in Syria), who had been one of Theophilus of Alexandria's most vigorous supporters against John Chrysostom but who at one hundred years was now the revered dean of eastern bishops, reproached Cyril for his unseemly attacks on Nestorius. In the minds of many, it was Cyril who was to be called to account before the council.

4. *The Divided Council*

Cyril was prepared. Although the imperial summons specified only a small number of bishops from each eparchy, Cyril gathered fifty of his bishops, a group of lesser clergy and a band of monks led by the famous Schenoudi, a great destroyer of pagan shrines, so fanatical that he once killed a monk while disciplining him. All these arrived at Ephesus a few days before Pentecost to find Nestorius already there with sixteen bishops, attendant clergy and a large armed bodyguard. Memnon of Ephesus had assembled twelve bishops from Pamphylia and fifty from the province of Asia, many opposed to Nestorius because of his attempts to enforce the jurisdiction of the See of Constantinople over them. Memnon closed the churches of Ephesus to Nestorius and his supporters. By June 12 Juvenal of Jerusalem arrived with fifteen Palestinian bishops and immediately attached his party to Cyril. While awaiting the arrival of other bishops and the papal legates, Cyril and Nestorius harangued their followers but refused to communicate with each other. Count Candidian, the commander of the imperial guard, was on hand to keep order, but his instructions forbade him to interfere with the debates of the bishops. Flavian of Philippi with a delegation from Macedonia finally arrived. But no bishops from farther West, apart from the papal legates, attended, though invited. Augustine of Hippo had died in the preceding August before his summons arrived, and the metropolitan of Carthage sent notice that the Vandal invasion had so disrupted Africa that none of his bishops could be expected; he was ultimately represented by a deacon. The Patriarch John of Antioch sent a message saying that he and his contingent were encountering difficulties but would arrive shortly.

Cyril would not wait. Armed with his commission from Pope Celestine, he announced on June 21 that he was calling the council into session on the following day. Immediately, sixty-eight bishops, among whom twenty-one were metropolitans, protested his action. Count Candidian vigorously supported the protesters. But on Monday, June 22, 431, Cyril opened the Council of Ephesus in the church called Mary with about 160 bishops in attendance. Candidian and some of Nestorius' supporters lodged a second protest, but they were firmly shown the door. The council was in session.

Nestorius was asked a second time to attend, then a third.

Like Chrysostom before him, he refused to face a court in which his accuser was his judge. The debates proceeded without him. They also proceeded without regard for the previous papal condemnation of Nestorius. Juvenal of Jerusalem moved that the faith of Nicaea be proclaimed, and the priest Peter of Alexandria, chief of the notaries, read out the Creed of the 318 Fathers. This was followed by a reading of Cyril's Second Letter to Nestorius. Cyril himself then rose and asked the fathers to declare his letter orthodox in conformity with the Nicene Creed. With Juvenal leading the chorus, all declared that this was their faith. Then Nestorius' reply to Cyril was read. The bishops voted that the doctrine of Nestorius was blasphemous and opposed to the faith of Nicaea. These two votes comprised the essential dogmatic statement of the Council — Cyril's Second Letter was declared to be in conformity with the Creed of Nicaea; Nestorius' reply not. Only later did the notary Peter read out Celestine's letter to Cyril and Cyril's Third Letter to Nestorius containing the Twelve Anathemas. These, however, were not voted upon but only included in the final acts of the Council.

The bishops of Melitene and Ancyra then reported a conversation they had had with Nestorius in the days preceding the opening of the Council. He had blasphemed, they charged, by saying that he could not call God a baby suckled by the Virgin nor believe in a God two or three months old. Nestorius, of course, was simply following his own rules for predication that human qualities could only be attributed to the manhood of Christ or to the *prosopon* of union but not to the Godhead. Next a dossier of patristic texts and extracts of Nestorius' writings made by Cyril were read through and ordered included in the official acts. At last, the Council proceeded to pass sentence on Nestorius. Constrained by the canons and the letter of Celestine, the bishops said, "Our Lord Jesus Christ, whom he has blasphemed, decrees through the Holy Synod here present that Nestorius is excluded from the episcopal dignity and every priestly assembly." In the end, 197 bishops signed the document. Nestorius was notified of their actions in the harshest terms:

"To Nestorius, new Judas. Know that by reason of your impious preachings and of your disobedience to the canons, on the twenty-second of this month of June, in conformity with the rules of the Church, you have been deposed by the Holy Synod, and that you now no longer have any rank in the Church." Well might Nestorius protest: "I was summoned by Cyril who assembled the Council, by Cyril who presided. Who was judge? Cyril. Who was accuser? Cyril. Who was bishop of Rome? Cyril. Cyril was everything." As the bishops came from the church called Mary after a long day's work, the people of Ephesus cheered them and led them to their lodgings in a torchlit procession. For the common people, Christ had defeated heresy ; Mary, Mother of God, had triumphed over Nestorius.

Victorious, Cyril sent off a report of the proceedings to Emperor Theodosius. Nestorius and ten of his supporters fired off a vigorous denunciation of the whole affair. Count Candidian declared all decisions null and void and appealed to the emperor for further instructions. While waiting for imperial approval, Cyril and his friends preached in the churches to the people of Ephesus. Then on June 26, John, Patriarch of Antioch, and the bishops of the Orient arrived. As they approached the city, they had been informed of the situation. With the dust of the road still on them, they indignantly convoked their own council in John's hotel and received an official report from Count Candidian. Ignoring the previous papal and conciliar action, forty-three bishops signed a creed drawn up by John of Antioch and excommunicated Cyril, Memnon of Ephesus and their adherents. These documents too were hurried off to the emperor in Constantinople. On June 29, an imperial rescript arrived annulling the action of Cyril's Council, forbidding any bishop to leave Ephesus and announcing the dispatch of a high court functionary to restore order. While the Council stood in abeyance in the increasing heat of the summer, John of Antioch tried to consecrate a new bishop of Ephesus in the Basilica of John the Evangelist, but was driven out.

By early July, the papal legates — two Italian bishops and the priest Philip — arrived with instructions not to enter into the debates but to act as judges and to defer in all things to Cyril. On July 10, Cyril's Council assembled in its second session in Memnon's episcopal residence and accepted the credentials of the legates and a letter from Pope Celestine. On the next day in a third session the proceedings of Cyril's Council were read to the legates. They approved what had been done and subscribed to the deposition of Nestorius. The priest Philip told the bishops: "There is no doubt, and in fact it has been known in all ages, that the holy and most blessed Peter, prince and head of the Apostles, pillar of the faith, and foundation of the Catholic Church, received the keys of the kingdom from our Lord Jesus Christ, the Savior and Redeemer of the human race, and that to him was given the power of loosing and binding sins: who down even to to-day and forever both lives and judges in his successors. The holy and most blessed pope Celestine, according to due order, is his successor and holds his place, and us he sent to supply his place in this holy synod, which the most humane and Christian Emperors have commanded to assemble, bearing in mind and continually watching over the Catholic faith. For they both have kept and are now keeping intact the apostolic doctrine handed down to them from their most pious and humane grandfathers and fathers of holy memory down to the present time." The bishops accepted the legates' subscription to the acts as expressing the adherence of the West to the Council's decisions and began to refer to their assembly as ecumenical.

In the fourth and fifth sessions of the Council held under Cyril with the papal legates present, the proceedings of John of Antioch's council were solemnly set aside. Though cited, John refused to appear before the Council, but he was not deposed, only forbidden to aid or harm others. At two further sessions it was determined that the Creed of the Council of Nicaea must be used in preference to all others and that the Church of Cyprus be allowed to leave the jurisdiction of the Bishop of Antioch. The Council also issued six canons dealing with problems associated with Nestorius. Metropolitans who joined the party of John of Antioch, supported Nestorius or adopted the theology of Celestius the

Pelagian were to be excommunicated and made liable to degradation from episcopal rank. Provincial bishops joining John of Antioch were to be degraded from priestly rank. Clergy, deposed by Nestorius and his adherents were allowed to resume their rank, and clergy were warned not to submit to bishops who did not adhere to the Council. Clergy holding with Nestorius or Celestius publicly or privately were to be deposed. Any attempt on the part of Nestorius and his supporters to restore deposed clergy was declared invalid. Clergy who unsettled the decisions of the Council were to be deposed; laymen, excommunicated. This business occupied the month of July.

Only in the early days of August did the imperial commissioner, Count John, minister of finance, finally arrive. Evidence of the emperor's confusion was that Count John bore letters for Celestine of Rome and Ruffinus of Thessalonika who were not in attendance and for Augustine of Hippo who had been dead for a year. Making no distinction between the councils of Cyril and of John, the commissioner confirmed the deposition of Nestorius, Cyril and Memnon of Ephesus, and called all factions together for discussion. All attempts at resolving the impasse came to nothing, so Count John put the three deposed bishops under house arrest. Then as bewildered as his predecessor, he appealed to the emperor for further instructions. All parties acknowledged the need of imperial confirmation validating their decisions. Nestorius dispatched one of his staunch followers, Count Irenaeus, a highly placed government official who had accompanied him to Ephesus in a private capacity, to the imperial court to lobby for his party. Cyril's personal physician approached important members of the imperial entourage and outdid his rival with liberal gifts from the patriarchical treasury — cloth, tapestries, ivory furniture, ostriches and a million in hard cash. Not unnaturally the court began to veer around to Cyril's way of thinking. More spectacularly, at the receipt of a letter smuggled out to him by Cyril, Dalmatius, a monk who had not left his cell for forty-six years, set out to approach the emperor personally on Cyril's behalf. Throngs of excited monks, among whom was the soon to be notorious Eutyches, joined him in the interview with Theodosius. After a hearing, the emperor simply dismissed them with a request for prayers.

The emperor then decided to convene a conference of eight delegates from each faction so that he could form his own opinion of the matter. Even before this meeting the matter of Theotokos, at least, had been settled. The bishops of the Orient had signified their acceptance of the term to Count John, and Nestorius too repeated in a creed drawn up for the purpose his acceptance of the term provided it was properly understood. He added that he would be willing to resign his see and return to his monastery if only orthodoxy could be restored. Somewhat to his dismay, he was taken at his word, and in September he was returned under guard to Antioch. Then the two delegations set out for Chalcedon across the Bosporus from Constantinople to meet with the emperor. In the party representing Cyril were two of the papal legates, who made no protest at his appeal to the emperor, and the chief theologian of the party, Acacius of Melitene. The Nestorian delegation was led by John of Antioch and included the noted theologian Theodoret of Cyrus. At Chalcedon the Nestorian party had to endure the enmity of the bishop who closed his churches to them and demonstrations by the local monks. The disputations, largely between Acacius and Theodoret, centered on the question of Cyril's Twelve Anathemas. Despite their efforts, the Nestorians failed to secure their condemnation. Finally, the emperor broke off the discussions and invited the Cyrillian party with the papal legates to the consecration of Nestorius' successor as patriarch of Constantinople, Maximian, who was well known at Rome. Not knowing how to wring a unified decision from the divided Council, Theodosius simply ordered it dissolved and the bishops dispersed, except for Cyril and Memnon who were to be held under arrest at Ephesus.

By this time Cyril had already fled back to Alexandria, and to save face, the court issued another rescript allowing him to stay at Alexandria and Memnon at Ephesus. Nothing further was said of their deposition. Cyril had come home to a people unimpressed by his intrigues. One of his bishops, Isidore of Pelusium told him quite frankly: "Favor obscures the view, but hatred blinds completely.... A number of those who have been at Ephesus represent you as a man burning to avenge an injury of his own, not to seek in orthodoxy the glory of Jesus Christ. He is, they say, a nephew of Theophilus.... The fury of the uncle was unleashed against John, the friend of God; the other too, though the cases are very different, has sought for a success about which he can boast." Still Nestorius had been deposed; once more Alexandria had triumphed over Constantinople.

Celestine of Rome was informed of the Cyrillian Council's decisions, but there is no record that the Council asked formal confirmation of its work from Celestine, nor did Sixtus III, his successor, ever formally confirm the Council. The very presence of the papal legates signified papal adherence and made the Council ecumenical in the minds of its participants. Full recognition of Cyril's Council as what we would today call ecumenical and acceptance of its doctrinal declarations came when the Council of Chalcedon in 451 reconfirmed the Creed of Nicaea and Cyril's Second Letter to Nestorius as the valid interpretation of its meaning. Cyril's Third Letter with its Anathemas was not, however, accepted even at Chalcedon.

5. *The Formula of Union*

With Maximian enthroned at Constantinople in the place of the expelled Nestorius, Cyril at home in Alexandria and Memnon recognized at Ephesus, the clouds of controversy seemed to be clearing. But the doctrinal question still loomed ominously. The quarrel now centered on Cyril's Twelve Anathemas which his opponents wanted withdrawn or condemned. At the urging of the aged dean of the Eastern episcopate, Acacius of Beroea who corresponded with each side, Cyril had sense enough to compromise. The Emperor Theodosius, intent on drastic measures, sent a tribune to

Antioch and Alexandria to order both bishops to a conference with him, but the bishops of the Orient assured him of their adherence to the faith of Nicaea and their refusal to add to it. Cyril responded to their declaration by asking his opponents to end the quarrel by agreeing to subscribe to the deposition of Nestorius and condemn his teaching. In a friendly fashion he assured them that he too wanted only orthodoxy and peace. Acacius to whom this letter was addressed wrote to Theodoret of Cyrus and Alexander of Hieropolis asking them to extend the hand of friendship to Cyril and to persuade John of Antioch to do likewise. Alexander haughtily refused, insisting that Cyril was Apollinarian and that Nestorius was no heretic. Theodoret acknowledged improvement in Cyril's attitude but refused to accept his doctrine or condemn Nestorius. His colleague, Andrew of Samosata, however, was more conciliatory and recommended mutual concessions. John of Antioch too wrote directly to Cyril and proposed a peaceful resolution to their difficulties. At Constantinople, the newly installed Maximian, not fully abreast of the situation, naively demanded to know why Cyril could not simply withdraw his anathemas and be done with it. Cyril again resorted to presents on a lavish scale to the imperial court and professed himself not fully satisfied with John of Antioch's letter. Fortunately, negotiations did not break down. John decided to accept the condemnation of Nestorius, for the moment leaving aside the question of the Twelve Anathemas. He sent Cyril the profession of faith that he and his supporters had drawn up during their council at Ephesus for Count John and the emperor in August, 431. It ran as follows:

> We confess, therefore, our Lord Jesus Christ, the only-begotten Son of God, perfect God and perfect Man, consisting of a rational soul and a body begotten of the Father before the ages as touching his Godhead, the same, in the last days, for us and for our salvation, born of the Virgin Mary, as touching his Manhood; the same of one substance with the Father as touching his Godhead, and of one substance with us as touching his Manhood. For of two natures a

union has been made. For this cause we confess one Christ, one Son, one Lord.

In accordance with this sense of the unconfused union, we confess the holy Virgin to be *Theotokos*, because God the Word became incarnate and was made man, and from the very conception united to himself the temple taken from her. And as to the expressions concerning the Lord in the Gospels and Epistles, we are aware that theologians understand some as common, as relating to one Person, and others they distinguish, as relating to two natures, explaining those that befit the divine nature according to the Godhead of Christ, and those of a humble sort according to his Manhood.

To this Cyril responded with a letter beginning: "Let the heavens rejoice and the earth be glad, for the wall of division is broken down." In it he accepted John's creed not as supplying some deficiency in the Creed of Nicaea but as fulfilling its meaning. Cyril argued that the solution to the whole controversy should be based on the affirmation that Mary is truly Theotokos because the Body of Christ did not come from heaven but from Mary. Mary bore Emmanuel, God with us, according to the flesh. The Lord Jesus Christ, perfect in Godhead, perfect in manhood, must be recognized as one person since different natures have been formed into an ineffable union. Yet there was no mixture nor confusion nor blending of God with the flesh. The divine nature of the Word was not susceptible of change; it remained always impassible. But the Savior of the world appropriated to Himself the sufferings of His own flesh. All parties must abide by the faith of Nicaea, for it was not the bishops who spoke but the Holy Spirit. Cyril did not insist on the acceptance of his Twelve Anathemas against Nestorius and he showed himself willing to accept a great deal of the opposition's theory. He made no objection to saying that the Word dwelt in the man as in a "temple" and that "of two natures a union has been made." He further allowed attributions of Scriptural expressions now to the divine, now to the manhood and commonly to the Person of Christ. Only after the two patriarchs had agreed to the Act of Union were Emperor Theodosius II and Pope Sixtus III, Celestine's successor, informed of the compromise.

Yet there were troubles still. Acacius of Melitene and some other bishops thought that Cyril had given up too much. At Antioch some who harbored Apollinarian views accused John of Nestorianism and one of his deacons refused communion with him. Theodoret of Cyrus and other Oriental bishops were horrified at John's surrender to Cyril who had not expressly withdrawn his Twelve Anathemas. The bishops of Tyana and Tarsus wrote directly to Pope Sixtus III begging that he do justice to the deposed Nestorius, a sign that in extreme urgency the Eastern Church looked to Rome for aid. There is no evidence of Sixtus' reply, but the pope who built the great basilica of St. Mary Major in Rome would not very likely be one to disparage the Virgin's prerogatives. With both John and Cyril troubled by rebellion in the ranks of their supporters, Maximian of Constantinople died and was replaced by Proclus, bishop of Cyzicus, who had twice been a candidate for the post. Meanwhile, the emperor began to pressure Theodoret of Cyrus to embrace the Act of Union. He was deluged with imperial letters and threats, petitions from his own people and even the intervention of the ascetic Simon Stylites from the top of the sixty foot pillar where he spent thirty-eight years. Finally, Theodoret relented and signed the Act. He wrote cordially to Cyril but refused to condemn Nestorius outright. With that most of the resistance collapsed. In the end, fifteen recalcitrant bishops favoring Nestorius were deposed, and Alexander of Hieropolis was condemned to the metal mines of Egypt, intransigent to the end. During this time Nestorius himself was sent from Antioch to Petra in the Arabian desert and then to the Great Oasis in Egypt. Though cut off from the theological world, he defended his position in a huge work published under a pseudonym — Tome of Heracleides. His supporters were forbidden to read or transcribe his books which were to be searched out and burnt.

6. *Grounds for a New Quarrel*

While the Nestorian controversy raged, the church in
Armenia was undergoing an intellectual renaissance under
its head the Catholicos Sahag and its principal theologian
Mesrub. Classics of the Greek and Syriac Fathers were being
translated into Armenian among them the works of the
Antiochene Theodore of Mopsuestia, the intellectual father
of Nestorius' doctrine. Some Apollinarists seeking refuge in
Armenia wrote against the Antiochenes. The staunch Cyrillians Acacius of Melitene and Rabulla of Edessa cautioned
the Armenians about accepting the teaching of a man connected with the heretic Nestorius. An Armenian synod
decided to send two priests to Constantinople to find out
where the truth lay. The new patriarch Proclus was clear-
headed in his views and had supported the term Theotokos
in a sermon preached before Nestorius himself years before.
In 437 he wrote a tome to the Armenian Church in which he
pointed out that "one and the same is with the Virgin and of
the Virgin." Even more clearly he anticipated the doctrine of
Chalcedon by affirming: "There is only one Son, for the
natures are not divided into two hypostases, rather the awe-
some economy of salvation has united the two natures into
one hypostasis." At last Proclus had distinguished between
nature and hypostasis, something that Cyril did not do, thereby mightily confusing the Christology of the period. Proclus was not content to send his letter only to the Armenians,
but decided to circulate it among the bishops of the Orient
asking for their signatures and express condemnation of passages taken from Theodore of Mopsuestia's writings and
appended to the letter. The Oriental bishops were thunderstruck; the affair of Nestorius was settled. John of Antioch
wrote on behalf of the bishops of the Orient that they had
condemned Nestorius and accepted the faith of Nicaea, but
that they would not condemn a man long dead. The emperor
himself ruled that it was a mistake to condemn posthumously a man who had died in full communion with the
Church. John wrote also to Cyril asking him to stop this
agitation. Loyal to the Act of Union, Cyril wrote to Proclus

asking him to withdraw his request to the bishops of the Orient. Proclus complied, and the issue was dropped for the moment.

Shortly afterward, however, Ibas succeeded to the see of Edessa left vacant by the death of Rabulla, a stout Cyrillian. While a professor at the catechetical school of Edessa, Ibas had translated the works of Diodorus of Tarsus into Syriac and was a warm admirer of Theodore of Mopsuestia. He expressed that admiration in a letter to Maris, a Persian living in Seleucia. The letter would later become notorious and grounds for a new quarrel. But the patriarchs of Constantinople, Alexandria and Antioch seconded by Emperor Theodosius calmed the rising spirits, and there was peace in the East from 438 to 446.

The patriarch Proclus used the time well to expand the jurisdiction of the see of Constantinople. In 437 Proclus had accepted a delegation from Illyricum which had hitherto applied to Rome for resolution of disputes and whose metropolitan at Thessalonika acted as vicar in the area for the bishop of Rome. Pope Sixtus III remonstrated with Proclus, but delegations continued to go to Constantinople from Illyricum. Proclus also continued to extend his jurisdiction into western Asia Minor at the expense of the metropolitan of Ephesus. Trouble would follow in the wake of a resurgent Constantinople. In 438 Proclus had the body of John Chrysostom triumphantly returned to the capital and buried in the basilica of the Apostles among his fellow bishops. Emperor Theodosius humbly kissed the casket of the man so unjustly exiled by his parents Arcadius and Eudoxia.

Gradually the principals of the Council of Ephesus passed from the scene. Pope Celestine had died the year after the Council to be succeeded by Sixtus III, and in 440 by Leo, the archdeacon of the Roman Church. John of Antioch died in 441/2 to be replaced by his nephew Domnus, an eager disciple of Theodoret of Cyrus. Cyril of Alexandria died in 444. A letter circulated under the name of Theodoret of Cyrus expressed the sentiments of the bishops of the Orient: "Tell the guild of undertakers to lay a heavy stone upon his grave, for fear he should come back again and show his changeable mind once more. Let him take his doctrine to the shades below." Cyril was replaced by his archdeacon Dioscurus who had been with him at Ephesus. The new patriarch broke sixty years of rule at Alexandria by Cyril's family. He promptly deposed Cyril's nephew from the priesthood and forced the family to disgorge its wealth. Supporters of Cyril were cleared out of the patriarchal administration, but even Dioscurus preserved Cyril's teaching. Theodoret of Cyrus lived on, an able and zealous administrator of the 800 parishes in his huge diocese, an admired preacher and counselor at Antioch, and an author of an excellent history of the Church. Irenaeus, the imperial count who was one of Nestorius' major supporters at Ephesus, was consecrated bishop of Tyre in Palestine, though he had been married twice. Nestorius too lived on in the depths of the Egyptian desert, derided by the fanatical Cyrillian monks and prisoner for a time of invading Bedouin tribes. Before his death, he would acclaim the work of the Council of Chalcedon as expressing his deepest beliefs.

Neostorianism itself had a long future ahead of it. Unlike the long-vanished Arians who dissented from the Council of Nicaea and the Macedonians and Apollinarians who opposed the Council of Constantinople, Nestorians still live on. After the Council Ibas continued to propagate Nestorius' view at Edessa. As the Monophysites, the more radical followers of Cyril, began to win over Syria, the Nestorians gradually moved into Persia and established a center at Nisibis. The shah of Persia encouraged their teaching among the Christians of Persia as a bar against imperial Roman interference in his land, and the Persian Church officially accepted Nestorianism in 486. In 489 Emperor Zeno expelled the Nestorians from their stronghold at Edessa. A bishopric was established in Persian Seleucia, today a part of Iraq and in 498, the bishop of Seleucia was proclaimed Catholicos of eastern Nestorians. As Babai the Great (569-628) systematized Nestorianism for his church, Nestorian missionaries were active in Arabia, on the Malabar coast of India and even in Turkestan on the borders of China. In 1625 there was discovered in northwest China the so-called Sigan-Fu stone set up in

781 which in Chinese describes the arrival of Nestorian missionaries in 635. The Church survived the Muslim Conquest, but the Catholicos was transferred to Baghdad. During the Mongol invasions of the thirteenth and fourteenth centuries, the Nestorians fled into the mountains of Kurdestan where they live today, known as Assyrian Christians. It is estimated that some 80,000 Nestorians live in the Mid-East, 5,000 in India, and 25,000 in North and South America. They refuse to accept the title of Mary as Mother of God and revere Nestorius as a saint. Among the Assyrians of Kurdestan was discovered in 1897 Nestorius' final work, the Tome of Heracleides, first printed in the West in 1910.

7. *Chronology*

385-412	Theophilus, bishop of Alexandria.
392	Suppression of pagan worship in public by Theodosius I.
395	Death of Theodosius I; Sons Arcadius in East, Honorius in West.
398-404	John Chrysostom, bishop of Constantinople, replaced Nectarius.
401	Synod of the Oak in which Theophilus of Alexandria deposed John Chrysostom.
407	Death of John Chrysostom in exile.
408-450	Accession of Theodosius II, son of Arcadius, in East.
406	Vandals, Alans and Sueves crossed the Rhine into Gaul.
410	Sack of Rome by Visigoth, Alaric.
412-444	Cyril of Alexandria succeeded his uncle Theophilus.

415	Pagans barred from military and civil offices.
422-432	Celestine, bishop of Rome.
428-431	Nestorius, Bishop of Constantinople; died in exile, c. 452.
429-441	John, bishop of Antioch.
429	First letter of Cyril to Nestorius.
430	Death of Augustine as Germanic Vandals besieged Hippo.
430	February: Cyril's second letter to Nestorius.
	August: Roman synod under Celestine condemned Nestorius; Cyril commissioned by pope.
	November: synod of Alexandria; Cyril cited Nestorius; third letter of Cyril.
	Theodosius II convoked Council to Ephesus for June 7, 431.
431	June 22: Cyril opened Council of Ephesus; Nestorius condemned and deposed.
	June 26: Council of John of Antioch.
	July 10: Arrival of papal legates.
	July 16, 17: Cyril's Council annuled acts of John's Council.
	July 22: Nicene Creed approved to exclusion of all others.
	August: Theodosius II dissolved the Council.
	September 3: Nestorius deposed and sent to Antioch.
432	Negotiations between Orientals and Cyril.
433	Formula of Union.
437	Tome of Proclus of Constantinople.

8. Select Bibliography

The events surrounding the controversy are clearly described in Duchesne, volume 3. The development of Antiochene thought is traced in D. S. Wallace-Hadrill, *Christian Antioch: A Study of Early Christian Thought in the East* (Cambridge, 1982). The history of Christology is masterfully analyzed in A. Grillmeier, *Christ in Christian Tradition* (London, 1965). More concise is the treatment of J. N. D. Kelly, *Early Christian Doctrines* (New York, 1960) and of Jaroslav Pelikan, *The Emergence of the Catholic Tradition* (Chicago, 1971). G. L. Prestige has two excellent chapters on Nestorius and Cyril in his *Fathers and Heretics* (London, 1940). R. V. Sellers examines the two in more detail in *Two Ancient Christologies* (London, 1940). R. A. Greer challenges Grillmeier's interpretation of Diodorus of Tarsus in "The Antiochene Christology of Diodore of Tarsus," *Journal of Theological Studies* 17 (1966), 327-341. Theodore of Mopsuestia is well covered in English by F. A. Sullivan, *The Christology of Theodore of Mopsuestia* (Rome, 1956), R. A. Greer, *Theodore of Mopsuestia Exegete and Theologian* (London, 1961), and R. A. Norris, *Manhood and Christ: A Study in the Christology of Theodore of Mopsuestia* (London, 1963). The standard work in English on Nestorius is F. Loofs, *Nestorius and His Place in the History of Christian Doctrine* (Cambridge, 1914). M. V. Anastos attempts to justify the complete orthodoxy of Nestorius in "Nestorius Was Orthodox," *Dumbarton Oaks Papers*, 16 (1962), 119-140. Unfortunately there is little in English on Cyril: Joseph van der Dries, *The Formula of St. Cyril of Alexandria* (Rome, 1939) and an article which excellently highlights one of Cyril's major concerns, H. Chadwick, "Eucharist and Christology in the Nestorian Controversy," *Journal of Theological Studies* 2 (1951), 145-164. On modern Nestorians, see J. Joseph, *The Nestorians and their Muslim Neighbors* (Princeton, 1961).

5

The Council of Chalcedon, 451

1. The Monk Eutyches

In 439 the historian Socrates ended his seven books with
the pious wish that peace continue to reign amid the flourish-
ing conditions in which the Church found itself, "for as long
as peace continues, those who desire to write histories will
find no materials for their purpose." Unfortunately, the condition of the Church for the rest of the century would provide ample material for the historian. Emperor Theodosius
II reigned on, but new influences within the court were
brought to bear on him. The cultured Empress Eudoxia had
fallen out with her husband and was living in Jerusalem. His
older sister Pulcheria too gradually lost favor. Into their
places stepped the Grand Chamberlain, the eunuch Chrysaphius. Among the chamberlain's intimates was Eutyches, his
godfather and spiritual adviser, the aging archimandrite of a
community of 300 monks in Constantinople. Eutyches was a
confirmed Cyrillian with wide connections in the monastic
world. One of his friends was the Syriac-speaking archimandrite Barsumas, who from his mountainside convent near
the Armenian border was busily drawing up indictments
against Domnus of Antioch and his theological adviser

Theodoret of Cyrus. Eutyches had influence among the bishops as well and supported the opposition at Edessa against the Nestorian Ibas.

Devoted to Cyril's theology and immersed in the pseude-pigraphical literature of Apollinarianism which he firmly believed was orthodox, Eutyches began to teach that before the Incarnation Christ was of two natures, but after it there was one Christ, one Son, one Lord in one *hypostasis* and one *prosopon*. Since he was a confused and muddled thinker, his doctrine was far from clear and consistent. He repudiated the existence of two natures after the Incarnation as opposed to the Scriptures and the teaching of the Fathers. "I worship," he insisted, "one nature, that of God made flesh and become man." Yet he conceded that Christ was born from the Virgin who was consubstantial with us and was perfect God and perfect man. However, the flesh of Christ was not in his view consubstantial with ordinary human flesh. Yet he acknowledged that Christ's humanity was a full humanity, not lacking a rational soul, as it was for the Apol-linarians. Nor was Christ's humanity a mere appearance as it was for the Docetists. Nor were the Word and the flesh fused into a mixed nature. Still he obstinately repeated that Christ is of two natures before the Incarnation, of only one after-wards. He feared to say that Christ's flesh was consubstan-tial with ours because he thought this really meant the Word assumed an individual subsistent man. He hated the idea of two natures in Christ after the Incarnation because he understood nature to mean concrete existence. To affirm two natures was for him to affirm two concrete existences, two *hypostases*, two persons in Christ. The genuine human-ity of Christ and the importance of his historical reality were in danger of being swept away by an imprecise terminology and an unbalanced emphasis on Christ's divinity.

Theodoret of Cyrus registered a caveat against Eutyches' views without mentioning him by name. "We acknowledge," Theodoret said, "such a union of Godhead and manhood that we perceive an individual person and know Him to be God and man." He insisted on distinction in natures, unity in *prosopon*. *Prosopon* meant for him a visible and tangible representation of the unity of God and man in Christ. In the single *prosopon* the divine became visible in its inwardness through the assumed manhood. Theodoret opposed any talk of natural union between body and soul because this implied necessity. In Christ unity was brought about by the gracious condescension of the Godhead, the loving obedience and subjection of the manhood. For Theodoret Christ, not the Word, was the common subject of the divine and human sayings of Scripture. To say that the Word suffered was to say that the Word suffered in His divine nature. To the end of his life Theodoret refused to say that the Word suffered, died and rose from the dead. Yet his theology evolved and by 449 he confessed that "The Lord's body is a body ..., yet it is not separated from the Godhead nor is it the body of anyone else. But it is that of the only begotten Son of God Himself. For it presents no other person but the Only Begotten Himself clothed with our nature." Beginning as an Antiochene, Theodoret ended by accepting Cyril's basic view that the Word is the sole person of Jesus Christ: "The Same is only-begotten in that He is God and First Born in that He is man." In 447 Theodoret wrote against those who, holding that Christ's humanity and divinity formed one nature, taught that the humanity had not really been derived of the Virgin and that the divinity suffered. He opposed the notion that in Christ the divinity absorbed the humanity as water absorbs a drop of honey. Especially he insisted throughout his work on the impassibility of the Godhead. Whether or not Eutyches really taught all these doctrines opposed by Theodoret, his view that Christ's humanity was not consubstantial with ours left the door open to wide misunderstanding.

Domnus of Antioch supported his suffragan Theodoret and wrote to the emperor accusing Eutyches of embracing Apollinarianism, of teaching one nature in Christ, of mingling the divine and the human and of attributing to God the sufferings of Christ. The court responded in 448 with a rescript once again condemning the writings of Nestorius and of all those not in conformity with the faith of Ephesus and of Cyril of pious memory. Nestorius' adherents, if clerics, were to be deposed; if laymen, excommunicated. Nestorius' old companion, Irenaeus, now bishop of Tyre, was summarily deposed. At Edessa, Ibas was charged with maladministration, calling Cyril a heretic and saying, "I do not envy Christ that He became God, for as far as He became this, I also have become the same." His recalcitrant clergy succeeded in deposing him. From Alexandria Dioscurus wrote arrogantly to Domnus of Antioch demanding an explanation of Theodoret's teaching and the immediate consecration of Irenaeus' successor at Tyre. At the urging of Dioscurus, the imperial court confined Theodoret to Cyrus and replaced Irenaeus at Tyre. Eutyches himself wrote to Leo at Rome urging him to take action against resurgent Nestorianism. The whole East was once more in ferment.

Eusebius, bishop of Dorylaeum, who as a layman had first raised the cry against Nestorius and whose "zeal made even fire seem cool," formally denounced Eutyches before the patriarch Flavian and the Home Synod, a semipermanent council of bishops at Constantinople. With considerable foreboding and hesitation, Flavian at last ordered Eutyches to appear before the Synod. While the Synod remained in session for two weeks, Eutyches repeatedly pleaded that his vow of seclusion and his ill health did not permit his coming before it. Finally, after the rumor spread that he was organizing the monks against the patriarch, he came in self-defense before the Synod escorted by a band of monks and, more ominously, by a group of court officials provided by the Grand Chamberlain Chrysaphius. Under questioning by the bishops, Eutyches admitted that though Christ took humanity from the Virgin, that humanity was not consubstantial with ours and entered in some way into the one nature of the Incarnate Word. Florentius, the imperial commissioner, urged him to admit two natures, but Eutyches obstinately refused. In all this, Florentius may have been playing a double game. It has been suggested that he was working for Eutyches' condemnation by Flavian in collusion with Dioscurus of Alexandria who was looking for an excuse to proceed against the patriarch. In the end, the Synod excommunicated Eutyches and deposed him as priest

and archimandrite. Twenty-three other archimandrites subscribed to the condemnation. Eutyches responded by appealing to the bishops of Rome, Alexandria, Jerusalem and
Thessalonika. At Antioch Domnus felt reassured; at Edessa
Ibas managed very briefly to regain his see.

Eutyches, Dioscurus and Chrysaphius now plotted to
overthrow this decision. Eutyches' protest, supported by a
letter from Emperor Theodosius, reached Rome where Pope
Leo, an able administrator (he once confided to his legate
that he had begun to answer his letters not only on the day
but at the very hour he received them) and a competent
theologian in his own right, enlisted the aid of Prosper of
Aquitaine to deal with the new controversy. To western
theologians Eutyches' position made no sense; before the
Incarnation there was only one nature and that divine; after,
there were the divine and human natures united without
confusion. For Leo, Eutyches was an imprudent and inexperienced old man. At Constantinople, Theodosius resolved to
settle the controversy immediately by calling a general council again to Ephesus in 449 with Dioscurus of Alexandria as
president assisted by Juvenal of Jerusalem and Thalassius of
Caesarea in Cappadocia. To represent the monks, the
emperor summoned to the council Barsumas, the fanatical
opponent of Theodoret of Cyrus. At Edessa Ibas was again
removed from office by an imperial commissioner. At Constantinople Flavian was accused of rigging the proceedings
of the Synod and doctoring its records. His resignation was
rejected, but he was called upon to submit a profession of
faith to the emperor.

Flavian submitted a strongly Cyrillian creed: "We proclaim Jesus Christ our Lord, born of God the Father without a beginning according to the Godhead, who for us and
for our salvation was born of Mary the Virgin in the last
days according to manhood, taking a rational soul and
body: perfect God and perfect man; the Same being consubstantial with the Father as to Godhead; the Same consubstantial with us as to manhood. Confessing, then, Christ to
form two after the Incarnation and humanization from the
holy Virgin, we affirm that He is one Christ, one Son, one

Lord in one *hypostasis* and one *prosopon*. We do not therefore refuse to maintain that He is one nature, God the Word
incarnate and made man, because he is one from both, the
Same being our Lord, Jesus Christ."

When Leo I at Rome received the summons to the Council, he excused himself on the grounds that it was against
precedent for the pope to attend. He added that Attila and
his Huns had thrown all Italy into turmoil. Leo agreed to
send legates and provided them with letters to the Emperor,
Flavian, the Council and the monks of Constantinople.
Among these letters was the famous Tome to Flavian in
which Leo summarized the Christology of the West. In his
Tome Leo shows himself less of a speculative theologian
than Cyril; he does not discuss or demonstrate; he judges and
settles difficulties, reproducing the teaching of Tertullian,
Augustine and the Antiochenes with uncommon precision
and vigor. The person of the God-man is for Leo identical
with that of the Divine Word: "He who became man in the
form of a servant is He who in the form of God created
man." The Word took to Himself a body from the body of
the Virgin: "Thus, in the whole and perfect nature of true
manhood true God was born — complete in what belonged
to Him, complete in what belonged to us." Though the
Incarnation involved a self-emptying, this should be understood as a stooping down whereby the Word underwent no
diminution of His omnipotence. The divine and human
natures existed in the one person without confusion or mixture. In uniting to form one person each nature retained its
natural properties unimpaired so that the form of God does
not abolish the form of a servant, nor does the form of a
servant diminish the form of God. For the redemption
required that "one and the same mediator between God and
man, the man Jesus Christ, should be able both to die in
respect of the one and not to die in respect of the other."
Each of these natures had its own principle of operation and
its own activity, which it did not, however, exercise inde-
pendently of the other nature nor apart from the union
which is permanent. "Each form accomplishes in concert
with the other what is appropriate to it, the Word perform-

ing what belongs to the Word, and the flesh carrying out what belongs to the flesh." The unity of person involved what was called the *communicatio idiomatum*, that is, "by reason of this unity of person, to be understood in both natures, the Son of Man is said to have come down from heaven when the Son of God took flesh from the Virgin from whom He was born; and again the Son of God is said to have been crucified and buried, though He suffered these things not in the Godhead itself, wherein the Only Begotten is coeternal and consubstantial with the Father, but in the weakness of human nature." Eutyches was called upon to acknowledge that "he whom he knows to have been subject to suffering was a man of like body to ours, since denial of His true flesh is denial also of His bodily Passion" which wrought the world's salvation. Eutyches' statement, "I acknowledge that our Lord was of two natures before the union, but after the union I acknowledge one nature," was branded as absurd and perverse, extremely foolish and blasphemous. For Leo, Eutyches "deserved a verdict of condemnation." Though Leo had by no means solved all the problems, he had at least laid out clearly the points to be considered. The Antiochenes could find here insistence on the reality and independence of the two natures; the Alexandrians, Cyril's basic insight that the person of the Incarnate is identical with that of the Divine Word.

2. The Robber Council of Ephesus

To represent him at the forthcoming Council at Ephesus, Leo named as legates Julius, bishop of Puteoli, the priest Renatus, the most capable of the four legates, who unfortunately died on the journey, the deacon Hilary, afterwards pope, and the notary Dulcitius. On landing at Ephesus the legates immediately presented themselves and their letters to Flavian, patriarch of Constantinople. The council was called into session on August 8, 449 with Dioscurus the president as designated by the Emperor. Presiding from a high throne in the church called Mary, scene of the previous Council of

Ephesus, he had at his side, Julius of Puteoli, the papal legate, and in order of seniority Juvenal of Jerusalem, Domnus of Antioch and Flavian of Constantinople. Present were about 170 bishops: some twenty from Egypt, fifteen from Palestine, all amenable to Dioscurus, and fifteen handpicked from the Orient in order to isolate their patriarch Domnus. The most prominent of Antiochene theologians, Theodoret, was interned by the government at Cyrus. Hilary and Dulcitius, not being bishops, were isolated from Julius at the foot of the assembly. The Count Helpidius and the tribune Eulogius were present to see that all went according to the prearranged program — the rehabilitation of Eutyches and the deposition of Flavian and all accused of Nestorianism.

Immediately the forty-two bishops who had been present at the Home Synod which had condemned Eutyches were denied the right to participate and were relegated to the position of spectators. After the imperial letters convoking the Council were read out, the legate Hilary rose to ask that Leo's letters too be read to the assembly. Dioscurus put off his repeated requests on one pretext or another. Julius, ignorant of Greek and isolated from his fellow legates, proved unequal to the situation, and Dioscurus maintained a firm hand on the discussions. Eutyches was brought in and presented his profession of faith which inspired renewed demands by Julius and Hilary for the reading of Leo's Tome. But in vain. The Council proceeded to the reading of the minutes of the Home Synod. As the account was read there of Eusebius of Dorylaeum's demand that Eutyches acknowledge two natures in the Incarnate, the bishops shouted, "Cut him in two who divides Christ." Then with Dioscurus leading the chorus, the assembly approved Eutyches' profession of two natures before the Incarnation, one afterward. By 111 votes out of 130, he was declared orthodox and restored to his offices of priest and archimandrite.

Next Dioscurus turned to other matters and had extracts of the preceding Council of Ephesus read in which it was forbidden under pain of deposition to put forward or teach a creed other than that of Nicaea. To this seemingly innocent declaration all, including the papal legates, signified assent. Then Dioscurus played an unexpected card; he denounced ·Flavian and Eusebius for violating this canon and demanded their immediate deposition. Flavian cried: "I disdain your authority." Hilary shouted in Latin: "I dissent emphatically." Other bishops approached Dioscurus and begged him to reconsider his motion. Pretending that he was being attacked, Dioscurus shouted for the imperial commissioner who ordered the church doors thrown open. The provincial governor entered with the military police, followed by a motley crowd of monks, Egyptian sailors and assorted toughs. Flavian tried to cling to the altar, and, after being roughed up, managed with Hilary to find refuge in the sacristy. Eusebius of Dorylaeum was put under arrest. Dioscurus forbade anyone to leave the church and despite anguished protests, all 170 bishops, including Domnus of Antioch, signed the official acts. For greater convenience, some of the bishops were induced to sign blank sheets to be filled in later by Dioscurus' notaries. The main business of the Council was now complete: Eutyches had been rehabilitated and restored; his accusers Flavian and Eusebius deposed.

While Dioscurus waited for imperial approval of his work, he determined to deal with the rest of his opponents. In a second session which the papal legates refused to attend, Ibas of Edessa and his two nephews who were his suffragan bishops were formally declared deposed; Irenaeus of Tyre and a suffragan he had consecrated were deprived of office, and even though Domnus of Antioch had cravenly agreed to all this, he too found himself deposed. To end the business the Council solemnly accepted the Twelve Anathemas of Cyril against Nestorius. Dioscurus with his henchmen Juvenal of Jerusalem, Eutyches and the monk Barsumas mightily aided by Chrysaphius, the Grand Chamberlain who had the Emperor's ear, had brought about the triumph of Cyril's theology. In 449, Alexandria was again victorious as it had been over John Chrysostom in 404 and over Nestorius in 431. However, what was designed to be an ecumenical council would not be accepted as such by the Church.

In the aftermath, the legate Hilary managed to slip through Chrysaphius' police and make his way to Rome where later as pope he erected a chapel to St. John in the Lateran Basilica in gratitude for having escaped alive from Ephesus. He brought with him an appeal to "the throne of the Apostolic See of Peter, Prince of the Apostles," which the unfortunate Flavian had written before his arrest and imprisonment. The impetuous Eusebius of Dorylaeum too managed to flee to Rome and lodge his protest against the Council with the pope. Soon priests from Cyrus arrived with a dignified appeal from Theodoret: "I await the sentence of your Apostolic See. I beseech and implore your Holiness to succour me in my appeal to your fair and righteous tribunal." Well informed of the events at Ephesus, Leo gathered a synod at Rome and annulled the proceedings of the Council, blaming Dioscurus as the chief culprit. He sent his protest to the Emperor, his sister Pulcheria, to Flavian and the clergy and monks of Constantinople demanding that a new council be held in the West to set things straight. From Rome the western Emperor Valentinian III, his wife, who was Theodosius' daughter, and the Dowager Empress Galla Placidia were induced to second the pope's appeal to their kinsfolk at Constantinople. But Theodosius formally approved the Council of Ephesus and assured the West that "peace reigned and pure truth was supreme." Imperial agents proceeded to carry out the decreed depositions. Flavian of Constantinople died while being taken into exile; Domnus of Antioch disappeared into a monastery at Jerusalem. Ibas, Eusebius and Flavian were soon provided with successors. But Leo now put his foot down. Branding the Council of Ephesus a *latrocinium*, a band of robbers, the pope refused to recognize Anatolius, the new patriarch of Constantinople, formerly Dioscurus' representative in the capital, until he signified acceptance of Cyril's Second Letter to Nestorius and his own Tome to Flavian. Four papal legates were dispatched to Constantinople to restore order. Suddenly the whole situation was radically changed when the Emperor Theodosius II died in July, 450, as a result of a fall from his horse while hunting. He had reigned forty-two years.

His older sister Pulcheria promptly seized power, ordered Chrysaphius executed and married the senator Marcian, an ex-military commander, associating him with herself as emperor. In one stroke, Eutyches and his party were without a protector, for Pulcheria's religious beliefs were those of Pope Leo and the brutalized Patriarch Flavian. Eutyches was promptly interned in a suburban monastery while Flavian's body was returned to Constantinople. The bishops quickly veered around; Anatolius of Constantinople received the papal legates and formally subscribed to Leo's Tome; Maximus of Antioch too fell into line. Only Dioscurus at Alexandria and Juvenal at Jerusalem, the chief agents of the Council of Ephesus, refused to recant. Since matters seemed to be righting themselves without a council, Leo now counseled against the assembly of another council, except perhaps at a later date and in the West. Emperor and Empress, however, wanted an immediate council in the East; one was called to Nicaea in 451. Reluctantly, Leo concurred and sent three legates whose leader Paschasinus, bishop of Marsala in Sicily, was designated as president of the forthcoming council, advised by Julian of Cos who tended to papal business in Constantinople.

3. The Council of Chalcedon

Hundreds of bishops had arrived at Nicaea by September 1, 451, and were waiting for Emperor Marcian to open the proceedings. In the interval, the redoubtable Dioscurus, backed by crowds of uninvited monks and many bishops from Egypt, Palestine and Illyricum, attempted another coup. On his own initiative he excommunicated Pope Leo for not accepting his Council of Ephesus. But he had misjudged the mood of the majority of bishops; even some of the Egyptian bishops balked at approving his action. Then, finding himself unable to leave Constantinople because of the Hunnish invasions, Emperor Marcian ordered the Council to reconvene at Chalcedon, just across the Bosporus from the capital.

So at Chalcedon on October 8, 451, the new Council opened with perhaps 500 bishops in attendance, though recent estimates would put the number as few as 350. In the center of the basilica of the great shrine of St. Euphemia, legendary martyr and virgin of the fourth century, stood an enshrined Book of the Gospels. No fewer than nineteen court functionaries led by the Patrician Anatolius occupied chairs lined up along the balustrade dividing the sanctuary from the nave. Down the left of the basilica sat the papal legates, Anatolius of Constantinople, Maximus of Antioch and the metropolitans and bishops of Thrace, Asia Minor and Syria. Across from them sat Dioscurus of Alexandria, Juvenal of Jerusalem and the representative of the bishop of Thessalonika with the bishops of Egypt, Palestine and Illyricum. The battle lines were drawn.

In accordance with their instructions, the papal legates summarily demanded the exclusion of Dioscurus, condemned by Leo, from the assembly without further discussion. But the court officials insisted on a formal trial before the Council, which the ever disputatious Eusebius of Dorylaeum opened with an attack on Dioscurus, now forced to sit as a defendant in the center of the nave. To expose the crimes of the accused, Eusebius demanded the reading of the acts of the Council of Ephesus of 449. At the mention of Theodoret of Cyrus in the acts, the imperial commissioners asked that he be admitted to the Council; he entered immediately to mingled shouts of acclaim and execration and took a seat in the assembly. Once order was restored, the reading of the acts continued to the mounting embarrassment of the former members of the Robber Council of Ephesus. One by one they sought to excuse themselves under the scornful eye and withering sarcasm of the increasingly isolated Dioscurus. The commissioners, at the request of Eusebius of Dorylaeum, next ordered the reading of the acts of the Home Synod which had originally condemned Eutyches. When the reader finished the letter of Cyril accepting the Formula of Union of John of Antioch quoted in the acts, the bishops cried out: "This we believe." Shouts were heard against Dioscurus, "murderer of Flavian." Confidently, Dioscurus too affirmed that he believed as Cyril did. Once the reader reached the doctrinal statement which Flavian had presented to the Emperor, the commissioners asked the bishops if they regarded it as orthodox. Beginning with the legate Paschasinus, the metropolitans on the left declared their agreement with Flavian. Juvenal of Jerusalem too rose, declared his agreement and led his Palestinian bishops across the nave to join the accusers of Dioscurus. The bishops of Illyricum, save Atticus of Nicopolis who developed a diplomatic illness, did the same. Finally, even four Egyptians crossed the hall, forsaking Dioscurus. Now almost alone, Dioscurus continued to insist that Flavian was justly condemned because he had spoken of two natures after the union. The only proper formula, he affirmed, is "one incarnate nature of the divine Logos." At nightfall, lights were brought in and the reading of all relevant documents was completed. The bishops of the Robber Council all declared they had erred and begged for pardon. The imperial commissioners announced that it seemed right to them to condemn Dioscurus, Juvenal and four other ringleaders from Ephesus, subject to the Emperor's consent. They then suggested that the bishops draw up a statement of their belief. But the assembly dispersed for the night as the bishops chanted, "Holy God, Holy and Mighty, Holy and Immortal, have mercy on us," the first mention in history of the Trisagion, until recently a hymn used in the Good Friday liturgy of the Roman rite.

On October 10 at the second session the imperial commissioners again asked the bishops to draw up a doctrinal statement. Instead, the bishops ordered read the Creeds of Nicaea and Constantinople together with Cyril's Second Letter to Nestorius, his letter to John of Antioch and Leo's Tome to Flavian. At the end, the bishops shouted: This is the faith of the Fathers and the Apostles; Peter has spoken through Leo; Cyril taught this too; Leo and Cyril taught the same. Atticus of Nicopolis, spokesman for the Illyrians, now restored to health, asked for time to compare the Tome with Cyril's Third Letter to Nestorius and appended Twelve

Anathemas, which, he noted, had been omitted. Most bishops opposed the delay, but Anatolius of Constantinople was finally charged with drawing up a statement to reassure the Illyrians. At the end of the session the Illyrians asked that all the leaders of the Robber Council be forgiven, even Dioscurus. Their request was denied and the session adjourned.

Three days later, the Council sat for a third time to take up the case of Dioscurus who refused to attend the session, if he were to be the only one tried. Since the imperial commissioners excused themselves as laymen from attending the trial of a bishop, the papal legate Paschasinus led the discussions. Three times Dioscurus was cited and three times he refused to come, telling the delegation sent to him that he had said all he had to say. Dioscurus was not in doctrine a follower of Eutyches but a staunch Cyrillian. He held, "that no one shall say that the holy flesh which Our Lord took from the Virgin by the operation of the Holy Spirit, in a manner which He himself knows, was different from and foreign to our body." "The flesh which was born of Mary was compacted with the soul of the Redeemer, that reasonable and intelligent soul.... For he was like us, for us, and with us, not in phantasy, not in mere semblance...but rather in actual reality from Mary the Theotokos. He became by the dispensation like us, that we in His tender mercy be like Him." Since the Eastern bishops were still hesitant to condemn one of their own, they asked the legates to decide the issue. Paschasinus conferred with his colleagues and summed up their indictment: Dioscurus had received Eutyches into communion though he had been condemned by his own bishop; he had not allowed Leo's Tome to be read; he had attempted to excommunicate the pope. Therefore, the legate concluded, "Leo through us and the present Holy Synod, together with St. Peter...who is the rock of the Church and the foundation of the orthodox faith, deprives him of his episcopal office and of all priestly dignity." Anatolius of Constantinople led 185 bishops in approving the sentence. Alexandria had been dealt a bitter blow. The other five ringleaders of the Robber Council were admitted to the Council after subscribing to Leo's Tome and the deposition of Dioscurus.

On October 17 at the fourth session, 305 bishops met to decide the fate of the recalcitrant Egyptian bishops. Eighteen of them presented the confession of their Church, but said nothing of Eutyches, Dioscurus or Leo's Tome. Under questioning they agreed to condemn Eutyches but begged not to be forced to subscribe to Leo's Tome nor to Dioscurus' deposition. If they did so, they claimed, they would be killed upon their return to Egypt. The Council ordered them to be interned at Constantinople until a new patriarch of Alexandria could be elected to give direction to the Egytian bishops. Next it was the turn of the monks who had supported Eutyches. Accompanied by the redoubtable Barsumas, they arrogantly demanded the restoration of Dioscurus and adherence solely to the Creed of Nicaea. Once the commissioners had quelled the outburst caused by this effrontery, the monks were asked to condemn Eutyches and accept the Tome. When they refused, they were handed over to the jurisdiction of the patriarch of Constantinople.

On October 22 at the fifth session, the imperial commissioners continued to press the bishops for a doctrinal statement. One had been drawn up in the quarters of Anatolius of Constantinople; this he now proposed to the Council. The text is no longer extant, but it was perhaps based on the creed Flavian of Constantinople had presented to the Emperor after having been rebuked for condemning Eutyches in the Home Synod (pp. 174-175). Anatolius' statement did not incorporate the Tome of Leo. The Council had reached a critical point. Most of the bishops acclaimed the statement, but the Orientals and the papal legates protested. Paschasinus insisted that Leo's Tome must be accepted. Anatolius countered that Dioscurus was condemned not for his doctrine but for the illegality of his actions at Ephesus. So acrimonious grew the proceedings that the legates asked leave to return to Rome. The imperial commissioners appealed to the Court for additional instructions. Back came the reply: either form a commission to draw up a new doctrinal statement or adjourn the Council to the West. The commissioners artfully put the question to the bishops: "Are you for Leo or Dioscurus?" "For Leo," they answered. So a commission consisting of the three legates, six Orientals, and three bishops from Asia, Pontus, Illyricum and Thrace met in the shrine of St. Euphemia and worked out the Definition of the Council of Chalcedon.

After a preamble expressing a desire for peace through the teaching of the truth of a common doctrine, the Definition solemnly presented the Creed of Nicaea ordering that "the Creed of the 318 Fathers remain inviolate." In the minds of the bishops this was the dogmatic foundation of Christian belief. Then after investigating the authenticity of the Creed of Constantinople I with which many bishops were not familiar, the Council accepted that Creed not as supplying any omission but as an authentic interpretation of the faith of Nicaea, thus raising the Council of Constantinople to the level of what today we would term an ecumenical council. "On account of those who impugn the Holy Spirit," the Definition continued, "it ratifies and confirms the doctrine delivered subsequently, concerning the essence of the Spirit by the 150 holy Fathers."

The bishops signified their adherence to the "order and formulas of the faith of the holy council formerly held at Ephesus, under the presidency of Celestine, bishop of Rome, and Cyril, bishop of Alexandria." With this declaration the Council accepted the sessions of the Council of Ephesus of 431 presided over by Cyril and confirmed by the papal legates on a par with the Councils of Nicaea and Constantinople. The definition also stated that the Council "has accepted the synodical letters of the blessed Cyril...to Nestorius and the Orientals, in keeping with those Creeds, for the confutation of the folly of Nestorius, and the explanation of the salutary Creed." Coupled with Cyril's letters was the Tome of Leo: "it has suitably joined for the confirmation of the orthodox faith the letter of the Ruler of the greatest and elder Rome, the most blessed and most holy Archbishop Leo, written to the saintly Archbishop Flavian...since it agrees with the confession of the great Peter, and is a pillar of support against the heterodox."

The reason the Council gave for making these declarations was that "some have uttered vain babblings," on one hand, denying the Theotokos; on the other, bringing in a confusion and mixing of natures, feigning one nature of flesh and Godhead and maintaining that the divine nature is passible. The Council declared itself opposed to those who affirmed a double Sonship, who said that the Godhead of the Only-Begotten is passible, who imagined a mixture or confusion of the two natures of Christ, who taught that the form of a servant, the flesh, of Christ is from heaven, and who feigned that the Lord had two natures before the union, but only one after. Clearly the bishops had Nestorius, Apollinaris and Eutyches in mind. Then followed the Definition proper:

> Wherefore, following the holy Fathers, we all with one voice confess our Lord Jesus Christ one and the same Son, the same perfect in Godhead, the same perfect in manhood, truly God and truly man, the same consisting of a reasonable soul and a body, of one substance with the Father as touching the Godhead, the same of one substance with us as touching the manhood, like us in all things apart from sin; begotten of the Father before the ages as touching the Godhead, the same in the last days, for us and for our salvation, born from the Virgin Mary, the Theotokos, as touching the manhood, one and the same Christ, Son, Lord, Only-begotten, to be acknowledged in two natures, without confusion, without change, without division, without separation; the distinction of natures being in no way abolished because of the union, but rather the characteristic property of each nature being preserved, and concurring into one Person and one subsistence, not as if Christ were parted or divided into two persons, but one and the same Son and only-begotten God, Word, Lord, Jesus Christ; even as the Prophets from the beginning spoke concerning him, and our Lord Jesus Christ instructed us, and the Creed of the Fathers has handed down to us.

The Definition ended, "it is unlawful for anyone to produce another faith, whether by writing, or composing, or holding, or teaching others," and provided suitable penalties for those who would attempt to do so.

In composing the Definition, the bishops drew upon Cyril's Second Letter to Nestorius and Letter to the Antiochenes, Flavian's Confession and Leo's Tome. J. Pelikan remarks that, even though it may be statistically accurate to say that the majority of the quotations came from the letters of Cyril, the contributions of Leo's Tome were the decisive ones. In their Definition the bishops at last clearly distinguished between person and nature; the person of Christ being one, his natures two. They rejected decisively the view that Christ is from two natures and in one by affirming that Christ subsists in two natures. The Apollinarian slogan — One Incarnate Nature of the Divine Word — thought by Cyril and his followers to be from Athanasius was opposed. The bishops thus renounced any notion of the hypostatic union which would jeopardize the differences of the natures or deny that their union was accomplished without confusion. But they insisted that Christ could not be divided or separated into two persons. By using a series of four Greek negative adverbs — without confusion, without change, without division, without separation — the bishops showed their concern for the mysterious and incomprehensible nature of the subject matter with which they were dealing.

Yet the Definition failed to do justice to certain concerns of the Cyrillians. To say that the differences of the two natures were preserved in the union could be understood to mean that human attributes of Christ must be predicated only of the human nature; the divine, only of the divine nature. "Without confusion, without change," terms which protect the immutability and impassibility of the divine nature, "could be read as an attack on the notion that because the salvation of man consisted in the transformation of his human nature into a divine one, the human nature of Christ had begun the process of salvation by its union with the divine nature," observes Pelikan.

Though the Definition insisted on the unity of person in Christ by repeating the adjective "same" eight times, it still left the concept of hypostatic union unclear. It did say that the natures combine in one person, that the Virgin is Theotokos, and that the natures are joined without division, without separation. But it did not specify the subject of suffering and crucifixion. Could one say with Cyril that the Word suffered, died and rose? Finally, the Definition did not clearly state argues Pelikan "that the ultimate deification of man had its inception in the union of the humanity of Christ with his divinity in an intimate and inseparable wholeness of person." The Definition by and large satisfied the West down to our own times. But the East found it wanting in clarity about the hypostatic union, the problems of predication, the single subject of suffering and death in Christ and the deification of the human begun in Christ. Since many thought that Cyril was a better guide to Christology than the Council of Chalcedon, new controversies were soon to follow.

Three days later, on October 25, the Emperor Marcian crossed the Bosporus to attend the ceremonies promulgating the Council's Definition of Faith. Solemnly, the papal legates and after them some 452 bishops affixed their signatures to the document. The Emperor asked the bishops to remain in session for a few more days to discuss matters of church discipline. Accordingly, from October 26 to 31 the bishops settled down to discuss matters of discipline. In a stormy session the Council debated the case of Theodoret of Cyrus, deposed by the Robber Council of Ephesus as Nestorian. Before the assembly he attempted to present his confession of faith, but the bishops howled him down, demanding that he anathematize Nestorius forthwith. With great reluctance he agreed: "Anathema to Nestorius and whoever denies that the Virgin is Theotokos or divides the only Son into two sons. I accept the Definition of Faith and the letter of Leo." Therewith the Council restored him to his see. Two whole days were given to the case of Ibas of Edessa, likewise deposed for Nestorianism. The legates ruled that what had been decided against him at the Robber Council should not prejudice the bishops against him. The bishops examined his letter to Maris the Persian. In answer to questions by the commissioners, Paschasinus and Maximus of Antioch testified that, from the reading of the letter, he was orthodox. Anatolius of Constantinople accepted him into communion because he agreed to the Definition of the Council and Leo's Tome. No official judgment was apparently voted on the letter itself, a point much debated in the next General Council at Constantinople in 553. Ibas, like Theodoret, was restored to his see.

The assembled Fathers then debated thirty disciplinary canons. Bishops themselves were enjoined not to sell ordinations, not to wander from place to place, not to receive another's clergy, not to delay the consecration of bishops in order to profit from the revenues of the vacant sees, not to intrigue with the government to divide sees. They were told to hold synods twice a year and to appoint stewards as auditors of episcopal finances. The clergy were ordered not to enter state service. All clerics were to be ordained for a definite charge and to stay under the jurisdiction of the ordaining bishop. They were to carry letters of commendation with them when traveling and to stay out of the city of Constantinople without permission. The staffs of various ecclesiastical institutions within a diocese were reminded that they were to remain subject to their bishop. Lectors and chanters were allowed to marry, but only women of orthodox faith. As for women, deaconesses were to be at least forty years old, properly examined, ordained (the word means ordination by imposition of hands) and celibate; consecrated virgins were not to marry but to be treated leniently if they did; women were not to be kidnapped for marriage. Monks were to be subject to the bishops and were forbidden to marry: the first official pronouncement about monastic celibacy. Monasteries once erected were not to be converted to secular use. All were warned about entering into conspiracies, about denouncing the clergy, about seizing the property of a bishop at his death and about failure to carry letters of peace and communion when traveling.

There was little to object to in all of this, but three other canons were decidedly controversial. The legates were not present at the discussion of these canons because, as they said, they lacked instructions to deal with such matters. Canon nine provided that bishops or clerics who had a dispute with their provincial metropolitan could appeal over his head to the exarch of the diocese or directly to the patriarch of Constantinople. Canon seventeen allowed anyone wronged by his metropolitan to appeal to the exarch of the diocese or to the patriarch of Constantinople. Further, it specified that ecclesiastical regions should correspond to the civil. The first two provisions were clearly innovations giving the patriarch of Constantinople jurisdiction over local bishops, bishops of metropolitan areas and even over bishops, called exarchs, of the groups of civil provinces called dioceses. In effect, the patriarch of Constantinople was made a court of appeal for all the East.

Most controversial of all, canon twenty-eight read that the Fathers of the Council of Constantinople "properly gave the primacy to the Throne of elder Rome, because that was the imperial city." And being moved by the same intention they now "gave equal privileges to the most holy Throne of New Rome, judging with reason, that the city which was honored with the sovereignty and senate, and which enjoyed equal privileges with the elder royal Rome, should also be magnified like her in ecclesiastical matters, being second after her." The canon also granted to the patriarch of Constantinople the right to ordain the duly elected metropolitans of the civil dioceses of Thrace, Asia and Pontus as well as the bishops in lands outside the Empire, though metropolitans continued to ordain the bishops subject to them. Thus, Constantinople was assigned a patriarchate comprising today's Turkey, eastern Bulgaria and Romania, giving it territory equal to Antioch and Alexandria. Besides it was declared, as the see of the capital of the Eastern Empire, to have equal privileges in ecclesiastical matters with the see of Rome but occupying second place to Rome in honor. Further, the patriarch of Constantinople could hear appeals over the heads of all the bishops, metropolitans and exarchs of the East. The intent of the Council Fathers in all of this was not to attack the bishop of Rome but to provide an ecclesiastical structure for the East to keep the Church in peace. In another declaration, the see of Jerusalem was proclaimed a fifth patriarchate along with Rome, Constantinople, Alexandria and Antioch.

The twenty-eighth canon was voted on October 21 with neither the papal legates nor the imperial commissioners present. Anatolius of Constantinople, Maximus of Antioch, Juvenal of Jerusalem and 182 bishops approved it. The next day the legate Paschasinus demanded the reading of the acts of the session. The bishops pointed out that he had refused to attend, but the notary read out the account of the proceedings. The papal legate Lucentius suggested that the bishops had been coerced into accepting the canon. This was vigorously denied. The legates then expressed amazement that the bishops had not followed the sixth canon of Nicaea which had said nothing of the authority of Constantinople. They insisted that their instructions were to resist any usurpation of the rights of the bishop of Rome. They refused to accept the third canon of the Council of Constantinople which decreed to Constantinople a primacy of honor after the bishop of Rome because Constantinople was new Rome. In vain the bishops of Pontus and Asia pointed out that the twenty-eighth canon merely sanctioned practice, for the patriarch of Constantinople had long ordained metropolitans in their civil dioceses. Eusebius of Dorylaeum said that he had personally read the third canon of Constantinople to Pope Leo and claimed that he had accepted it. The imperial commissioners approved the canon; the bishops acclaimed their decision over the protests of the papal legates. On this sour note, the Council ended. In February, 452, Emperor Marcian promulgated the decrees: "All therefore shall be bound to hold the decisions of the sacred council of Chalcedon and indulge no further doubts. Take heed therefore to this edict of our Serenity: abstain from profane words and cease all further discussion of religion."

4. The Response of the West

The letter of the Council to Pope Leo gave him good news and bad. "We were all delighted," they said, "as at an imperial banquet, reveling in the spiritual food, which Christ supplied to His invited guests through your letter." "You were the chief, as head to the members. . . while our religious Emperors presided to the furtherance of due order, inviting us to restore the doctrinal fabric of the Church. . . . " They then informed the pope that they had ratified the long-prevailing custom whereby the bishop of Constantinople ordained the metropolitans of Asia, Pontus and Thrace, not to confer a privilege on Constantinople but to provide for good government. They acknowledged that they had ratified as well the third canon of the Council of Constantinople despite the vehement protests of the papal legates. Accordingly, they entreated him to honor their decision, "as we have yielded to the head of our agreement on things honorably so may the head also fulfill for the children what is fitting." The Emperor Marcian and the Patriarch Anatolius wrote asking Leo to approve canon twenty-eight which merely sanctioned a custom of 60 to 70 years in the dioceses of Pontus, Asia and Thrace.

The Eastern bishops' appeal that Leo accept the twenty-eighth canon with its underlying theory that the importance of an episcopal see depended on the status of the city which it embraced was fated to fall on deaf ears. For Leo had a very different view of the prerogatives of the Roman See. As J. G. Jalland observes, Leo was not the creator of the theory of papal government but a mason cementing into a solid whole the traditions of his see. In Leo's view, Peter was chosen to rule over "all whom Christ also rules originally." Nor does Peter cease to preside over the whole Church, "for the stability which the rock himself was given by that Rock, Christ, he conveyed also to his successors." Those successors are the bishops of Rome, because Peter was sent "to the citadel of the Roman Empire that thus the light of Truth, which as being made known for the salvation of all the nations, might shine forth with greater efficacy throughout the whole world from the very capital itself." Thus the Church "ever finds Peter in Peter's see." So if anything is rightly done and rightly decreed by the bishop of Rome, "it is of his work and merit whose power lives and whose authority prevails in his see." Moreover, the authority of all Christian bishops is mediated from Christ through Peter and his successors, "so that from him as from the head His gifts should be conveyed to the whole body, so that whoever dares to secede from the foundation of Peter may know that he is excluded from...the divine mystery." Leo concluded: "Through the most blessed Peter, chief of the Apostles, the Holy Roman Church holds the principate over all the churches of the world." In a dispute with Hilary, bishop of Arles, Leo had his claims supported in the West by the decree of Emperor Valentinian III: "We decree by this perpetual edict that it shall not be lawful for the bishops of Gaul or of the other provinces, contrary to ancient custom, to do aught without the authority of the venerable Pope of the Eternal City; and whatsoever the authority of the Apostolic See has enacted, or may hereafter enact, shall be the law for all."

For six months after the receipt of the Council's letter Leo, usually so prompt in answering, delayed his reply. Finally, on May 22, 452, the Pope responded, declaring himself happy over the extirpation of error but reproaching Anatolius of Constantinople for ambition. Leo insisted on the apostolic foundation of the major sees and, to wipe out the insult to Alexandria and Antioch, the implementation of canon six of the Council of Nicaea in which Constantinople was not mentioned. To the Emperor Marcian, Leo wrote counseling Anatolius to be content with the see of Constantinople granted to him by the aid of the emperor and the favor of the pope, even though it was not an apostolic see. In a letter to the Empress Pulcheria, the pope said that the regulations of bishops repugnant to the canons of Nicaea "we dismiss as invalid, and by the authority of Peter, the blessed apostle, we absolutely disannul." On February 15, 453, Marcian wrote to the Pope urging acceptance of the Council because the followers of Eutyches were profiting from his silence. The emperor proposed separating the definition from the canons. On March 21, 453, Leo accepted this diplomatic gesture and accepted the faith but not the canons of Chalcedon, while again expressing his displeasure with Anatolius. Anatolius replied with a humble letter reserving the conciliar decrees to the Pope's authority. Leo allowed himself to be reconciled while still rejecting the canons and insisting on the validity of the sixth canon of Nicaea. There matters rested. Only in the sixth century was the twenty-eighth canon admitted into the official canonical collections of the Greek East and in 1274 at the Second Council of Lyons accepted by the Catholic West.

5. Aftermath in the East

As with the Creed of Nicaea, one hundred and twenty-five years before, the definition of Chalcedon was not the end but the intensification of controversy. No sooner was the Council closed than the monk Theodosius hurried back to Palestine to give out a jaundiced view of its proceedings and the treatment meted out to the Patriarch Dioscurus, standard bearer of the Cyrillians. Juvenal of Jerusalem who had broken with Dioscurus in the midst of the Council was the special object of the monk's fury. The widowed Empress Eudoxia, living in Jerusalem, resenting the overthrow of her husband Theodosius II's Robber Council of Ephesus with the support of her sister-in-law Empress Pulcheria, joined the ranks of the dissidents. Gerontius, abbot of a famous double monastery on the Mount of Olives, shared the dismay of the followers of Cyril. These and others resolved that the traitor Juvenal be replaced as bishop of Jerusalem. Juvenal returned to his see to face a riot. One of his suffragans was murdered, and the monk Theodosius managed to get himself elected patriarch of Jerusalem. The new patriarch began installing his own bishops to replace the traitors returning from Chalcedon. Still, when Eutyches passed through Palestine on his way to an unknown place of exile, the bishops and monks had nothing to do with him. Their objections to Chalcedon were not centered on the condemnation of Eutyches but on the apparent failure of the Council to accept the full Cyrillian theological program. Juvenal was finally restored to his see by the military in a city sullen under martial law. Imperial and papal letters urging reconciliation rained on the city. Leo wrote to the Palestinian monks: "Although from that beginning whereby 'the Word was made flesh' in the Virgin's womb, no division ever existed between the divine and the human substance, and through all the bodily growth the actions were of the One Person all the time, yet we do not by any mixture confound these very things which were done inseparably; but we perceive from the character of the acts what belongs to either form. For neither do the divine acts damage the validity of the human, nor the human acts that of the divine, since both so concur, and that for this very purpose, that between them neither is the property absorbed nor the Person doubled." The usurping monk Theodosius was interned in Constantinople, but the widowed Empress gave up her resistance only in 455 at the news that her son-in-law, the western emperor Valentinian III, had been assassinated, Rome pillaged by the Vandals, and her daughter and grand-daughters carried off as captives to Africa by the Vandal king. In Syria and Cappadocia too there were instances of strong objections to the conciliar definition. At Constantinople, firm measures had to be taken against certain recalcitrant monks.

At Alexandria, as might be expected, resistance was even more fanatical. With Dioscurus in exile, the ecclesiastical and civil authorities selected as the new patriarch, Proterius, the archpriest to whom Dioscurus had entrusted the administration of the see in his absence at Chalcedon. The city broke out in revolt at this news; troops driven into the ruins of a pagan temple were burnt alive. The government responded by interdicting food supplies and closing the baths and theatres. Even under military occupation the mass of the people resolutely refused to accept Proterius. At the death of Dioscurus in exile three years later, riots broke out again, and even the dispatch of an imperial ambassador could not reconcile the populace. Resistance centered in a

faction headed by the priest Timothy (Aelurus) the Cat and
the deacon Peter (Mongus) the Hoarse. They had no sympathy with the muddled theology of Eutyches but were stal-
wart Cyrillians. This party came to be known as Monophysite, for adhering to the Cyrillian formula — one incarnate
nature (*physis*) of the Divine Word.

Timothy and other Cyrillians were convinced that the
Definition of Chalcedon was positively Nestorian for reasons already indicated. They also complained about what
the Definition had omitted. There was no mention of Cyril's
central doctrine: one incarnate nature of the Divine Word.
Timothy drew up a compendium of patristic texts justifying
the phrase, but these were largely drawn from pseude-
pigraphical Apollinarist texts passing as the writings of
Athanasius, Pope Julius I and others, names that were
designed to guarantee their orthodoxy. Timothy complained
that in the Definition of Chalcedon no mention was made of
hypostatic union; nor of the phrase "out of two" to show
that Christ existed out of two disparate elements, the divine
and the human, but not "in two" natures which would be to
separate the One Christ into two persons, as did Nestorius.
Timothy taught that "we anathematize those who speak of
two natures or of two *ousiai* in respect of Christ," for "Nestorius was deposed because he spoke of 'two natures.'"
Nature for Timothy and the Cyrillians was almost synonymous with person: "There is no nature which does not
have its *hypostasis* and there is no *hypostasis* which exists
without its person (*prosopon*); if then there are two natures,
there are of necessity two persons, but if there are two persons, there are two Christs." The use of Leo's Tome further
convinced Timothy that the Definition of Chalcedon was
Nestorian, for Leo had said that "Jesus Christ was capable
of death in the one nature and incapable of death in the
other," that "each form, in communion with the other, performs the function proper to it; that is, the Word performing
what belongs to the Word, the flesh carrying out what
belongs to the flesh," and that "it does not belong to the
same nature to say 'I and my Father are one' and to say 'My
Father is greater than I.'" This sort of language was simply

blasphemy to the Cyrillians, indicating division in Christ and therefore clearly Nestorian. The restoration of the Nestorian-tainted Theodoret of Cyrus and Ibas of Edessa to their sees was further indication that the Council of Chalcedon was Nestorian. Finally, Chalcedon had added to the faith of Nicaea, something that the Cyrillian Council of Ephesus had forbidden.

Positively, Timothy and the Cyrillians believed that without change in His divinity the eternal Word, consubstantial with the Father, truly became man in Jesus Christ. The Word was one and the same person before and after the Incarnation, for the same person became through a personal, a hypostatic union, incarnate. This is what the Council of Chalcedon had not clearly declared: that the person of the union was the pre-existent person of the Word. The Word was united to flesh consubstantial with ours, consisting of body and rational soul, for we could not have been saved if the Savior were not in all things, sin alone excepted, like to His brethren. Jesus Christ is thus "out of two," out of Godhead and out of manhood, and in their union in His one person, each remains in its reality, inseparable, but perceived as different through intellectual analysis.

Secular politics soon complicated theological controversy even more. With the death of Empress Pulcheria in 453 and of Emperor Marcian in 457, the Theodosian line became extinct except for the princesses, captives of the Vandals in Africa. The Arian German general Aspar, the real power in Constantinople, handed the crown on to the quartermaster general of the army, Leo I. For the first time, the patriarch Anatolius presided at the coronation, hitherto a purely civil function, to give Leo's accession an added air of legitimacy. With the change in government in the capital and the provincial governor occupied elsewhere, the Monophysites at Alexandria seized the opportunity to have Timothy the Cat consecrated as patriarch. The governor soon restored order and banished Timothy, but on Holy Thursday, two weeks later, the imperial patriarch Proterius was surprised during the liturgy and torn to pieces by a mob. Timothy returned and quickly consolidated his position by deposing Chalcedonian bishops and clergy throughout Egypt. Anatolius of Constantinople countered Timothy's diplomatic negotiations with the imperial court and upheld the Council of Chalcedon. But Emperor Leo took Timothy's case under advisement. Deciding not to call yet another council, the emperor proceeded to poll the 65 metropolitans and 1600 bishops of the East on two questions: Should the Council of Chalcedon be upheld? Should Timothy be recognized at Alexandria? The answer was a resounding yes to the first question, no to the second. Still the Court delayed action against Timothy. From Rome Pope Leo intervened and sent two legates to the East armed with a conciliatory letter, omitting the phrase "in two natures," and a dossier of patristic texts in which Cyril's works figured prominently. These were forwarded to Timothy, but he remained unmoved at these efforts toward compromise even in the face of the terrible consequences to the unity of the Church and eventually to the stability of the Empire itself.

In 458 Anatolius was followed in the see of Constantinople by Gennadius who was more firmly Chalcedonian, not to say Nestorian. The new patriarch translated Chalcedonian terminology in a way that the Monophysites could not accept. He avoided any mention of Theotokos and hypostatic union, emphasizing the particular identity of each nature which entered into union in a single *prosopon*. This only stiffened the Monophysites in their belief that the Council of Chalcedon was at base Nestorian. The Duke of Egypt was ordered to oust Timothy. Blood flowed, but Timothy was at last arrested and exiled to the Crimea on the Black Sea. Here he remained for the next seventeen years, fulminating against Eutyches and the Council of Chalcedon alike. Elected in his place was Timothy of the White Turban, a gentle and kindly man who went so far as to replace Dioscurus' name on the diptychs but who failed nonetheless to reconcile the fanatical Cyrillians who clung to their watchword — One Incarnate Nature of the Divine Word.

In Syria, the ancient stronghold of Antiochene theology, the doctrines of Cyril were making surprising headway. The monks particularly became zealous propagators of his teaching. Among the people too the Cyrillian emphasis on the divinity of Jesus grew in appeal. The rising power in the East, Zeno, a Romanized Isaurian, a people long known for brigandage in eastern Asia Minor, married Emperor Leo's daughter and settled into Antioch as vice-emperor. One of his associates was a priest, Peter, surnamed the Fuller. Peter had previously been a monk among the strongly Chalcedonian religious called the Sleepless Monks (Acoemetae) noted for their absolute poverty and perpetual prayer. At Antioch Peter took the lead of the Cyrillians and with Zeno's approval installed himself as patriarch. Gennadius of Constantinople had Peter ousted, but the imperially appointed bishop soon retired in disgust at a "rebellious clergy, an unruly people, a church defiled." Peter the Fuller returned, but only briefly. Driven out again by Gennadius, he returned again in 475 only to be exiled once more. His successor was stabbed to death by fanatics in 481. Since the election of a Chalcedonian patriarch had been impossible, the Patriarch of Constantinople imposed the Chalcedonian priest Calendion as patriarch on a thoroughly alienated Antioch.

At the death of Emperor Leo I in 474, Zeno the Isaurian managed to seize the imperial throne. Neither his origins, private life or government endeared him to the people. His mother-in-law, the redoubtable Dowager Empress Verina led the faction that replaced him with her own brother Basilicus. Determined to end religious strife, the new emperor overruled his patriarch Acacius who had replaced Gennadius in 471 and called from exile the aging Monophysite Timothy the Cat. On his own initiative and without the concurrence of an ecclesiastical synod, Basilicus entrusted Timothy with an Encyclical in which the Tome of Leo and all things done at Chalcedon in innovation of the faith of the 318 Fathers of Nicaea were anathematized. Timothy was to promulgate this imperial fiat throughout the East. Failure to subscribe to it carried the penalty of deposition for the clergy, exile and confiscation of property for the laity. Timothy the Cat made a triumphal entry into Constantinople, though Chalcedonian monks barred his way into the cathedral. The patriarch of the capital, Acacius, gave

Timothy a cold reception and refused to sign the Encyclical. Remarkably enough he was left unmolested. Vainly the Chalcedonians of Constantinple protested Timothy's reappointment as patriarch of Alexandria to which he soon returned, stopping to celebrate his triumph at Ephesus, scene of the victories of Cyril and Dioscurus years before. In defiance of Acacius of Constantinople Timothy recalled a Monophysite bishop to Ephesus and even pronounced the deposition of Acacius himself. Triumphant too at Alexandria, he reinstalled himself as patriarch, granting a pension of a penny a day to his predecessor Timothy of the White Turban, who had retired to a monastery. Monophysitism was in the ascendant all over the East.

However, at Constantinople Acacius still stood firm for Chalcedon. Gradually he won over the people, partly by inducing a famous pillar-sitting ascetic Daniel to descend from his perch and join a demonstration with him in the city against the Monophysites. The people's enthusiasm grew to fever pitch. Threatened, Emperor Basilicus withdrew his Encyclical. But treason against him was abroad, and in 476 Zeno retook the capital and the throne. Basilicus and his children were allowed to die of starvation in exile.The bishops, between 500 to 700 of whom had subscribed to the Encyclical rejecting Chalcedon, now quickly veered back to its support. Thunderstruck, Timothy the Cat watched his triumph evaporate. The imperial commissioner who came to depose him found him old and ill and he was allowed to die in peace in 477. At his death one of his suffragan bishops, Theodore, hastily imposed hands on the deacon Peter the Hoarse as the new patriarch. But Peter had time only to bury Timothy and flee Alexandria one step ahead of the imperial police. The gentle Timothy of the White Turban was recalled to the patriarchal throne from monastic exile to restore order.

By 482 Acacius of Constantinople was beginning to have second thoughts about the Definition of Chalcedon. Since the majority of Eastern bishops resisted it, he started to plan for compromise. The reaction of the West had begun to mean less. It had ceased de facto to be a part of the Empire.

Roman legions and administration had long withdrawn from Britain, and pagan Angles, Saxons and Jutes were pushing the Christian Celts into the western and northern hills. Pagan Franks were striking south from the Rhine against the weakening independent kingdom of the Roman Syagrius in Gaul. Arian Alamanns and Burgundians had occupied western Gaul, while Arian Visigoths had seized southern Gaul and shared the Iberian peninsula with the Arian Sueves. Arian Vandals had for forty years maintained a kingdom based at Carthage in North Africa and in 467 had repulsed a Roman army and fleet sent to dislodge them. In Italy a Germanic chieftain Odovacar had made himself king, nominally subject to the emperor in Constantinople, and in 476 had sent the imperial regalia to Zeno, since the West had no need of it any longer. The bishop of Rome and his Chalcedonian associates were surrounded by Arians and pagans of alien races.

At Alexandria, the Chalcedonian patriarch Timothy of the White Turban, was feeling the onset of old age. Eager to insure an orthodox successor against his rival, Peter the Hoarse, Timothy sent one of his priests, John Talaia, to Constantinople to arrange the succession. The imperial court agreed to protect the interests of the Chalcedonians; John, for his part, agreed not to seek the patriarchal throne himself. But at the death of the patriarch Timothy, John Talaia accepted election as his successor. Acacius, who was seeking to pacify Alexandrian resistance to Chalcedon and wanted someone less controversial than the intriguing John, refused to recognize his election. John Talaia, like many before him, fled from Alexandria to Rome, while Acacius entered into negotiations with Peter the Hoarse about conditions for his recognition as the legitimate patriarch. A decree of union, the Henotikon, was drawn up probably by Acacius himself and with the sanction of Emperor Zeno sent to Egypt and Libya. In the Henotikon, no new form of faith was proposed, for "the only right and true belief" was that of Nicaea as confirmed at Constantinople and followed at Ephesus. The Twelve Anathemas of Cyril against Nestorius were accepted and no mention was made of "two natures."

The core of the document read:

> We confess that the only-begotten Son of God, himself
> God, who truly became man, our Lord Jesus Christ, who,
> *homoousios* with the Father according to Godhead and the
> Same *homoousios* with us according to manhood, came
> down and was incarnate of the Holy Spirit and of Mary the
> Virgin and 'Theotokos,' is one and not two; for we affirm
> that both the miracles and the sufferings which he voluntar-
> ily endured in the flesh are those of one Person. We alto-
> gether reject those who divide or confuse or introduce a
> phantom, since this true incarnation which was without sin
> of the 'Theotokos' did not bring about an addition of a Son;
> for the Trinity remained a Trinity even when One of the
> Trinity, the divine Logos, became incarnate.

Nestorius, Eutyches and those who think with them or who
have held any other opinion than that proposed in the Henotikon, whether at Chalcedon or in any other synod, were
condemned. Neither the Definition of Chalcedon nor the
Tome of Leo was mentioned.

Peter the Hoarse promptly accepted the Henotikon and
was recognized by Acacius as the legitimate patriarch of
Alexandria. But many Monophysites wanted more — the
outright repudiation of Chalcedon and the Tome. Peter
played a double game, protesting to Acacius his respect for
the Council while conciliating the Monophysites with propaganda kept carefully hidden from the hostile eyes of the
civil authorities. Since the Monophysites remained restive,
an imperial commissioner was sent to investigate. The
Monophysites under Theodore, the bishop who had originally consecrated Peter, organized a demonstration of
monks said to have numbered 30,000. Under the suspicious
eye of the imperial commissioner, Peter walked the theological tightrope with amazing adroitness; he convinced the
monks that he reprobated Leo and Chalcedon without
antagonizing the commissioner. Peter remained patriarch,
but the monks and others refused in the end to be concil-
iated. The Monophysite dissidents, called Acephali (the

Headless) because they were without their own bishop, continued their protests.

At Antioch the Chalcedonian patriarch Calendion,
imposed on the Monophysite-sympathizing city, refused to
accept the Henotikon. But soon he was surrounded by political intrigue. Isaurians who had fallen out with Emperor
Zeno prepared a coup against him and declared an army
commander emperor. When Zeno drove the usurper from
Antioch, the Chalcedonian Calendion, suspected of treason,
was sent into exile in Egypt. The Monophysite Peter the
Fuller found himself for the fourth time patriarch of Antioch. He promptly accepted the Henotikon which apparently
satisfied the Monophysites of the Orient. To the venerated
Trisagion — Holy God, Holy and Mighty, Holy and
Immortal — Peter added the phrase: crucified for us. This
plain profession of the one nature of the Incarnate Word
became a rallying cry for the Monophysites from now on.
Chalcedonians were hounded from office throughout the
Orient and bishops subscribed wholesale to the Henotikon.
In Palestine too the Patriarch of Jerusalem imposed the
Henotikon on Chalcedonians and Monophysites alike.

At Rome, Pope Simplicius received with horror the news
of the elevation of Peter the Hoarse as patriarch of Alexandria. Vainly he deluged Acacius of Constantinople with protests and requests for further explanation. By the time of his
death in 483, the pope had received no satisfactory reply
from Acacius. Simplicius' successor, Pope Felix III, tackled
the question with greater resolution. Acting on the information of John Talaia, who had fled to Rome, he sent a delegation to Constantinople citing Acacius to answer charges
brought against him by John. Acacius managed to isolate
the legates and compel them to accept his explanations. The
legates even attended the solemn inscription of the name of
Peter the Hoarse on the diptychs of Constantinople. But the
Sleepless Monks, loyal to Chalcedon, sent reports of the
situation to Rome. Outraged, Felix III convened a synod of
seventy-seven bishops in Rome in 484 at which both Acacius
and the legates were deposed. The pope in synod decreed:
"Acacius, who in spite of two warnings has not ceased to

disregard salutary ordinances, who has dared to imprison me in the person of my representatives, God, by a sentence pronounced from heaven, has ejected from the priestly office." Any who held communion with Acacius, whether bishop, cleric, monk or layman, were likewise condemned "by command of the Holy Spirit." Another papal official was sent to Constantinople to deliver the sentence, but he apparently succumbed to bribery and failed in his duties. However, monks, loyal to the pope, succeeded in pinning the decree to the patriarch's vestments during the liturgy in the cathedral. Whereupon, Acacius erased the name of Pope Felix from his church's diptychs. Thirty-three years after the Council of Chalcedon, the result of its Definition was outright schism between Eastern and Western churches.

6. *Chronology*

448 Condemnation of Eutyches by Home Synod and Flavian of Constantinople.

449 Tome of Leo the Great to Flavian of Constantinople.

449 Robber Council of Ephesus led by Dioscurus of Alexandria and Juvenal of Jerusalem; Flavian of Constantinople and Domnus of Antioch deposed.

450 Theodosius II died; succeeded by sister Pulcheria and Marcian.

451 Council convoked to Nicaea, then transferred to Chalcedon; legate Paschasinus president.
   COUNCIL OF CHALCEDON

   October 8 - Trial of Dioscurus of Alexandria
       10 - Council accepted Creeds of Nicaea and Constantinople I; Cyril and Leo declared to agree with one another and with Creeds.
       13 - Dioscurus deposed.

17 - Dissident Egyptians remanded to custody of new Patriarch of Alexandria; dissident monks, to Patriarch of Constantinople.
22 - Proposed creed rejected by legates because Tome of Leo not included.
25 - Definition promulgated and signed in presence of Emperor Marcian.
26-31 Theodoret of Cyrus and Ibas of Edessa reconciled; canons drawn up.

453   Leo the Great accepted conciliar definition but not canons.

457   Death of Emperor Marcian; succeeded by Leo I. Timothy the Cat, Monophysite, bishop of Alexandria.

458   Chalcedonian Gennadius, patriarch of Constantinople replacing Anatolius.

460   Exile of Timothy the Cat from Alexandria.

461   Death of Leo the Great; former legate Hilary elected bishop of Rome.

468   Simplicius elected pope following Hilary.

471   Acacius, patriarch of Constantinople, following Gennadius.

474   Death of Emperor Leo I, succeeded by Zeno until 491.

475   Usurper Basilicus drove out Zeno and issued anti-Chalcedonian Encyclical promulgated by Timothy the Cat.
Peter the Fuller, Monophysite bishop of Antioch, three times exiled.

476   Zeno restored.
End of Western Empire under German Odovacar.

477   Timothy the Cat, restored to Alexandria, died; Peter the Hoarse consecrated and immediately exiled from Alexandria.

482   Peter the Hoarse restored to Alexandria; Peter the Fuller, to Antioch.
       Henotikon of Emperor Zeno issued.
483   Resolute Pope Felix III sent legates to Constantinople to try Acacius.
484   Mutual excommunications of Felix of Rome and Acacius of Constantinople; beginning of Acacian Schism which will last to 518.

7. Select Bibliography

The events surrounding Chalcedon are well described by L. Duchesne, *The Early History of the Church* (London, 1912), vol. 3, chapters 11 and 12. Useful documentary material is in J. Stevenson, *Creeds, Councils and Controversies* (London, 1966). A. Grillmeier, *Christ in Christian Thought* (Atlanta, 1975) is a masterly treatment of Christology up to the Council of Chalcedon; J. N. D. Kelly, *Early Christian Doctrines* (New York, 1959) and J. Pelikan, *Emergence of the Catholic Tradition* (Chicago, 1971) are shorter treatments. J. Meyendorff, *Christ in Eastern Christian Thought* (Crestwood, N.Y., 1975) perceptively analyzes Christology after the Council. R. V. Sellars, *The Council of Chalcedon* (London, 1953) is a fine survey of history and doctrine. A good treatment of the relations between the patriarchates is N. H. Baynes, "Alexandria and Constantinople: A Study in Ecclesiastical Diplomacy," in *Byzantine Studies* (London, 1955), 97-116. W. H. C. Frend, *Rise of the Monophysite Movement* (Cambridge, 1972) is a massive study of the whole question. T. G. Jalland, *Life of and Times of St. Leo the Great* (London, 1941) and *The Church and the Papacy* (London, 1944) are standard works. Francis Dvornik, *Byzantium and the Roman Papacy* (New York, 1966) is a splendid little book by a great scholar. Gerald O'Collins, *What are They Saying about Jesus?* (New York, 1977) outlines the questions modern theologians are raising about the work of the Council. Useful too is J. Richards, *The Popes and the Papacy in the Early Middle Ages, 476-752* (London, 1979).

6

Council of Constantinople II, 553

1. Development of Monophysitism

The period following the Council of Chalcedon was much like that following the Council of Nicaea: at both councils a basically Western solution to an Eastern problem had been intruded into the theological diet of the East. After both councils it took the East considerable time and effort to digest and assimilate an alien morsel. In the case of Nicaea, the Roman World gradually accepted its Creed. Arianism lingered on largely among the German tribes, but here too slowly succumbed to Nicaea. In the case of both Ephesus and Chalcedon, sections of the Roman World and beyond went into schism rather than accept their decisions and would continue in schism down to our day. The Council of Constantinople II was an effort to show the (by then) schismatic Monophysites that Chalcedon really did preserve the theological values they held dear.

In the last chapter we outlined the resistance to Chalcedon by moderate Cyrillians and outright Monophysites resulting in the Acacian schism of 484. By this date almost everywhere in the East the Henotikon of Emperor Zeno and the Patriarch Acacius was accepted by the bishops, at least formally, as the definition of orthodox faith. By 492 the first set of protagonists in this controversy had dropped from the scene. Peter the Fuller died at Antioch in 488; Acacius, at Constantinople in 489; Peter the Hoarse, at Alexandria in 490; Emperor Zeno, in 491, and Felix III, at Rome in 492. The new patriarch of Constantinople, Fravita, in 489 had entered into a conciliatory correspondence with Felix III and Peter the Hoarse. Before anything could come of his somewhat tentative attempts at conciliation, Fravita too died, to be replaced by the Syrian Euphemius. A convinced Chalcedonian, the new patriarch of Constantinople notified Felix III of his election and refused communion with Peter the Hoarse in Alexandria. Euphemius planned a synod to depose Peter, when Peter died and was replaced at Alexandria by the Monophysite Athanasius II. As the price of full communion with Rome, Felix demanded that Euphemius expunge the name of Acacius from the diptychs. Though Chalcedonian in faith, the patriarch was in a political situation which would not permit him to do this.

These initial moves toward healing the schism were further frustrated by the accession to the imperial throne in 491 of Anastasius I. A Slav by birth, the new emperor was so noted for his piety and charity that, even though a layman, he had been proposed for the patriarchate of Antioch at the death of Peter the Fuller. Unfortunately for the peace of Christendom, Anastasius was an ardent Monophysite. At the age of sixty this surprising emperor married Zeno's widow and was crowned by Euphemius of Constantinople, who first requested him to make a profession of faith in favor of Chalcedon. This Anastasius consented to do in writing. Once crowned, Anastasius showed amazing energy: the revolt of the Isaurians loyal to the dead Emperor Zeno was put down; imperial finances, the judiciary and the police were reformed; the Empire's defenses strengthened. In the West, still in the emperor's mind a part of the Empire, Anastasius sent consular insignia to the rising Frankish king Clovis, newly converted to orthodox Catholicism from paganism, who was in the process of occupying all Gaul, turning it into Frankland, France. In Italy, Anastasius recognized as king Theodoric, the Arian Ostrogoth who had in 493 conquered the peninsula. The emperor's religious policy was, however, less fortunate. In Egypt, successive patriarchs of Alexandria to 518 consistently anathematized the Tome of Leo and the Definition of Chalcedon. At Jerusalem the patriarch continued to adhere to the Henotikon while the Palestinian monastery near Gaza headed by Peter of Iberia remained a hotbed of radical Monophysitism. In Syria, the Patriarch of Antioch, Palladius, was strengthened in his anti-Chalcedonian position by one of the principal theologians of Monophysitism, Philoxenus of Mabbough.

Philoxenus had been trained in the theological schools of Edessa, where he early showed himself a determined opponent of the Nestorian-leaning Ibas. During the rule of Calendion, the Chalcedonian patriarch of Antioch, he had been expelled from the city because of his preaching. In return he helped engineer the deposition of Calendion. Recalled to Antioch by Peter the Fuller, he was made bishop of Mabbough, about 100 miles east of Antioch. Under the patriarch Palladius, he became an indefatigable preacher of Monophysite doctrines throughout the Orient, though he spoke only Syriac. The Monophysitism of Philoxenus was a basically Cyrillian Christology clothed in a somewhat primitive materialist philosophy and monastic spirituality but without the flexibility to recognize the Cyrillian elements of the Definition of Chalcedon. For Philoxenus, Jesus Christ "is God, and if He became what He was not, it is not from man that He became God, but from God that He became man, while remaining God as He was." "He became and underwent no change, for He remained [what He was] even in His becoming." At the heart of Philoxenus' position was his view of nature and person: "There is no nature without person, just as there is no person without nature. If there are two natures, there must be two persons and two sons." To admit two natures was for Philoxenus to admit two concrete, complete beings in Christ, destroying the unity of Christ and thus the very basis of human salvation. The Incarnate Word was a single nature that took to Himself changing humanity, becoming with it one nature. But Philoxenus was neither

Eutychian nor Apollinarian: "He has become perfect man as to the soul, the body, and the intelligence, in order to renew the whole man. True God by nature, by essence and eternity, He made Himself...with the exception of sin...true man and according to the flesh, consubstantial with us." There was in Christ no real "mingling" of Godhead and manhood, though Philoxenus used the term in deference to Syriac custom: "The Word was not changed into flesh when He took a body from it, and the flesh was not transformed into the Word's nature when it was united to it. The natures were not mixed among themselves as water and wine which by commixture lose their natures." Still, as John Meyendorff observes, "the weakness of Philoxenus' position resides...in the fact that in his Christology there exists no formula radically opposed to Eutychianism." Stubbornly viewing the statements of Chalcedon of one person, two natures as Nestorian, Philoxenus preached a rigidly Cyrillian doctrine of One Incarnate Nature of the Divine Word.

Meanwhile, the struggle between Chalcedonians and Monophysites centered in Constantinople. The Patriarch Euphemius demonstrated his loyalty to Chalcedon by confirming its decrees in a synod in 492 and by opening correspondence with Pope Gelasius, Felix III's successor. Patriarch and emperor were now at loggerheads. Anastasius was further angered when Euphemius refused to return the emperor's written confession in the faith of Chalcedon made before his coronation. Two attempts were made on the patriarch's life. Then Euphemius made the mistake of complaining about the emperor's treatment of the rebel Isaurians. He was accused of treason and deposed. Despite the lively protests of the people, he was exiled and replaced by Macedonius, nephew of the former patriarch Gennadius. Macedonius promptly subscribed to the Henotikon, much to the scandal of the Sleepless Monks and other Chalcedonians. To conciliate them he confirmed in synod the decrees of Chaldedon without mentioning the Henotikon. Emperor Anastasius allowed this ambiguity to stand. Nothing now seemed to hinder rapprochement with the West. But at Rome, the new pope Gelasius, an African by birth, was a tough and vigorous man with a taste for controversy. As long as Gelasius was pope, ambiguous compromise was impossible. Contemptuous of Greeks in general, he regarded the bishop of Constantinople as a mere suffragan of Heraclea according to the canons of Nicaea. When Anastasius sent ambassadors to the German king of Italy, they were instructed to have no relations with the pope. On the other hand, ambassadors sent from Italy to the imperial court were warned not to treat with the Patriarch Macedonius. The pope made every effort to urge the Latin-speaking bishops of Illyria to erase the hated name of Acacius from their diptychs.

Before and during his pontificate Gelasius wrote theological works developing his arguments against Acacius. He pointed out that the Roman See above all was bound to carry out the decrees of councils, "since it ratifies each council by its authority, and safeguards it by ceaseless oversight, in virtue of its leadership, which the blessed Peter the Apostle received by word of the Lord, and which by common agreement of the Church he has always possessed and still retains." The pope wrote as well to Anastasius: "There are in fact two, August Emperor, by whom this world is originally governed; the consecrated authority (*auctoritas*) of bishops and the royal power (*potestas*). Of these, the responsibility of the bishops is the more weighty, since even for the rulers of men they will have to give account at the judgment seat of God." Here Gelasius assigns to bishops *auctoritas,* a term consecrated in Roman law and belonging to the ideal and moral sphere whose force was derived from tradition and public opinion; to the emperor, *potestas,* the power granted to Roman magistrates for the carrying out of their executive duties during their term of office. Thus in the mind of the pope episcopal authority is higher in some undefined degree to imperial power just as moral influence is superior to physical force. In another letter he commented, "It is his [Emperor's] business to learn what is the content of religion, not teach." Though the bishops of southern France counseled moderation, the schism between East and West dragged on throughout Gelasius' pontificate.

Pope Anastasius II who succeeded Gelasius in 496 was more conciliatory. He sent two legates to Emperor Anastasius urging peaceful settlement of the issues. The legates also entered into negotiation with the patriarchs of Constantinople and Alexandria. These promising developments were disrupted by the premature death of the pope. After a tumultuous double election in Rome which had to be arbitrated by the Arian king and which was followed by a scandalous schism, the next pope Symmachus returned to the hardline policies of Gelasius. When asked by the emperor to approve the consecration of Peter the Fuller, Symmachus answered that a penitent's stool, not a bishop's throne, was the place for that heretic.

Throughout the East, Zeno's Henotikon remained the imperially imposed official declaration of faith. But, outside of Egypt, partisans of Chalcedon were to be found everywhere. At Antioch the Chalcedonian Flavian succeeded the Monophysite Palladius as patriarch. At Jerusalem the Chalcedonian Elias, a hermit who had fled Egypt during the persecution of Timothy the Cat, became patriarch, subscribing to the Henotikon as a pure formality. He had the support of Sabas, abbot of some 400 monks in the Kedron valley and superior of all the hermits of Palestine. Chalcedon thus had the support of Macedonius at Constantinople, Flavian at Antioch and Elias at Jerusalem. But Anastasius, till now distracted by the task of defending his throne and empire, had time to turn to the religious question. In these matters he had the aid of vigorous Philoxenus of Mabbough and the new intellectual leader of Monophysitism, Severus.

Scion of an aristocratic family whose grandfather had been a bishop at the Council of Ephesus and had voted to condemn Nestorius, Severus studied literature and rhetoric at Alexandria. He continued his studies in law at the celebrated school in Beirut before presenting himself for baptism. Baptized in 488 he became a monk in a house near Gaza in Palestine among the fanatical Monophysite disciples of Peter of Iberia. After a rigorous ascetic life in the desert, he founded a monastery, largely with his own money, and was ordained priest. He now put his education, brilliance and zeal wholly into the Monophysite cause.

In his Christology Severus was purely and simply Cyrillian, though more rigorous and obstinate in presentation. He opposed any mingling of natures in Christ, any manhood as a distinct nature. But though there was but a single nature in Christ, it possessed all the natural qualities of manhood. "We are not allowed," he said, "to anathematize those who speak of natural properties, the divinity and the humanity that make the single Christ. The flesh does not cease to exist as flesh, even if it becomes God's flesh, and the Word does not abandon His own nature, even if He unites himself hypostatically to the flesh which possesses a rational and intelligent soul. But the difference is also preserved as well as the identity under the form of the natural characteristics of the natures which make up the Emmanuel [God with us], since the flesh is not transformed into the Word's nature and the Word is not changed into flesh." Christ was for Severus not a single essence, a single *ousia*, for to say this would be to deny all duality in the qualities and Christ's consubstantiality with us. Christ was rather a single nature. Severus taught a real duality within the one nature while avoiding all confusion between humanity and divinity. Before the Incarnation, the Word was a simple nature; after He became a composite nature in regard to the flesh. *Hypostasis* and *physis* Severus regarded as synonymous in the case of Christ, for He was one concrete, unique being sharing in the essence of God and the essence of man. Intellectually, it is possible to discern in Christ two natures, but the union of divinity and humanity is such that Christ is out of two natures and in one nature. "In two natures" meant for Severus a duality signifying separation; "from two natures" indicated composition and union without confusion. He refused ever to admit two natures after the Incarnation except through contemplation by the intellect. This resolute insistence on one nature led him to insist as well on one agent and one activity in Christ. Thus Leo the Great's statement in his Tome that each nature does what is proper to it in communion with the other was anathema to Severus: "One is the agent, one the activity, but the works are varied." He added, "We do not have the right because of the brilliance of the divine miracles and of the things that transcend the law of nature, to deny that His sufferings of redemption and His death occurred in accordance with the law of nature. He is the Logos incarnate without being changed. He performed the miracles as is appropriate for God, and He voluntarily permitted the laws of the flesh to operate in His parts while He bore His sufferings in a human way."

John Meyendorff brings out quite well the basis of the disagreement between the Chalcedonians and Monophysites:

> Severus's position on the single energy is a good illustration of the very basis of the disagreement. The two opposing parties followed conflicting arguments. The Monophysites contemplated the Logos in his new "state," the incarnate state, and insisted on the absolute unity of subject, expressed by them with the word *physis* in both states. No human energy could thus be found in the action accomplished by the Logos alone in the incarnation. The Chalcedonian argument, while admitting the soteriological inspiration of the Cyrillian theology and, evidently, the identity between the pre-existing Logos and the incarnate Word, was also preoccupied with the human aspect of salvation. It could not be satisfied with a manhood conceived only *en theoria* as a "state" of the Logos, which was expressed in human acts without human existence. Severus, of course, admitted this existence, but only *en sunthesei* and he refused to designate it by the terms *physis/energeia,* which according to him were necessarily linked to an existence that was separate, concrete, and hypostatic. But is a human nature without human energy a true human nature?

Severus criticized the Chalcedonian definition for its neglect of Cyrillian terminology and its insistence on two natures which meant for him two concrete and distinct beings. Even though Chalcedon had used the term one *hypostasis,* some of its supporters interpreted it as a synonym for the Antiochene *prosopon* of union, a fact which did not encourage Monophysite allegiance to Chalcedon.

Especially, by neglecting to emphasize the hypostatic union, Chalcedon did not stress firmly enough for Severus that the hypostasis of union is the pre-existent hypostasis of the Logos. The Antiochene prosopic union for Severus is like the union existing between Peter and Paul on the basis of their both being apostles. In such a union, two beings exist in their union. Hypostatic union can only be out of two natures, never in two natures. After the union, though the two hypostases remain, they have no individual separate existence of their own; there is only one countable entity. There is only one center of activity, one source of operation out of which arise all the actions of the one incarnate nature of the divine Word.

In the years 506/7, Philoxenus opened the Monophysite campaign against the resurgent Chalcedonians. He condemned the older proponents of Antiochene theology — Diodorus of Tarsus, Theodore of Mopsuestia, Theodoret of Cyrus and Ibas of Edessa — and stirred up the Monophysites against the patriarch, Flavian of Antioch. The lingering problem at Antioch is well described by Meyendorff:

> The Antiochene theologians admitted, no doubt, that God had appropriated the flesh by becoming fully man; but their training, going back to Theodore of Mopsuestia, still forbade them to say that 'God died in the flesh' and, by implication, that Christ's single hypostasis was not a 'hypostasis of union' newly appeared at the moment of the incarnation but the very hypostasis of the Logos; that it designated not only the concrete being of Christ but the *personal and pre-existent identity* of the eternal and incarnate Word. The pre-existent Word is the *subject* of the death of Christ, for in Christ there is no other personal subject apart from the Word; only *someone* can die, not something, or a nature, or the flesh. Here lay the subject matter of the debate. Antiochene thought was still unable to admit a distinction between nature and hypostasis.

Flavian defended himself by condemning Nestorius once again, but Philoxenus insisted on explicit condemnation of

all who held the doctrine of two natures. But when Philoxenus attempted to carry the struggle to Constantinople, he
met with a cold reception from the Patriarch Macedonius
and the people and was forced to leave the city. Severus
himself soon arrived at Constantinople from Palestine at the
head of two hundred monks and opened a campaign against
the Chalcedonian monks of Palestine. Some two hundred of
these journeyed to the capital to defend themselves. The
quarrel died down, but Severus remained in the city for
some time using every means at his disposal to advance the
Monophysite cause. The Patriarch Macedonius was caught
between the Monophysite Severus and the Chalcedonian
monks whom he had alienated by adhering to the Henotikon. Soon he incurred imperial displeasure by calling
Anastasius a Manichean.

After neutralizing Macedonius' supporters and alerting
the army, the emperor deposed the patriarch in 511. The
Monophysites seized the cathedral and celebrated the
liturgy, omitting the patriarch's name. Later an imperial
official found the dejected Macedonius alone in a corner of
the cathedral and informed him of the imperial decree of
exile. The cathedral treasurer, Timothy, a moderate
Monophysite who did not condemn Chalcedon, was made
patriarch, much to the anger of some Monophysites who
wanted Severus. It took the firm support of the emperor to
ensure Timothy's survival.

Resistance to the Monophysites and the Patriarch Timothy
grew at Constantinople among the monks and people and
more ominously among the emperor's own family and that
of Areobindus, his principal military commander. The
emperor himself stood firm. In 512 he allowed a demonstration in favor of the Monophysites in which the modified
Trisagion — Holy God, Holy Immortal One, crucified for us
— was chanted publicly in the streets. The Chalcedonian
monks incited a riot: statues of Anastasius were overthrown;
houses of prominent Monophysites were burned. Finally,
the mob fortified the forum of Constantine and drove away
with stones the imperial commissioners sent to negotiate

with them. Three days later, Anastasius, simply dressed and bareheaded, appeared in the circus where the common people customarily gathered to express their political opinions. The crowd met him chanting the orthodox Trisagion. The emperor promised reform and even offered to abdicate in the interest of peace. Impressed by the emperor's humility and sincerity, the crowd veered round to his support. The crisis had passed for the moment.

At Antioch, Philoxenus continued his attack on the Patriarch Flavian. Even though Flavian subscribed to the Typos, a statement of Monophysite belief prepared by Severus, condemned the whole Antiochene School, the Definition of Chalcedon excepting only the rejection of Nestorius and Eutyches, and all who held two natures in Christ, Philoxenus still pursued him. In 512 Flavian called a synod at Sidon in an attempt to calm Syria. About eighty bishops, including Severus and Philoxenus, attended. The orthodox firmly resisted the Monophysites, throwing them into confusion by revealing letters of communion sent by the Monophysite patriarch of Alexandria to bishops who had accepted the Henotikon but without condemning Chalcedon or Leo's Tome. The imperial commissioner promptly dissolved the synod. To conciliate the imperial court, Flavian of Antioch and Elias of Jerusalem wrote to assure the emperor of their acceptance of the Henotikon. Still Philoxenus tirelessly attacked Flavian, rousing the monks, winning over bishops, until Emperor Anastasius resolved on Flavian's deposition despite his reiterated condemnation of Chalcedon. Flavian was exiled to Petra in southern Palestine. In his place Severus himself was chosen patriarch. At his consecration, he solemnly professed the faith of Nicaea, Constantinople and Ephesus, and accepted the Henotikon, while condemning Nestorius, Eutyches, the Council of Chalcedon, Leo's Tome and all who held two natures in Christ. Severus succeeded in imposing his views at a provincial synod held in Antioch in 513. Again at a larger synod at Tyre, he succeeded in giving the Henotikon a clearly anti-Chalcedonian interpretation. But Severus had opposition from both sides. Extreme

Monophysites reproached him for moderation. Others now labored to show that Chalcedon really did express the deepest insights of Cyril's theology.

These theologians have come to be called Neo-Chalcedonians. They worked to counter the widespread interpretation of the Definition of Chalcedon in an Antiochene fashion by reconciling it with Cyrillian Christology. They went beyond Cyril's Second Letter to Nestorius and Letter to the Orientals to include his Third Letter with its Twelve Anathemas passed over at Ephesus and Chalcedon. They circulated florilegia of Cyril's writings to show that his teaching was not opposed to Chalcedon. R. V. Sellers lists examples of their argument:

> Thus — to make use of but one or two of the citations from Cyril — they could point out that the great authority had said that the flesh is flesh and that the Logos is Logos, that 'Godhead is one thing according to its nature, and manhood another thing,' and that 'each remains and is perceived in its natural property'; moreover, he had affirmed that, like that of the natures, the difference of the sayings was not to be abolished. Again, they could show that he had emphatically rejected the notion of a 'mixture' of Godhead and manhood in Jesus Christ. He had expressly stated that in respect of his Godhead 'the Lord is immutable and impassible, and that in respect of the nature of the flesh,' or in the 'earthly nature,' he is *homoousios* with us, and suffered for us. And, going farther, they could ask whether it was not indisputable that the champion of orthodoxy had accepted the 'two natures.' For, besides allowing that one could speak of the 'nature' of the manhood and of the Godhead of Emmanuel, had he not taught that 'two natures' are to be 'seen' in the one Christ, and accepted the formula, 'a union of two natures,' when he entered into communion with the Orientals in the year 433? The inference, then, was obvious: Cyril himself could have confessed with Chalcedon that Jesus Christ is one Person, 'in two natures' —and this 'after the union' —since he taught in the same way.

Palestine was the home of several theologians who promoted this synthesis. No actual writings of John of Scythopolis survive, but he seems to have been a pioneer in exposing the fraudulent Apollinarian writings, especially those attributed to Pope Julius. Somewhat more is known of John the Grammarian of Caesarea who was active between 514 and 518. John accepted the Cyrillian formula of the hypostatic union and showed it excluded any notion that Christ's humanity ever existed apart from His divinity. He accepted too the Monophysite battle cry: One Incarnate Nature of the Divine Word. But he went on to show that one nature in Christ does not mean one substance, for in Christ there is a double consubstantiality — with the Father and with us. He accepted the Monophysite Trisagion: Holy God. . . crucified for us, as showing that all predication of attributes applies to the one *hypostasis* in Christ. Unfortunately Severus dismissed his efforts as "womanish fables and absurdities."

As Severus defended Monophysitism at Antioch, his cohorts mounted the opposition against Elias of Jerusalem. The Chalcedonian monks of Palestine staunchly supported him until the government divulged a letter in which he had expressed certain reservations about Chalcedon. With his support waning, Elias was exiled in 516. To replace Elias, John, a deacon and guardian of the Holy Cross, was chosen patriarch after he had agreed to condemn Leo's Tome and Chalcedon. But the Chalcedonian monks resisted the new patriarch under the leadership of Sabas, the Archimandrite of all Palestinian hermits, an admirer of the godfather of Nestorianism, Theodore of Mopsuestia. As the quarrel grew in intensity, the new patriarch appeared before an immense crowd of clergy and laity in the Church of St. Stephen in Jerusalem. Much to everyone's surprise, at his side stood the Archimandrite Sabas. The crowd exploded into acclamations for Chalcedon. When the patriarch could speak at last, it was to condemn the Monophysites and proclaim his adherence to the Four Councils as to the Four Gospels. For the moment Chalcedon was in the saddle at Jerusalem.

From 513, Emperor Anastasius had to face the challenge

of Vitalian, an officer of the Danubian garrison, who appeared before the capital with a ragtag force of some 60,000 men. To rally those discontented with Anastasius to his attempt to gain a more important command, Vitalian declared his adherence to the Council of Chalcedon. At first Anastasius fended him off with vague promises of promotion, but after Vitalian defeated two detachments of the regular army, the emperor gave him command of the legions in Thrace. Anastasius and Vitalian then agreed to the convocation of a council at Heraclea under the presidency of the pope to resolve the religious question. Anastasius dispatched a conciliatory letter to Pope Hormisdas, successor to Symmachus who had died in 514. An able diplomat, Hormisdas encouraged communication while insisting on the recognition of Chalcedon and the condemnation of Acacius. In 515 the pope sent legates to Constantinople for further negotiations. But Vitalian's revolt soon collapsed and Anastasius resumed his policy of supporting the Monophysites. When the pope reproached him, the emperor responded: "You may injure me and condemn me but you cannot give me orders."

Still the bishops of Illyria and Macedonia declared for Chalcedon and union with the bishop of Rome. The tide was turning against the Monophysite policy of Anastasius. In Egypt Monophysitism was strongest, sinking deep roots among clergy and people. At Antioch Severus survived as patriarch, but faced stiff opposition from the rising Neo-Chalcedonians. At Constantinople, Timothy remained a moderate Monophysite. At Jerusalem the patriarch John had declared his allegiance to Chalcedon. Chalcedonians and Monophysites had fought each other to a standstill, while the Neo-Chalcedonians labored at a theology which could resolve their differences. Then in 518, Anastasius died after a twenty-seven year reign.

2. Orthodox Reaction under Justin I

The new emperor, Justin I, had been the elderly commander of the palace guard. A semi-literate Illyrian peasant in origin and married to an ex-slave, Justin was an orthodox Chalcedonian. At his side stood his able, well-educated and orthodox nephew Justinian. The stage was now set for an orthodox reaction. Six days after the coronation of the new emperor, a crowd in the cathedral tumultuously demanded that the new patriarch John, who had just replaced Timothy, recognize Chalcedon and condemn Severus of Antioch. The next day John presided at a public ceremony in honor of Chalcedon. Soon after, a synod of forty bishops accepted an appeal from the monks of Constantinople for the recall of exiled Chalcedonians. Justin then publicly ordered the bishops to accept Chalcedon and barred all heretics from the army and the civil service. At Jerusalem and Tyre, synods recognized Chalcedon, but northern Syria and Egypt remained intransigent. Severus fled from Antioch to Monophysite Alexandria. His court-appointed successor Paul opened an exceptionally bitter persecution of Syrian Monophysites, especially among the monks.

The emperor then proceeded to open negotiations with Pope Hormisdas in an effort to end the twenty-four year Acacian Schism. Justin invited Hormisdas to Constantinople to restore orthodoxy in the East. The pope sent five legates to Constantinople, among them the Greek deacon, Dioscurus, an able diplomat. Hormisdas was firm about the terms of reunion: recognition of the faith conserved at Rome, condemnation of Nestorius, Eutyches and their followers, acceptance of the dogmatic letters of Pope Leo, deletion from the diptychs of the names of Acacius, his successors and all in communion with them, as well as excommunication of Emperors Zeno and Anastasius. In 519 Justin welcomed the papal legates with all possible honor and offered to discuss terms. When the legates refused all discussion, the emperor acceded to their demands. The patriarch, all the bishops present in Constantinople and the heads of monasteries signed the papal formula of reunion. The Acacian Schism was over at last. The legates remained at Constantinople until the next year to see to the full implementation of the terms of reunion.

During these negotiations, a new dogmatic difficulty

arose. Scythian monks from the area at the mouth of the Danube associated with the rebel commander Vitalian began to circulate a formula by which they hoped to reconcile the teachings of Leo and Cyril and exclude any Nestorian interpretation of the Definition of Chalcedon. They proposed as the basis of reconciliation the Theopaschite Formula — One of the Trinity suffered for us. This they interpreted according to the twelfth anathema of Cyril against Nestorius. The refusal to accept the formula became the best proof of crypto-Nestorianism because it meant the rejection of the union of divinity and humanity in the hypostasis of the pre-existing Logos. (It will be remembered that the Antiochene Theodoret of Cyrus refused to the end of his life to admit that the Word suffered in the flesh.) By showing their acceptance of a fundamentally Cyrillian tenet, they hoped to reconcile Severus and his Monophysites. The Chalcedonian Sleepless Monks who refused to accept Cyril's rule for the predication of divine and human attributes to the Logos and were suspicious of the term Theotokos, opposed the Theopaschite Formula. They warned the papal legates to avoid discussion with the Scythian monks on their arrival in Constantinople. But Justin's nephew Justinian supported the formula and recommended the monks to Pope Hormisdas.

The pope thought the formula unwise and put them off. But the Roman canonist Denis the Short aided them by translating the Third Letter of Cyril with its twelve anathemas against Nestorius into Latin. The African bishops in exile in Sicily led by Fulgentius of Ruspe wrote in approval of the formula. When the monks, thus encouraged, again approached the pope, he ordered them from Rome. On their return to Constantinople, they accused the papal legate Dioscurus of heresy and their leader John Maxentius wrote a violent letter to the pope. For the time being, however, the quarrel died down and the Scythians were taken under the protection of Justinian, the all-powerful imperial nephew and heir to the throne.

The Hormisdan formula of reunion received a poor welcome in many places. At Ephesus, the Council of Chalcedon was repudiated. At Thessalonika, the legate who sought the bishop's signature was attacked. At Antioch, the imperial patriarch Paul had so alienated the populace by his severity against the Monophysites that he had to be removed. His successor was killed in the earthquake that destroyed Antioch in 526, and his successor, in turn, Ephrem of Amida, had to resort to armed force to install orthodox bishops in place of the exiled Monophysites. The situation was made more difficult when the bishop of Cyrus allowed a procession in honor of Theodoret and celebrated a feast in honor of the great Antiochene theologians and "Saint" Nestorius. He was deposed by imperial intervention. From exile Severus remained in constant contact with the Syrian people still faithful to him and with his fellow Monophysite bishops in exile. He poured out writings in defense of his position. Since the sharp eye of the imperial police hindered the ordination of priests loyal to the Monophysite cause, Severus authorized the exiled bishop John of Tella in Callinicum, far away to the East on the Euphrates to ordain Monophysite priests and deacons. Denounced to the authorities, John was arrested and imprisoned at Antioch, the list of those ordained confiscated by the police.

In Egypt, resistance was even stronger. At the death of the Monophysite bishop in 518, Pope Hormisdas urged the installation of his legate-deacon, Dioscurus. Instead, in deference to the strong feelings in Egypt, Justin authorized the consecration of Timothy III, an intransigent Monophysite who had refused to accept even Zeno's Henotikon. Justin went so far as to employ Timothy as a negotiator with the Monophysite king of Axoum, modern Ethiopia. Egypt was soon filled with Monophysite bishops fleeing from imperial persecution elsewhere, among whom the leader and principal theologian was Severus, held in great veneration by the Egyptians.

But the Monophysites of Egypt were soon riven by factions. One group of disputing monks addressed a question to Severus and his fellow bishop in exile, Julian of Halicarnassus: was the flesh taken up by Christ corruptible? Severus answered yes; Julian, no. For Julian, pushing the doctrine of

one nature in Christ to extremes, by nature Christ could not
suffer. From the union of Word and flesh in Mary's womb,
Christ was impassible. He admitted, however, that Christ
had suffered, because He willed to do so for the sake of the
economy of redemption, not because His body was subjected to the necessity of natural laws. In Julian's view, the
capacity to suffer is a result of sin; Christ's body was consubstantial with the body of Adam before his fall into sin and
not with man in his present sinful state. Many bishops and
especially monks embraced Julian's view. Severus worked
hard to convince Julian and his increasing followers that
their view undermined the whole economy of redemption.
But by the 530's most of Lower Egypt was Julianist or, as
they were called, Aphthartodocetists. On the other hand,
one of Severus' own followers drew the conclusion that if
Jesus' body were by nature corruptible and passible, then he
must have been subject to the same degree of ignorance as
other men. This gave rise to yet another sect known as
Agnoetes.

One other heresy still held on in the East among the
Gothic soldiers in the Roman army — Arianism. Justin
ordered the closure of Arian churches in Constantinople and
the exclusion of Arians from civil and military office. This
brought a protest from the Arian king of the Ostrogoths,
Theodoric, who regarded himself as an ally, ruling Italy with
imperial approval. A sincere admirer of Roman culture,
Theodoric administered Italy in collaboration with the
Roman aristocracy and granted toleration to his orthodox
subjects. To intercede for his fellow Arians, Theodoric sent
Pope John to Constantinople, accompanied by five bishops
and four senators of highest Roman nobility. In 525 the
delegation was received with greatest ceremony, the emperor
prostrating himself at the pope's feet. The pope acceded to
Justin's request and recrowned him emperor. In 526, Pope
John celebrated the Easter liturgy in Latin in the place of
honor above the patriarch. Justin granted Theodoric's
request in part, authorizing the return of their churches to
the Arians but refusing permission for Arians converted to
Catholicism to return to their first faith. This did not please

the king, and the pope's return met a hostile reception. John was imprisoned where he soon died; an edict was prepared to allow Arians to seize Catholic churches. But before it could be implemented, Theodoric himself died, succeeded by his daughter, Amalasuntha, as regent.

3. Emperor Justinian I

In the spring of 527, Emperor Justin, nearing eighty, fell ill and had his nephew Justinian proclaimed emperor and crowned together with his wife Theodora by the patriarch. By fall, Justin was dead, and Justinian entered upon his sole reign without incident. A native of Macedonia, Justinian was about 45 years of age at his accession, well educated though of peasant descent and long associated with his uncle in every aspect of imperial administration. He was orthodox and deeply pious with a taste for theological discussion. Though surrounded by elaborate court ceremonial, he was frugal in his personal habits, and in his untiring devotion to his duties, seemed never to sleep. Raised as a great Roman aristocrat, Justinian had married before his accession Theodora, a woman from the lowest rung of society, circus bear-keeper's daughter, night-club entertainer and call girl. Once married to Justinian in what seems to have been a genuine love match, she was every inch the empress, strong-willed, charitable, and in religion a Monophysite. Under the rule of this remarkable and devoted couple Roman law was codified with authoritative commentary in the *Corpus Juris Civilis*, art flourished in all forms, culminating in the great domed basilica of Hagia Sophia, the Empire preserved in the face of onslaughts by the Slavs, Persians and Avars, and the West — Africa, Italy and Southern Spain — brought under direct imperial administration. Unfortunately, the reconquest of the West would strain the empire's strength and complicate its religious policy, as Justinian was forced to reconcile the Chalcedonian West with the Monophysite East.

In order to guarantee the well-being of his empire, Justinian was deeply interested in the integrity of its faith. He wrote to his patriarch:

> The two greatest gifts which God in His infinite goodness has granted to men are the *Sacerdotium* and the *Imperium*. The priesthood takes care of divine interests and the empire of human interests of which it has supervision. Both powers emanate from the same principle and bring human life to its perfection. It is for this reason that the emperors have nothing closer to their hearts than the honor of priests because they pray continually to God for the emperors. When the clergy shows a proper spirit and devotes itself entirely to God, and the emperor governs the state which is entrusted to him, then a harmony results which is most profitable to the human race. So it is then that the true divine teachings and the honor of the clergy are the first among our preoccupations.

To this end, Justinian intervened in ecclesiastical matters more forcefully and systematically than any of his predecessors. Even more than Zeno and Anastasius he sought to impose doctrine directly on clergy and people without reference to ecclesiastical authority. Still the emperor was deeply conscious of the place that Old Rome played both in State and Church. "The old city of Rome," he declared in one of his laws, "has the honor to be the mother of laws and no one can doubt that it is there that we must find the summit of the sovereign pontificate." He included in his revised code of laws an enactment from the time of Valentinian III: "Since the primacy of the Apostolic See has been confirmed by the merits of St. Peter, the prince and the crown of the episcopacy, by the dignity of the city of Rome, and also by the authority of the holy synods, no one should presume to attempt to do anything illicit outside the authority of this see. For the peace of the churches will finally be preserved everywhere when the whole church is subject to its supreme ruler." In order to stabilize the relations between the sees of Rome and Constantinople, he declared in law that "...in accord with the decisons of the Council,...the most holy

Pope of Ancient Rome is first of all the hierarchs and that the holy bishop of Constantinople — the New Rome — occupies the second see, after the holy and apostolic see of Rome but with precedence over all other sees."

Justinian's efforts on behalf of the true faith were far reaching. With great vigor he sought to wipe out the not inconsiderable remnants of paganism in the East. Going beyond any of his predecessors he decreed that all pagans undergo religious instruction and, under pain of confiscation of their goods, receive baptism. Backsliders into paganism were to be put to death. Missions to the pagans were organized among the monks led by the well-educated and austere John of Asia. He and his monks worked in the hills of western Asia Minor and one chronicler credits them with 100,000 conversions, the erection of 100 churches and a dozen monasteries. At Constantinople itself John pursued the remaining pagans where at least two were put to death. In Egypt missionary work was less effective; pagan ceremonies continued there well into the seventh century, and the University of Alexandria in Justinian's time counted pagans among its professors, especially the Aristotelian philosopher John Philoponus. More sensational was the closure in 529 of the largely pagan University at Athens, which mistakenly prided itself on dating to the time of Plato, but which was by now in full decline. Some of its pagan professors fled to Persia where they put the Dialogues of Plato into the native language for the Shah Chosroes himself.

Justinian tolerated the Jews but forbade them to testify against Christians or buy the lands and goods of Christian churches, and though taxed like the municipal middle class, they could not share its privileges. He even interfered to dictate Jewish doctrine forbidding teaching against the Last Judgment, resurrection of the dead and existence of angels. Rabbis were compelled to allow reading of the Bible in the synagogues in Greek or Latin, along with Hebrew. Toward the always restive and frequently rebellious Samaritans still remaining in Palestine, Justinian was merciless. Their synagogues were seized and their subsequent revolts were put down ruthlessly by the army, their leaders crucified. Remnants fled to Persia or remained hidden in the hills of the Holy Land. To his credit, the bishop of Caesarea intervened to protect the Samaritans.

Toward heretics of all kinds Justinian was severe. They were rigidly excluded from civil and military office and from the liberal professions. They could not testify in court nor inherit. All manifestations of their cult were forbidden; their churches closed. Manicheans were condemned to death; Montanist churches were burned by the indefatigable John of Asia, sometimes when occupied by the sectaries. After the capture of Vandal Africa, the Arians there were chased from their churches which were turned over to the Catholics, their priests exiled, their civil rights denied.

All these measures, however, dealt with relatively small numbers of people. By far the largest heterodox group in the empire was the Monophysite movement. Toward them the emperor was more wary, not in the least because his empress Theodora, who exercised real power, was Monophysite in sympathy; her palace of Hormisdas was a place of refuge for as many as 500 Monophysite monks and many exiled bishops. Justinian's policy toward the Monophysites was based on two principles: to hold to the Definition of Chalcedon, but to interpret it according to the mind of Cyril of Alexandria, thus clearly disavowing any Nestorian interpretation and thereby winning over the Monophysites. After the great uprising of 532, the Nika riots, which almost cost the emperor his throne, he called a colloquy of six Monophysite and six orthodox bishops at the Palace of Hormisdas. Severus was invited but excused himself. At the first session presided over by an imperial count, the Monophysites firmly condemned the doctrine of Eutyches. At the second session, the results were less fortuitous; the Monophyites expressed dismay that the Council of Chalcedon had not accepted Cyril's Twelve Anathemas against Nestorius but had restored Theodoret of Cyrus and Ibas of Edessa to communion. Hypatius of Ephesus threw the Monophysites into confusion by attacking the authenticity of the Pseudo-Apollinarian books. Justinian himself presided at the third session in which the Monophysites objected again about the reception of Theodoret and Ibas and about the orthodox Catholics' refusal to accept the Scythian Theopaschite Formula. In the end only one Monophysite bishop was converted.

The colloquy seemed to have convinced Justinian that the Theopaschite Formula — One of the Trinity suffered for us — a formula designed to integrate Chalcedon and Cyril, was the key to the reconciliation of the Monophysites. On his own initiative he promulgated two decrees defining the formula as the faith of Chalcedon, sending one to the people of Constantinople and the cities of Asia, the second to the patriarch Epiphanius. When the Sleepless Monks who interpreted the Definition of Chalcedon in a strongly Nestorian sense objected to the edict, Justinian sent the edict to the pope, John II. After consultation with the African deacon Ferrandus, the pope approved the formula. When the Sleepless monks still refused to accept the imperial formula, John, calling them Nestorians, condemned them and notified the emperor of his acceptance of Cyril's Twelve Anathemas.

The emperor began to be looked upon favorably by the Monophysites, and Theodora acted boldly on their behalf. In 535, at the death of Timothy III, patriarch of Alexandria, Theodora dispatched one of her own chamberlains to Egypt, apparently without the emperor's knowledge, to engineer the election of Theodosius, an ardent Monophysite and friend of Severus. Later the same year Theodora secured the election of Anthimus, already bishop of Trebizond, to the vacant see of Constantinople. Though Anthimus had attended the colloquy of 533 as an orthodox participant and had promised the emperor to follow the Bishop of Rome, he was secretly in sympathy with the Monophysites and sent a profession of faith to Severus in exile in Egypt. Monophysite fortunes were on the rise with patriarchs of their persuasion at Constantinople and Alexandria because of the patronage of the empress.

Increasingly hopeful of conciliating the Monophysites, Justinian invited Severus himself to Constantinople for conferences in 535. For a year Severus worked in the city to further the Monophysite cause. To the scandal of the Chalcedonians, Monophysites publicly baptized the children of leading families of the court and the city on Holy Saturday in 536. But the situation in Egypt began to disintegrate. Theodosius, who owed his election at Alexandria to Theodora, was vigorously opposed by the more radical Aphthartodocetist followers of Julian of Halicarnassus. He was deposed by the people and Gaianus, a friend of Julian, was installed as patriarch. The eunuch Narses, later conqueror of Italy, was dispatched to Egypt with 6,000 men. He restored Theodosius after extensive street fighting in which some 3,000 were said to have been killed. Gaianus was exiled to Africa.

As Justinian's program to conciliate the Monophysites began to break down, Pope Agapetus arrived at Constantinople. He came as an ambassador from the ephemeral Ostrogothic king of Italy Theodatus, successor of Theodoric, who was disturbed at the reports of Justinian's plans for the reconquest of Italy. But during his brief stay in the capital, religious questions were more to the fore than diplomacy. The pope promptly refused to communicate with the patriarch Anthimus unless he confessed two natures in Christ and denounced his elevation to the patriarchate as illegal according to the Canons of Nicaea, since he had been previously the bishop of Trebizond. After the emperor notified Anthimus of this development, the patriarch resigned and disappeared into Theodora's palace where he lived in secret the life of an ascetic for the next twelve years. With his own hands, Pope Agapetus consecrated Anthimus' successor, Menas, as the new patriarch. The pope then called for a synod to condemn the deposed Anthimus and presented the emperor with a petition from the monasteries of Syria and Palestine asking for the expulsion of all Monophysites from Constantinople. Before the synod could meet, the pope died. But Menas presided over the synod with the dead pope's entourage representing the Holy See; Anthimus and Severus were condemned. In accordance with the wishes of the synod, Justinian expelled Severus and the leading Monophysites from the city. Severus fled again to Egypt where his followers had to protect him from the Julianists. He died there, his cause in eclipse, in 538, to be canonized by the Egyptians. The Roman deacon, Pelagius, remained in Constantinople as representatitve of the new pope, Severius, and became increasingly the emperor's chief theological adviser. Ephrem of Antioch proceeded against the Monophysites in his huge diocese. Theodosius, the Monophysite patriarch of Alexandria, was summoned to Constantinople and, when he refused to recant, was deposed and exiled. In his place, the monk Paul was consecrated patriarch and imposed on a stubborn Alexandria by armed force. When Paul attempted to compromise with the recalcitrant Monophysites, he too was deposed at a synod presided over by the Roman deacon Pelagius. Imperial policy was now fully Neo-Chalcedonian and anti-Monophysite.

Imperial police were instructed to prevent the ordination of Monophysite priests so that their clergy would gradually die off. But Theodora herself frustrated this policy. She allowed the Monophysite ex-patriarch of Alexandria, Theodosius, interned in her palace, to travel secretly through Asia Minor to fill the ranks of the thinning Monophysite clergy. In 543, when the prince of the Ghassinid Arabs, allied to the empire, asked Theodora for a Monophysite bishop, she sent him to Theodosius, who ordained an archbishop for Bostra in Arab territory and, more importantly, appointed Jacob Bar'adai bishop of Edessa with the task of building a Monophysite hierarchy in the East. Until his death in 578, Jacob roamed over the East in secret ordaining bishops and priests. He claimed to have ordained in all two patriarchs, twenty-seven bishops and 100,000 clerics. Monophysitism had passed from heresy to open schism. The Monophysite church would repay its debt to Jacob Bar'adai by calling itself Jacobite, because he was in everything "an imitator of the battles of the great St. Jacob (James), the archbishop and martyr and brother of Our Lord Jesus Christ."

Between 532 and 536 Leontius of Jerusalem further developed the Neo-Chalcedonian case. He insisted on the identification of the hypostasis of union with the pre-existent hypostasis of the Word. Resolutely he rejected any notion of the pre-existence of Christ's manhood. "The Word," he said, "in the latter times, having himself clothed with flesh his hypostasis and his nature, which existed before his human nature, and which, before the worlds, were without flesh, hypostatized human nature into his own hypostasis." The single hypostasis in Christ was hypostasis of both the divine and human natures. Christ's humanity had no separate hypostasis. Moreover, added Leontius, "Christ does not possess a human hypostasis which, like ours, is particularized and distinct in relationship to all beings of the same species or of different species, but the Word's hypostasis, which is common to and inseparable from both his human nature and the divine nature which is greater." Thus Christ unites not just an individual but all of mankind to the divinity. Leontius rejected Apollinarianism, insisted that Christ's human nature included a soul and accepted the full historical reality of Christ's manhood. Still he is a bit muddled in his definition of hypostasis, terming it "a nature with limiting characteristics." Yet the hypostasis of the Incarnate Word, possessing all divine characteristics, assumed new characteristics, human characteristics having been added to the divine after the Incarnation. In accepting the Theopaschite Formula — One of the Trinity suffered for us — Leontius established the distinction between hypostasis and nature. "The Word," he says, "is said to have suffered according to the hypostasis, for within his hypostasis he assumed a passible essence beside his own impassible essence, and what can be asserted of the passible essence can be asserted of the hypostasis." Leontius clarified the Definition of Chalcedon which asserted the union of two natures into one hypostasis by identifying that hypostasis as the pre-existent hypostasis of the Divine Word. Leontius does justice to the dynamism of salvation through Christ upheld by the Cyrillians: "Because of the organic union with God, effected in an immediate way by an intimate union on the level of hypostasis, the wealth of deification entered the man who was the Lord in his particular human nature; as for the rest of mankind...the Body of the Church...they only partake by way of mediation in the natural union with the man who was the Lord...the only

Mediator between God and men, the man Jesus Christ Our Lord."

While Justinian's attempts to reconcile the Monophysites were running out of steam, still another theological crisis broke out. In 531, the Archimandrite Sabas, at the age of ninety-two, arrived in Constantinople to complain of attacks on the Palestinian monks by the Samaritans and to request the expulsion of monks who were teaching Origenist doctrines. These monks had already broken away from Sabas' Great Laura, or hermit community, and had founded their own New Laura south of Bethlehem. Origenist teaching remained popular even in the Great Laura and forty monks had been expelled. A monk favorable to Origen, Theodore Askidas, was named bishop of Cappadocian Caesarea and had found favor with Justinian as his theological adviser. By 539, when the Roman legate Pelagius stopped in Palestine while tending to the deposition of Paul of Alexandria, he denounced Origenism, and on his return to the capital again requested Justinian to take measures against it. In 540, Ephrem of Antioch condemned Origenism in a provincial synod, and in the next year Peter of Jerusalem complained to the emperor about the continuing problem. Finally, Justinian took the matter in hand and in 543 issued a theological tract in the form of an edict accompanied by excerpts from Origen's *On First Principles* and ten anathemas, probably at the instigation of Pelagius, the papal legate attached to the imperial court. Even Theodore Askidas swallowed his beliefs and subscribed to the condemnation. The condemnation of Origenism will be repeated in the anathemas of the Second Council of Constantinople.

Origenism has been associated with the monk Leontius of Byzantium, an influential theologian active between 532 and 544, three of whose works survive. However, the final verdict of the nature of Leontius' Christology is not yet in. Some see him as Origenist, teaching a doctrine of Christ like that outlined further on (see p. 247) and condemned by the Council of Constantinople II. Others argue that he is merely Cyrillian. Rather than enter into the technicalities of the dispute, here we shall simply indicate one concept developed by Leontius which will become a staple of subsequent Christology—his description of Christ's humanity as a *enhypostaton*. Leontius distinguishes between nature and hypostasis: nature situates a being in a genus; hypostasis denotes individuality. An hypostasis always has a nature, but a nature does not always have an hypostasis. For things can be united in three ways. An example of the first is the Nestorian juxtaposition of two natures and two hypostases in Christ. Secondly, the distinction between two natures may be so merged that a third results as Eutyches argued in his Christology. Thirdly, two natures may subsist in one hypostasis. Thus body and soul are united in a single hypostasis called man, and all operations of body and of soul are attributed to this one hypostasis. So in Christ, his human nature subsists in the hypostasis of the divine nature. Human nature in Christ is an *enhypostaton*, that which subsists in an hypostasis of another nature. The single hypostasis of Christ is the Eternal Word in which subsist two natures divine and human. All operations of the two natures are attributed to the hypostasis of the Divine Word. But in Christ the divinity remains uncircumscribed and unaffected by the human nature, while in humans, the soul is circumscribed and therefore affected by the body. Moreover, Christ is unique, but men are not. This clarification of the relation of the human nature to the Divine Word as an *enhypostaton*, subsisting only in the divine hypostasis will have a long history ahead of it.

When later in 543 the legate Pelagius was recalled to Rome, the Origenist Theodore Askidas became the emperor's chief theological adviser. Though he had signed the emperor's anti-Origenist edict, he remained a convinced Origenist and harbored a grudge against the Palestinian monks of the Great Laura. Since these monks favored Antiochene theology, Askidas slyly suggested to the emperor the condemnation of the sources of Antiochene theology as a means of reconciling the Monophysites, thus neatly killing two birds with one stone. Justinian welcomed the opportunity to undertake another campaign of reconciliation of the

Monophysites. After consultation, it was agreed to condemn the person and whole works of Theodore of Mopsuestia (d. 428), the writings of Theodoret of Cyrus (d. 458) against the Cyrillians and the Letter to Maris the Persian of Ibas of Edessa (d. 457). It will be remembered that the last two bishops had been personally restored to the orthodox communion by the Council of Chalcedon. A compendium of the writings of these Antiochenes was drawn up under three headings; the document came to be known as the Three Chapters. In 543 Justinian issued an edict embodying the condemnations. The patriarch of Constantinople Menas signed provisionally, dependent on papal approval. The bishops of the Home Synod at Constantinople signed, as they told the papal legate, under constraint. The patriarchs of Antioch and Alexandria too sent their approval, but Peter of Jerusalem had to be called to Constantinople and threatened with deposition before he gave his approval. The rest of the eastern episcopate fell in to line, but for the West it was a different story. The papal representative at Constantinople refused his approval and broke off relations with all who signed the condemnation. At Rome the wily Pope Vigilius, who was imposed on the Romans as pope through the influence of Empress Theodora after the Byzantine general Belisarius had removed Pope Severius on a trumped up charge of treason, hesitated. But his deacons, Pelagius and Anatolius, wrote to Deacon Ferrandus in Carthage urging him to alert the African episcopate to the danger of the edict which, in their view, cast doubt on the actions of the Council of Chalcedon. Dacius, bishop of Milan, who was in Constantinople when the edict was published, refused his approval, and hurried back to Italy to warn the pope. Exasperated at Pope Vigilius' shilly-shallying, Justinian had the pope forcibly removed from Rome, and then unaccountably allowed him to remain for the next ten months at Syracuse in Sicily. From Sicily the pope urged the western bishops to resist the Edict against the Three Chapters. Resistance mounted; Deacon Ferrandus of Carthage rallied the African bishops; bishops of Sardinia declared against the edict, and Zoilus, patriarch of Alexandria, sent legates to inform the pope that his approval was obtained by force and that he had retracted it.

By January, 547, Pope Vigilius arrived in Constantinople to be greeted ceremoniously and lodged in the palace of Placidia, the customary residence of the permanent papal legate. Vigilius, however, refused to enter into communion with the patriarch Menas or any other bishops approving the edict. Menas promptly erased Vigilius' name from the diptychs. In the meantime the deacon Pelagius arrived in Constantinople on a peace mission from the Ostrogothic king Totila (542-552) who had just retaken the city of Rome from the imperial armies. For the moment he helped keep the pope firm against the edict, before returning to Italy on his diplomatic mission. The pope and his entourage were battered by continual arguments to accept the imperial edict and condemn the Three Chapters. Except for the African bishop Facundus of Hermiane and the Roman deacon Pelagius, the group around the pope was not particularly distinguished or strong-willed. By June Vigilius was beginning to give way; he received Menas into communion and was himself restored to the diptychs. At this time he sent to the emperor a secret letter professing his belief in the faith of Chalcedon but promising to condemn the Three Chapters. Still the pope energetically refused the imperial request for public approval of the edict.

Next the Pope convoked a conference of seventy bishops who had not signed the edict. Facundus pointed out forcefully that in his opinion the Letter of Ibas had been pronounced orthodox at Chalcedon. The pope broke off the debates and asked each bishop to write out his own opinion and submit it to him. Imperial officials allowed the bishops seven days to reply. On the basis of this information, the pope drew up his decision — the Judicatum — which he sent to the Patriarch Menas in April, 548. Vigilius thereby condemned the Three Chapters but with reservations, keeping intact the decisions of the Council of Chalcedon. His action brought a storm of protest from the West, even less tempered than before, since the powerful Monophysite-sympathizing empress Theodora had died in June of the same year. His own papal entourage opposed him; protests poured in from Italy, Dalmatia, Illyria, Africa, even from Gaul. To recoup his authority, the pope reprimanded and suspended members of his entourage, including his own nephew, the deacon Rusticus who broke with him publicly at Christmas Mass in 549. Matters began to move beyond mere protest. In Illyria, the bishops in synod deposed a metropolitan who accepted the Judicatum; Aurelian of Arles, vicar apostolic for Gaul, sent one of his priests to investigate the situation at Constantinople; the priest returned strongly opposed to acceptance of the imperial edict against the Three Chapters. More forcefully, Reparatus of Carthage presided over a council of African bishops who excommunicated the pope himself, until he would withdraw the Judicatum.

In the face of such opposition, the emperor allowed the pope to retract his Judicatum and explain to the West the need for a council to examine the reasoning of the East on the subject. Justinian compelled the pope to take a secret oath on the Gospels that he would work toward the condemnation of the Three Chapters, and both pope and emperor undertook not to discuss the question further until the convocation of the proposed general council.

Justinian proceeded to lay plans for the convocation of the Council. He ordered a provincial synod to investigate the veneration paid to Theodore at his former see of Mopsuestia in order to pave the way for the condemnation of the dead bishop. The synod reported that Theodore's name had never been placed on the diptychs there. Reparatus, bishop of Carthage, and several other African bishops who had recently excommunicated the pope because of his Judicatum were brought to Constantinople. When Reparatus refused to condemn the Three Chapters, he was deposed and exiled on trumped-up charges; the others who refused were interned in monasteries. An Arian turned Catholic in favor at court was sent to Africa to recruit for the forthcoming Council bishops amenable to the imperial policy. The bishops of Illyria refused to come to the Council. When Zoilus of Alexandria refused to condemn the Chapters, he was deposed; his successor, Apollinaris, recognized by the pope after an initial refusal, would sit at the Council as patriarch of Alexandria. To make sure the bishops understood what was expected of them, Justinian, breaking his agreement with the pope to remain silent, published an edict at Askidas' urging, explaining his own view of the matter.

The emperor insisted on the Theopaschite Formula but not to the detriment of the Definition of Chalcedon. He warned against the confusion of the divinity and humanity in Christ. He recognized the distinction between nature and person; the natures being two united in one person. Drawing on the insights of Leontius of Byzantium, the Emperor stressed that the natures could exist only within the person; by the person of the Word the humanity of Christ received existence in Mary's womb. Thus within the single person, Christ is God and man. The two natures are not complementary as are soul and body and were not simultaneously created, since the uncreated divinity pre-existed the Incarnation. Yet the two natures of Christ can only be distinguished "by way of speech and thought and not as two distinct things." Justinian accepted Cyril's formula of one incarnate nature of the divine Word but pointed out that nature here really meant person. In the attached anathemas it was shown that the Chalcedonian Definition was not Nestorian. Repeatedly the unity of subject in the Incarnate Word was stressed; the Theopaschite Formula proclaimed; Cyril's Twelve Anathemas accepted. Again it was emphasized that the one nature of Cyril's formula must be understood as one person. Only in thought can the two natures of Christ be distinguished. Thus the emperor sought to reconcile Cyril and Chalcedon.

The emperor's confession of faith stirred Vigilius to action. He insisted on its withdrawal, and Dacius of Milan protested against it in the name of the bishops of Gaul and North Italy. When these protests were ignored, Vigilius broke off relations with Menas and prepared to depose Theodore Askidas and all who subscribed to the new edict. Fearing reprisals against his person, Vigilius fled in August, 551, from the Palace of Placidia to the church of St. Peter in the

Palace of Hormisdas, where he signed but did not publish the deposition of Askidas. The imperial police soon broke into the church and arrested the papal entourage when they attempted to protect the pope. Vigilius, who was advanced in years but tall and strong, seized the columns of the altar and refused to leave the church. The soldiers attempted to dislodge him by pulling at his beard and feet. In the ensuing struggle the altar collapsed and the disconcerted police were forced to leave, their mission unaccomplished, amid the shouts of the hostile crowd which filled the church. After this incredible scene, Justinian sent a delegation led by his great general Belisarius who had fought in Italy to negotiate with the pope. The imperial commissioners swore on relics to ensure the pope's safety, and he returned to his quarters in the Palace of Placidia.

But at imperial orders the pope was isolated from his advisers and even from his personal servants, his palace filled with spies. His notaries were bribed to send forged letters from the pope to Italy. But some of the papal entourage managed to send a true account of affairs at Constantinople back to Italy through Ostrogothic ambassadors sent to the emperor to negotiate peace in Italy. By December, 551, the pope's situation had become impossible. By night he escaped from the Palace of Placidia over the roofs of neighboring buildings and fled across the Bosporus to the sanctuary of St. Euphemia at Chalcedon; there, worn out and ill, he took refuge in the crypt of the church where 100 years before the Council of Chalcedon had deliberated. Vainly, Belisarius attempted to convince the pope to return to Constantinople. Not trusting the emperor, Vigilius issued an encyclical letter to all Christian people, narrating the measures taken against him and outlining the faith of the four general councils. He published the deposition of Askidas and excommunicated Menas and all bishops loyal to him. When the pope again refused the emperor's request to return to Constantinople, Justinian had ten Italian and two African bishops arrested and had the pope's principal adviser, the deacon Pelagius forcibly removed from St. Euphemia. Nothing daunted, Vigilius had his Sentences against Askidas and Menas posted in public places throughout Constantinople.

In view of the approaching council, Justinian decided to compromise. He ordered Askidas and Menas to Chalcedon where they professed unqualified faith in the four councils and humbly begged the pope's pardon. Satisfied, the pope returned to Constantinople where death soon removed from the scene Dacius of Milan, the pope's comrade in arms, and Menas, the patriarch of Constantinople. The new patriarch, Eutychius, in January, 553, submitted to Vigilius an orthodox profession of faith signed by himself together with Apollinaris of Alexandria, Domninus of Antioch , and Elias of Thessalonika. Vigilius accepted their profession and gave his approval for the convocation of a General Council under the presidency of Eutychius of Constantinople. The pope added a proviso — that a Council be held in Sicily or Italy in order to guarantee the presence of western bishops, but the emperor refused. Over papal protests, it was announced that 150 eastern and some twenty-five western bishops would attend the Council. None were to be present from Illyria, Gaul and Spain, though a handpicked delegation would represent Africa. Pleading illness, the pope asked for time to consider his approval of these measures. Still hoping to avoid an eastern Council, the pope proposed instead a small conference attended by himself with three Italian bishops and the four Eastern patriarchs. When the emperor refused to accept this, proposing instead equal representation from each patriarchate, thus outnumbering the West, the pope proposed that the Council deliberate according to his own instructions, retaining the authority himself to publish the conciliar decisions. This too the emperor refused.

4. Council of Constantinople II

Accordingly, the Council convened on May 5, 553, in the great hall attached to the patriarchal palace in Constantinople. Eutychius of Constantinople flanked by the patriarchs of Alexandria and Antioch presided; present were the representatives of the patriarch of Jerusalem; in all 151 to 168 bishops attended, including six to nine from Africa. At the opening session, an imperial commissioner read a letter from the absent Justinian in which he pointed out the solicitude of his predecessors for sound doctrine at the previous four general councils, stressed the papal condemnation of the Three Chapters in Vigilius' Judicatum, and remarked on the pope's hesitations in calling the Council. The bishops were asked to review the opinions of Theodore of Mopsuestia, Theodoret of Cyrus and Ibas of Edessa by which the Nestorians wished to impose their views on the Church, to consider the absurd assertion that heretics might not be condemned after their death and to act with all due speed. With that Justinian left the bishops to their work without the presence of lay commissioners. At the close of the first session the bishops decided to send a delegation to the pope inviting him to attend the Council. The next day a number of bishops led by the three patriarchs duly called on the pope. Pleading illness, Vigilius asked for time before deciding. Again on the following day the patriarchs and three high civil officials repeated the invitation. The pope notified them that he would not attend the Council until some Italian bishops were admitted and asked for three weeks to draw up a statement on the Three Chapters.

On May 8, at the second session, the bishops were informed of Vigilius' refusal to attend, and at the third session they proceeded to elaborate their profession of faith in which they accepted the decisions of the first four councils and a long synopsis of the teachings of the Fathers. At a fourth session, May 12/13, they discussed the person and teachings of Theodore of Mopsuestia and condemned them. By May 14 Vigilius had finished his definitive decision in the matter of the Three Chapters but delayed its publication. The Council Fathers continued in their fifth and sixth sessions with the condemnation of certain writings of Theodoret of Cyrus and the Letter to Maris said to have been written by Ibas of Edessa. Then on May 24, Vigilius intervened with his Constitutum I, largely the work of the deacon Pelagius. In a dignified and moderate tone and with consid-

erable literary elegance, the pope resolutely refused to condemn the persons of the three great Antiochenes because
they had died in communion with the orthodox church. He
did condemn 59 of the 71 propositions of Theodore of Mopsuestia presented to him and added one more proposition on
his own. He refused to condemn any of Theodoret's views
but condemned four propositions of Nestorius. Lastly, he
refused to condemn Ibas' letter which, he said, had been
declared orthodox at Chalcedon. Along with the pope, sixteen bishops and six clerics, including Pelagius, signed Constitutum I. When the judgment was delivered to the
emperor, he refused to accept it, saying that the Three Chapters had already been condemned by the assembled Council.

In early June, the Council responded by declaring the
need for a collegial decision on the question of the Three
Chapters. For his part, Justinian sent to the bishops at their
seventh session a dossier of documents designed to destroy
the pope's credibility. Included were Vigilius' letters to the
western bishops urging them to support his Judicatum in
which he had previously condemned the Three Chapters
together with his private letters and solemn oath to work
with the emperor for the acceptance of the condemnation of
the Chapters. In the face of such evidence, the emperor
asked that Vigilius' name be erased from the diptychs of
Constantinople and the churches of the world. In reply, the
bishops praised the emperor's zeal for the purity of the faith
and broke off communion with Vigilius personally because
he had set himself against the universal church represented
by a council, but without separating themselves from the
Holy See itself. Later the bishops declared that it was legitimate to condemn heretics who had died in error. All was
prepared for the eighth and final session, in which the
bishops approved their Sentence, to which they added four-
teen anathemas.

In their Sentence, the council Fathers expressed their conviction that to do nothing in the face of attacks on the faith
would be a dereliction of their duty. They observed that "the
most religious Vigilius" was in the city and "was present at
all the discussions with regard to the Three Chapters, and

had often condemned them orally and in writing, nevertheless he gave his consent in writing to be present at the Council and examine together with us the Three Chapters." However, in spite of the invitation of the emperor and the
bishops, Vigilius did not attend the Council. Notwithstand-
ing this, the bishops met following the example of the Apostles in each of whom abounded the grace of the Holy Spirit
"so that no one of them needed the counsel of another in the
execution of his work, yet they were not willing to define on
the question then raised...until being gathered together
they had confirmed their own several sayings by the testi-
mony of the divine Scriptures." Vigilius, not responding to
the requests of bishops and emperor to deliberate among
them, promised to pass sentence on the Three Chapters himself. But the bishops, fearing to give scandal to the emperor
and the people, gathered to confess their faith. They confessed the faith and creed of the 318 Fathers of Nicaea, the
explanation of that faith made by the 150 of Constantinople,
the consent to that faith of the 200 of Ephesus and that one
and same faith defined by the 630 gathered at Chalcedon.

The bishops then recounted how they reviewed the writings of Theodore of Mopsuestia which had proved so
blasphemous that they had hesitated to have them read
through. But they finished their work to bring confusion on
those "who gloried in such blasphemies." They then "took
care to have recited and inserted in our acts a few of these
things which had been impiously written by Theodoret
against the right faith and the Twelve Chapters of St. Cyril
and against the First Council of Ephesus, and also certain
things written by him in defense of those impious ones
Theodore and Nestorius." In the third place, they examined
"the letter which is said to have been written by Ibas to
Maris the Persian," whose "impiety was manifest to all."
Reviewing the Council of Chalcedon, the bishops said that it
was impossible that such a letter could have been approved
there because its contents were wholly opposed to the faith
of Chalcedon. What may have been approved, they added,
was a letter of the Edessan clergy defending Ibas. They
remarked that Ibas himself had been restored at Chalcedon

after condemning Nestorius and his teaching and so had Theodoret after anathematizing "those things of which he was accused." Concluding, the bishops condemned Theodore of Mopsuestia and his writings, certain writings of Theodoret and the letter said to have been written by Ibas.

In the Anathemas appended to their Sentence the bishops condemned first of all those refusing to confess a consubstantial Trinity, one Godhead to be worshipped in three subsistences or Persons. Secondly, they rejected anyone who does not admit that the Word of God had two births, one from all eternity of the Father, the other in these last days being made flesh of Mary, Mother of God and always a virgin. In canon three they were condemned who do not say that one and the same Lord Jesus Christ, the Word of God incarnate, one Person worked miracles and endured sufferings in His flesh. The fourth canon bade all to say that "the union of God the Word is made with the flesh animated by a reasonable and living soul, and that such union is made synthetically and hypostatically, and therefore there is only one Person, to wit: Our Lord Jesus Christ, one of the Holy Trinity." The union of divinity and humanity proposed by Apollinaris and Eutyches which produced a mixture of natures was rejected as was the relative union proposed by the followers of Theodore and Nestorius. "In the mystery of Christ," canon four continued, "the synthetical union not only preserves unconfusedly the natures which are united, but allows no separation." Canon five rejected any who "will not recognize...that the Word of God is united with the flesh hypostatically , and that therefore there is but one hypostasis or only one person, and that the holy Council of Chalcedon has professed in this sense the one Person of Our Lord Jesus Christ." In canon six he was reprobated who will not confess that Mary "is exactly and truly the Mother of God, because that God the Word who before all ages was begotten of the Father was in these last days made flesh and born of her," and that in this sense the Council of Chalcedon called Mary Mother of God.

So far the emphasis had been on the unity of Person in Christ; next the bishops turned to the duality of natures. The seventh canon condemned those who divide the natures, making of them two persons, or attempt to number the natures as if they were two wholly distinct entities. Rather one should recognize through intellectual analysis alone a difference of the natures of which an ineffable union is unconfusedly made, the union being hypostatic. The eighth canon dealt with the Cyrillian battle cry: One Incarnate Nature of the Divine Word. This expression, the bishops warned, should not be used to introduce one nature or substance made by a mixture of the Godhead and manhood in Christ, "for in teaching that the only-begotten Word was united hypostatically to humanity we do not mean to say that there was made a mutual confusion of natures but rather each nature remaining what it was, we understand that the Word was united to flesh. Wherefore, there is one Christ, both God and man, consubstantial with the Father as touching his Godhead, and consubstantial with us as touching his manhood." The ninth canon prescribed worship of Christ by one adoration, God the Word made man together with his flesh, and the tenth canon approved the expression that "Jesus Christ who was crucified in the flesh is true God and the Lord of Glory and one of the Holy Trinity."

The eleventh canon gathered up the heretics of the previous three hundred years in a blanket condemnation — Arius, Eunomius, Macedonius, Apollinaris, Nestorius, Eutyches and Origen. Finally in the last three canons the person and works of Theodore of Mopsuestia, certain works of Theodoret of Cyrus and the letter said to be written by Ibas of Edessa were again anathematized. The work of the Council was complete. The Council of Chalcedon, the bishops hoped, was rid of its Nestorian incubus and shown to safeguard Cyril's deepest insights, while Cyril's borrowing from pseudepigraphical Apollinarian literature was explained as not denying the differences in the natures. The work of the Neo-Chalcedonians was crowned with success in an ecumenical council.

Associated with the Second Council of Constantinople are fifteen anathemas directed against Origenist doctrine.

These anathemas present two problems. Firstly, scholars are not agreed on how these anathemas became connected with the Council. Some say that the bishops gathered for the Council approved the anathemas presented to them by the emperor before the actual opening of the official proceedings. Others argue that the anathemas were approved at some point during the conciliar discussions. At any rate, they are continually linked to the work of the Council. Secondly, scholars have long debated whether the doctrines condemned were actually those of Origen. Now it is becoming increasingly clear that some of the condemned doctrines dealing with cosmology, anthropology and eschatology are really those of Origen drawn from his theological treatise — On First Principles. Doctrines dealing with Christology, however, seem to have come from Evagrius of Pontus (346-399) who had been ordained deacon by Gregory of Nazianzus and spent the latter part of his life as a monk in the Egyptian desert. He was deeply influenced by Origenist thought. The teachings of Origen and Evagrius were eagerly studied by many monks who embraced theories of Platonic spiritualism, endeavoring by asceticism and prayer to escape the prison of the material body.

Influenced by Hellenic thought Origen taught that because the good God always needed objects toward whom he could exercise His goodness He created from all eternity, spiritual, intellectual beings, all equal among themselves. These beings became diversified and fell into matter in varying degrees through the exercise of their free will. Thus spiritual beings fallen from their primal perfection became angels, demons, human beings, even heavenly bodies. Anathemas 2, 3, 4 and 5 condemn this view. Origen's cosmological views necessarily included an insistence on the pre-existence of human souls; though fallen into matter from their primal state, they have existed as creatures from all eternity and will, if good, return to their primal state. Anathemas 1 and 15 condemn these opinions. All these fallen beings — even Satan himself — are capable of escaping their fallen state and regaining their primal perfection. At the end of this world matter will be no more. Anathemas 12 and 11 condemn these doctrines.

Anathemas 6, 7, 8, 9, 12 and 13 condemn the Christology of Evagrius. He distinguished between the Word and Christ. The Word is the second person of the Trinity, God Himself. Christ is a created intellect, the only spiritual being who remained firm in contemplation of God, who never fell from primal perfection into matter. In the Incarnation, God-Word was joined to Christ-Mind who abased himself in relation to a material body in order to save fallen spiritual creatures and restore them to their primal state. The final restoration of the fallen will result in their having the same relation to God-Word as does the unfallen Christ-Mind. One other anathema — the tenth — condemned the strange view, perhaps coming from the Alexandrian theologian Didymus the Blind (313-398), a staunch Nicene, who held that after His resurrection Christ's body took a spherical shape, the sphere being for Hellenic thinkers the perfect shape.

J. Meyendorff comments on the effects of these anathemas:

> The importance of the condemnation of Origenism at the Fifth Ecumenical Council was overwhelming for the later development of thought and spirituality in the Byzantine world. The anathematisms directed against Origen and Evagrius attacked spiritual authorities who had left their mark on whole generations and who continued to have numerous followers, especially among the monks. It therefore is not surprising that for many later Byzantine writers the decisons concerning Origen took first place in the work of the council of 553; their essential character underlined once more, perhaps permanently as far as Byzantium was concerned, the inner incompatibility between Hellenism and the Gospel.

5. Aftermath

Once the Council had completed its work, Justinian sent the acts to all the bishops for their signatures. Those in the papal entourage who resisted the conciliar decrees were exiled to the Egyptian desert; the deacon Pelagius was impris-

oned at Constantinople. The ailing Vigilius remained in
Constantinople. Since Rome had been occupied by the
imperial armies, the Romans requested the return of their
bishop who had not been in the city since 545. Justinian
agreed to Vigilius' return provided he recognized the Council. Vigilius held out for six months. In February, 554,
declaring that he had been misled by his advisers, Vigilius
capitulated. In his Constitutum II, he reversed his earlier
stand and accepted the Sentence and anathemas of the
Council, condemning the person and works of Theodore of
Mopsuestia and some of the works of Theodoret. He still
had reservations about Ibas' letter but in the end condemned
the letter said to have been written by him. To sweeten the
bitter pill Justinian had forced the pope to swallow, he
granted a Pragmatic Sanction reorganizing the government
of Rome and Italy and conferring on them greater powers of
self-government. The pope was allowed to return home but
died on his journey at Syracuse in Italy in 555.

In the West, opposition to the Council was strong and
widespread. In Africa, the metropolitan of Carthage, an
imperial appointee, who had forcibly replaced the exiled
Reparatus, was not recognized by his suffragans, and Vigilius was regarded as a traitor. All over Africa, recalcitrant
bishops and clergy were deposed and exiled. In Illyria, which
had refused to send representatives to the Council, there was
a stonewall of resistance. In prison, the deacon Pelagius
wrote tracts criticizing Vigilius' weakness yet pointing the
way to a compromise between the acts of Chalcedon and
those of Constantinople. Justinian resolved to use him to
conciliate the West and imposed him as pope on the
Romans after the death of Vigilius. Under the protection of
the imperial general Narses, Pelagius was consecrated
bishop in 556 by the only two bishops found willing to do so.
In order to stem the growing tide of resistance, Pelagius,
while assuring the emperor of his acceptance of the Council,
issued a profession of faith in the four Councils of the West
omitting all reference to the fifth, Constantinople II. This
calmed Rome, but the bishops of Northern Italy and Dalmatia, under the leadership of the metropolitan of Aquileia,

broke off communion with him. The imperial commander in Italy, Narses, refused to intervene.

To the end of his life, Justinian sought means to conciliate the Monophysites of Egypt and Syria, even though his Council had failed so signally to do so. At last he pinned his hopes on Aphthartodocetism, the theory that Christ, though by nature impervious to suffering because of His single nature, miraculously willed to suffer His passion and death. When the Patriarch Eutychius, former president of the Council, refused to sanction an edict imposing this doctrine, he was deposed. At Antioch the patriarch and 197 bishops informed the Emperor they would resign their sees rather than accept the doctrine. While the patriarch of Antioch was preparing his speech of farewell to his people, Emperor Justinian died at the age of eighty-two, after thirty-seven momentous years of rule. He left an empire amid all its artistic splendor overextended and economically weakened, a people despite their newly codified system of law restive under the extortionate taxation of a corrupt bureaucracy, a church expanded by its missionary activity, but in which relations between East and West were badly strained, the Syrian and Egyptian Monophysites unreconciled.

After the death of Justinian, his ablest nephew Justin II was proclaimed emperor by the Senate and acclaimed by the people in the Hippodrome. Married to the Monophysite-sympathizing Sophia, a niece of Justinian's wife Theodora, Justin made an effort to conciliate all parties by recalling the bishops exiled by Justinian. The leaders of the Monophysites continued to be the ex-patriarch of Alexandria, Theodosius, who from his exile in Thrace corresponded with the faithful in Egypt, and Jacob Bar'adai whose work was now largely confined to Arab territory, east of Palestine. Large pockets of Syriac-speaking schismatics were found in the outskirts of Antioch and Apamea and others in the hills of western Asia Minor. They had lost ground in Egypt where the orthodox patriarch Apollinaris had confiscated their church in Alexandria and barred their clergy from the city. At the death of Theodosius in 566, they were without a leader. They began to fragment into numerous sects; one contemporary tract lists twenty. The largest to which most of the bishops adhered was that of Aphthartodocetists, but it too was subdivided into three parties disagreeing over the manner of Christ's ability to suffer. The strangest was that of Halacephalites, who believed that by hanging head down for a number of hours for twenty days, one could become impassible and purified of evil. Even the Monophysites were horrified by the new heresy of the Tritheists, who held that there were as many natures as persons in God, and thus that there were three gods. The philosopher John Philoponos of the University of Alexandria supported the doctrine with principles drawn from Aristotle. It spread throughout Egypt and reached even into Italy.

After a whole year of discussion with Monophysite leaders, the new Emperor Justin II issued an Henotikon in which he renewed Zeno's Henotikon, condemned the Three Chapters without mentioning Chalcedon, and declared an amnesty for all condemned Monophysites. But the Monophysites assembled at Callinicum in 567 quarreled among themselves and refused to accept the imperial Henotikon. Nothing daunted, Justin prepared a new Henotikon in 571, which recognized one sole incarnate nature, and a difference only in thought between the two natures, divine and human. Chalcedon was again ignored. This second Henotikon was applied by force under the direction of the patriarch of Constantinople John the Scholastic. But by 573 Justin II began to show signs of mental instability. As his illness grew worse, the empress Sophia persuaded him to appoint as his heir Count Tiberius. Justin, incapacitated, lingered on until 578, but effective power was in the hands of Tiberius from 576 on.

Tiberius released Jacob Bar'adai, the Monophysite leader, from a three-year imprisonment and called off the persecution of the Monophysite party. Eutychius, former patriarch of Constantinople in exile since 565, was restored to office in 577 at the death of John the Scholastic. The theological confusion of the period is well illustrated in the restored patriarch's support of a heresy denying the possibility of the resurrection of the body. The future pope, Gregory the Great, resident papal legate at the imperial court, protested to

Emperor Tiberius, who forced Eutychius to burn the book he had written on this latest theological novelty. At Tiberius' death in 582, the general Maurice (582-602) succeeded to the imperial throne and continued the moderate religious policies of his precedessor, maintaining a close friendship with the legate Gregory the Great.

During the period of moderation in Justinian's last years, the Monophysite Jacobites seized the opportunity to strengthen their position. In 575, after the efforts of Justin II, all the bishops of the East adhered to the imperial orthodoxy and the Monophysites were in hiding. But under Tiberius and Maurice the orthodox imperial bishops called now Melkites increasingly lost their congregations to the Jacobites. In 575, the Monophysites of Alexandria rejected a Syrian candidate to the patriarchate and elected as patriarch Peter, an unlearned but vigorous old Monophysite. Peter promptly ordained 70 Jacobite bishops and, despite the objections of Jacob Bar'adai, deposed Paul, Monophysite patriarch of Antioch, then in exile in Egypt, in order to weaken Syrian influence on the Egyptian church. This act further embroiled the Syrian Monophysites in controversy. Peter of Alexandria then proceeded to act as ecumenical patriarch over all the eastern Monophysites. At his death in 577, the divisions among the Monophysites in Egypt were so great that it took them a year to agree on his successor, Damian, a theologically learned monk of Syrian origin.

Damian continued his predecessor's authoritarian manner over the Monophysites, but the sect remained badly divided by episcopal rivalries and doctrinal differences. In 578, Jacob Bar'adai died in the midst of a mission to reconcile the Syrian Monophysite supporters of the deposed Paul and the Egyptians ruled by the strong hand of Damian. With the respected Jacob gone, Damian set a bolder course and traveled with a group of bishops to Antioch where he attempted to install a Monophysite patriarch amenable to his authority. Discovered by the police, Damian fled to Constantinople. There, at the urging of the Monophysite emir of the Ghassinid Arabs, the Monophysite leaders met in council to work out their differences. But the peace-making council was not well received in Egypt nor in Syria, and quarrels broke out again. The Syrian Monophysites were further divided when the clergy of Antioch elected Peter of Callinicum patriarch in opposition to Paul. Peter and Damian in turn soon quarreled over Damian's attempt to deal with the Tritheists. He argued that the properties of the three persons were really the persons themselves, each participating in the common God. When Peter vigorously refuted this latest theological confusion, Syrian and Egyptian Monophysites remained at war with each other, though both parties resolutely opposed imperial attempts to impose the decrees of Constantinople II.

In the East outside of the confines of the empire, the Persian church remained Nestorian under the able direction of Mar-aba, elected Catholicos in 540, who pacified and organized the church until his death in 552. Jacob Bar'adai had attempted to spread Monophysite doctrines into Persia by consecrating a Monophysite bishop who succeeded in baptizing a son of the Shah Chosroes into the sect. Monophysite monks had some success in propagating their doctrines along the trade routes leading through Persia. By 585 the Catholicos convened a Nestorian council at Seleucia which condemned the Monophysites.

In Armenia, the church had declared itself officially Monophysite in 491. Repeatedly the Council of Chalcedon was firmly rejected. When Armenia was divided politically between Emperor Maurice and the Shah Chosroes, the Catholicos of the Persian-controlled area remained staunchly Monophysite, while Maurice imposed an orthodox Catholicos in his area, in which the rank and file of the population remained firmly Monophysite.

In the West, bishops of northern Italy and Illyria continued in their refusal to accept the decisions of Constantinople II. Even when the Lombard invasion, beginning in 568, forced the archbishop of Milan to flee to Genoa and the patriarch of Aquileia to take refuge at Grado, the schism lingered on, despite sporadic efforts of the Byzantine governor at Ravenna to stamp it out by force. The popes in Rome were further caught up in the attempts of the eastern emperor to negotiate with the Franks as a counterweight against the expansion of Lombard power in Italy. But by 590, Rome was encircled by Lombard dukes at Spoleto and Benevento. In northern Italy, occupied by the Arian Lombards, many bishops continued the schism with the Bishop of Rome, still politically subject to the imperial governor at Ravenna, down into the seventh century. Only under Pope Sergius I (687-701) did the schism end.

During this time, Popes Pelagius I (556-561), Pelagius II (579-590) and Gregory I the Great (590-604) all accepted the definitions of Constantinople II, but all had reservations about the condemnations of the Three Chapters, thinking that they did not deal with the substance of the faith. The Lateran Synod of 649 held under Pope Martin I (649-653) demanded the West's acceptance of the Council. In 680/81, the Third Council of Constantinople declared its acceptance of all five previous general councils.

6. *Chronology*

485   Philoxenus (d. 523), bishop of Mabbough consecrated by Peter the Fuller.

489   Acacius succeeded by Fravita.

490   Negotiations with Felix III by Fravita and Zeno.

491   Death of Zeno; accession of Anastasius I.

492   Gelasius (d. 496) pope, opposed Emperor Anastasius I.

506/7   Philoxenus opened Monophysite campaign against Chalcedon.

508   Severus wrote Typos of Anastasius.

509   Synod at Antioch condemned writings of Theodore of Mopsuestia, Diodorus of Tarsus, Theodoret of Cyrus and Ibas of Edessa.

512   Severus, patriarch of Antioch.

514   Hormisdas I (d. 523) pope.
Synod at Tyre rejected Chalcedon.

518   Death of Anastasius; Justin I emperor.
Flight of Severus and Julian of Halicarnassus to Egypt.

519   Signing of Formula of Hormisdas; end of Acacian Schism.
Feast of "Saint" Nestorius at Cyrus.

520   Scythian monks present Theopaschite Formula at Rome.

527   Coronation of Justinian and Theodora.
Death of Justin I.

531   Sabas at Constantinople to oppose Origenist monks.

532   Colloquy between six orthodox and six Monophysite bishops.

533   Theopaschite Formula proclaimed by Justinian.

534   John II (d. 535) accepted formula and condemned Sleepless Monks.

535   Theodosius, Monophysite, patriarch of Alexandria.

536   Agapetus at Constantinople; deposition of Anthimus; Menas, patriarch of Constantinople.
Severus and Monophysites condemned and expelled from Constantinople.

537   Vigilius (d. 555) pope.

538   Pelagius, papal legate at Constantinople.
Death of Severus.

543   Ten Anathemas against Origen.
Three Chapters.

544   Menas forced to sign Three Chapters; Western resistance.

545   Vigilius taken from Rome; stays at Sicily.

546/7   Totila the Ostrogoth retakes Rome.

547   Vigilius at Constantinople; Menas excommunicated (January).
Reconciliation with Menas; secret agreement to condemn Three Chapters (June).
Facundus of Hermiane rejected condemnation of Three Chapters.

548   Judicatum I accepted edict condemning Three Chapters; violent reaction in West.
Death of Theodora.

549   Roman deacons repudiated Vigilius.

550   Secret assurances between Vigilius and Justinian.
Deposition of Reparatus of Carthage.

551   Flight of Vigilius to Chalcedon in autumn.

552   Encyclical of Vigilius; condemnation of Menas and Theodore Askidas.
Convocation of Council.

553   Vigilius accepted council to be called in West; confession of faith in Chalcedon by eastern patriarchs.
Fifteen anathemas against Origenism.
Pre-conciliar discussions between Justinian and Vigilius.
Opening of Council (May 5).

May 8	Second session — negotiations with Vigilius.
May 9	Third Session - Profession of Faith.
May 12/13	Fourth session — Anathemas against Theodore of Mopsuestia.
May 14	Vigilius finishes Constitutum I.

May 19	Sixth session — discussion of Ibas' Letter to Maris.
May 24	Publication of Constitutum I.
May 26	Seventh Session—Justinian rejects Constitutum I; reveals secret promises of pope; bishops condemn Vigilius.
June 2	Eighth session—condemnation of Three Chapters; fourteen anathemas.
June 14	Publication of Anathemas.
July 14	Justinian publicizes perjury of Vigilius.

554   Publication of Constitutum II of Vigilius — condemns Three Chapters (February).
Pragmatic Sanction of Justinian dealing with Italy.

555   Death of Vigilius in Sicily.

556   Pelagius consecrated; resistance in Africa, Gaul and Italy.

565   Death of Justinian; accession of Justin II (d. 578).

568   Lombards entered Italy.

576   Tiberius regent; emperor in 578.

582   Maurice succeeded Tiberius. Maurice murdered by Phocas in 602.

7. Bibliography

The standard political history of the Eastern Roman Empire is G. Ostrogorsky, *History of the Byzantine State* (New Brunswick, 1957); broader in scope is A. A. Vasiliev, *History of the Byzantine Empire*, 2 vols. (Madison, 1964). The ecclesiastical history of this period is covered in H. Jedin, editor, *History of the Church*, vol. 2 (New York, 1980). Two more detailed books are P. Charanis, *Church*

and State in the Later Roman Empire: The Religious Policy
of Anastasius I (Thessalonica, 1974) and A. A. Vasiliev,
Justin I (Cambridge, 1950). Perhaps the best short life of
Justinian is P. N. Ure, *Justinian and His Age* (Baltimore,
1951). The documents dealing with the Council can be found
in English in H. M. Percival, editor, *The Seven Ecumenical
Councils*, volume 14 of *A Select Library of Nicene and Post-
Nicene Fathers* (New York and Oxford, 1900). The best
book on the Monophysites is now W. H. C. Frend, *The Rise
of the Monophysite Movement* (Cambridge, 1972). A
detailed study of Monophysite theology is R. C. Chesnut,
Three Monophysite Christologies (Oxford, 1976). The Origenist influence is studied in D. Evans, *Leontius of Byzantium: An Origenist Christology* (Washington, 1969). However, Evans' conclusions are not accepted by John J. Lynch,
"Christology of Leontius," *Theological Studies*, 36 (1975),
455-471. The best book on the whole question of Christology is J. Meyendorff, *Christ in Eastern Christian Thought*
(St. Vladimir's Seminary, 1975). The general theology of the
period is outlined in J. Pelikan, *The Emergence of the
Catholic Tradition* (Chicago, 1971). Relations of the Eastern
Church with the Papacy are masterfully treated in F. Dvornik, *Byzantium and the Roman Papacy* (New York, 1966).
Of interest too is J.A. McGukin, "The Theopaschite Confession," *Journal of Ecclesiastical History,* 35 (1984), 239-255.

7

Council of Constantinople III, 680

1. Reign of Heraclius (610-641)

When Heraclius, son of the governor of Africa, sailed from Carthage in 610 and overthrew the anarchic rule of the usurper Phocas (602-610), who had murdered Emperor Maurice and his family, the Empire lay in ruins, its people demoralized, its finances exhausted, its army and administration in disarray, its frontiers in east and west overrun by alien peoples. So desperate was its plight that at one point Heraclius thought of moving his headquarters to the relative safety of Carthage in North Africa. From this he was dissuaded by the people of Constantinople and its patriarch, Sergius. During the first two decades of his long reign, the Avars, a fierce nomadic people from the steppes of central Asia spread destruction in the Danubian provinces. An ocean of Slavic peoples surged into the Balkan peninsula reaching even to southern Greece, destroying the mixed Latin and Greek civil and ecclesiastical diocese of Illyricum and with it a vital connecting link between East and West — a situation that would lead to increasing alienation between Greek and Latin churches.

At the same time the Empire was engaged in a mortal

struggle in the East with Sassanid Persia under Chosroes. In 611 the imperial army was heavily defeated at Antioch and in 613 the Persians forced their way south to capture Damascus and north to take Tarsus in southern Asia Minor. Armenia in eastern Asia Minor soon fell as well. Most horrifying to the Christians of the Empire was the Persian sack of Jerusalem in 614, when after ravaging the Constantinian basilica of the Holy Sepulchre, the Zoroastrians carried off the Holy Cross in triumph to their capital at Ctesiphon. By 619 Egypt, the granary of the Empire, was occupied by the Persians. They reached even the Bosporus to threaten Constantinople itself.

But slowly the heads of State and Church, Emperor Heraclius and Patriarch Sergius rallied their people. This remarkable pair well complemented each other. When Heraclius lost heart, Sergius fanned his hopes. The patriarch poured the wealth of the Church into the empty coffers of the Empire. As the emperor led his armies on the frontiers, the patriarch as regent rallied the capital and warded off the attacks of its enemies. When the emperor needed a theological basis for the reunion of dissident Christians, Sergius provided it in Monoenergism and Monothelitism. To strengthen the structure of the state Heraclius reorganized the remnant of his Empire into military districts, the themes, headed by generals, and rebuilt his armies on the basis of effective native levies of sturdy farmers from Asia Minor. The central administration, especially its financial departments, was overhauled. With the sinews of government strengthened, church wealth put at the service of the state, and religious fervor fanned into flame, Heraclius was ready to launch a Holy War to rewin the Cross from the infidel Persians. The Avars in the West were neutralized by treaty and tribute, the Patriarch Sergius and the Patrician Bonus were appointed regents, and the emperor himself assumed command of his armies. After a solemn liturgy in Hagia Sophia, the emperor and his army marched from the capital on Easter Monday, 622. By fall, Heraclius was victorious in Armenia; Asia Minor was cleared of Persians. He then drove south into the Persian city of Ganzak where he demolished the great Zoroastrian fire temple in revenge for the destruction of Christian shrines in Jerusalem. The Shah Chosroes was forced to retreat deep into Persia. But on Heraclius' rear, Constantinople itself was threatened in 626 by hordes of Persians, Avars, Slavs and Bulgars. The Patriarch Sergius rallied the capital behind its great walls, and Byzantine sea power broke the encircling armies. They fell back on all fronts, and Heraclius prepared to launch a great counter-offensive. By the autumn of 627 he advanced into the heart of Persia and before the ancient city of Nineveh destroyed the Persian army. In 628, after the Shah Chosroes had been deposed and murdered, his son sued for peace. In the Persian heartland, Heraclius dictated his terms: Armenia, Roman Mesopotamia, Syria and Egypt were restored to Byzantine control. In 630 the emperor personally restored the Holy Cross to its place in Jerusalem. His people, the Patriarch Sergius at their head, exultantly welcomed him home. Though the great wedge of Slavic peoples remained firmly ensconced in the Balkans, and far to the west southern Spain was reoccupied by Visigoths, Heraclius had in twenty years humbled his enemies and largely restored his Empire.

During this time the Empire became more strongly Hellenized. Greek was proclaimed the official language of the administration replacing Latin. By the next generation knowledge of Latin was rare even in educated circles. Thus another barrier was raised to the interchange of ideas between the Greek East and the West, where, through the instrumentality of the Church, Latin had become the language of the learned. The old Roman titles of imperator, caesar and augustus were abandoned in the East; the head of state became the Basileus; succession to the title was well on its way to becoming hereditary.

2. Religious Controversy

As the eastern and southern provinces — Armenia, Syria and Egypt — were regained to the Empire, the emperor had to face once again the religious question, how to reconcile the dissident Monophysites without alienating Chalcedonian Asia Minor, Italy and Africa. This task was made more urgent after a Persian-sponsored meeting of the Monophysite leaders at Ctesiphon in 614. It fell to the Patriarch Sergius to provide the theological basis for ecclesiastical reconciliation. As early as 617/18 Sergius wrote to George Arsas, a leader of the Monophysites in Egypt, asking for texts referring to the unique activity of Christ. Severus of Antioch, the earlier great theologian of the Monophysite movement, had already insisted on one nature, one will, one activity in Christ. What Sergius evidently had in mind was to hold to the Chalcedonian definition of "in two natures" but to reconcile this with a declaration of one activity in Christ. Sergius wrote as well to Theodore, bishop of Pharan near Mount Sinai, a Chalcedonian. He forwarded to him a letter supposedly written by Menas, the Justinianic patriarch of Constantinople, to Pope Vigilius containing several testimonies from the Fathers to one energy and one will in Christ. This letter would later be shown to be a forgery at the Council of Constantinople III, but Theodore was won over. Moreover, it seems to have been Theodore who supplied the metaphysical justification of Monoenergism, the theory that there is in Christ only one activity. In Theodore's view, in Christ, the body was the instrument of the soul and both were the instrument of the Word. All activity proceeded from the Word as agent. Whatever was done by the Incarnate Word was done by Him as Creator and God, and that therefore all the things that were said of Him either as God or in a human way were the action of the divinity of the Word. As mediator between God and man, Christ was the subject who carried out human acts in an ineffable way by means of the flesh that He had assumed. Because Christ had by a divine and wise economy taken upon Himself such human needs as sleep, work, hunger and thirst, it was necessary to attribute these things to the single action of one and the same Christ. The Incarnate Word was thus the agent and subject of all action, whether this was appropriate to his divine or human nature. In a letter to Paul the Blind, chief of the Cypriot Monophysites, Sergius commissioned him to forbid the archbishop of Cyprus to speak of two activities in Christ after the Incarnation. Cyrus, bishop of Phasis in the Caucasus on the Black Sea, raised the question of how this doctrine could be reconciled with the statement in Pope Leo's Tome that in Christ each form (nature) performs the function that is proper to it in communion with the other. Sergius' response was to reread Leo's statement, putting form not in the nominative but in the ablative case to the effect that the Word does *by means* of each form, the acts that belong to it. Cyrus, too, was won to Monoenergism and was to be employed later in the struggle to propagate the doctrine in Egypt.

With his wars at an end for the moment, Heraclius met with Ezra, the Catholicos of the Monophysite Armenians in 630. His efforts at conciliation bore fruit when a synod of Armenians in 633 decided to accept the Council of Chalcedon. This proved an ephemeral decision, mainly, it seems, because the Armenians were opposed to Chalcedon's subjection of the Armenian Church to the patriarch of Constantinople. In 629, when Heraclius had reoccupied Syria, he found Antioch without a Chalcedonian patriarch. He opened negotiations with the Monophysite patriarch, Athanasius Gammala, and won him to his side. Armed with texts supplied by Sergius, including the forged letter of Menas, Heraclius met the patriarch and twelve of his suffragans at Mabbough and the Syrians accepted Monoenergism and its later variant Monothelitism so firmly that its proponents at Constantinople III will be largely Syrian. At Alexandria, there was a double hierarchy, the Chalcedonian Melkite patriarch heading a small congregation in the city and the Monophysite Coptic patriarch controlling the rest of Egypt. In 630/31 Heraclius sent Cyrus of Phasis to Egypt as patriarch armed with ecclesiastical, civil and military powers to effect a union with the Copts. Benjamin, the Coptic patriarch, fled from Alexandria at Cyrus' approach. After Cyrus instituted a reign of terror in which Benjamin's brother, among others, was tortured to death, he managed in 633 to negotiate a Pact of Union embodied in nine chapters. The seventh chapter formed the theological center of the Pact. It anathematized all who did not hold the doctrine of the two natures in Christ, perfect in His divinity and humanity, the natures remaining unconfused and undivided after a natural and hypostatic union, but attributed all activity in Christ to the one person not to the natures. "There was but one and the same Christ, working both the divine and human actions by one theandrical operation" as Dionysius taught. Cyrus was referring here to an author whose name carried great weight in these controversies — Dionysius, supposedly a disciple of St. Paul himself who is mentioned in Acts 17:34. He was first cited by Severus of Antioch and may have been none other than the much exiled Monophysite patriarch of Antioch, Peter the Fuller. Dionysius had maintained that Christ had "done divine things as God and human things as man," but that there had been "a certain divine-human (theandric) action of God made man." As Cyrus explained, it was no longer permissible to speak of two actions after the union but only of a single dominant action, which directed everything that the Incarnate Word said or did or experienced in mind or body. The alternative position which ascribed a distinct action to each of the two natures, would be obliged to go on to posit a distinct action for the body of Christ's humanity and another for his soul, which by reduction would lead to three actions in the incarnate Christ. For what do we attribute to the whole Christ if we do not give to the whole the single action through the union? From the pulpit of the patriarchal basilica in Alexandria Cyrus promulgated the Pact of Union and all parties entered in communion at the Eucharist. Cyrus triumphantly announced his success to Heraclius and Sergius who approved his formulation, especially the seventh chapter. The Monophysites meanwhile congratulated themselves that acceptance of one operation was the equivalent of the recognition of one nature in Christ. By 633 the emperor seemed to have triumphed over his foreign foes and reconciled all the Monophysites — the Armenians, the Syrian Jacobites and the Egyptian Copts.

But there was in Alexandria at the time a monk who

would make a shambles of this attempt at union by revealing its unorthodox theological foundation — Sophronius of Jerusalem. Sophronius came originally from Damascus and had lived as a monk near Jerusalem. He had been in contact with the orthodox party of Alexandria around the Chalcedonian patriarch John the Almsgiver (d. 619). He had visited Rome in 614, but returned to Palestine in 619 to bury his friend John Moschus, an influential spiritual writer. His wanderings took him to Carthage where he met the monk Maximus the Confessor, who would take up his battle against imperial Monoenergism. By 633 Sophronius was in Alexandria in time to protest the theology of Cyrus' Pact of Union. Sophronius insisted that activity proceeds not from the person of Christ as the sole agent but from the two natures. Cyrus promptly sent Sophronius on to Sergius at Constantinople. There Sergius persuaded Sophronius to cease from numbering the activities in Christ, whereupon the monk left Constantinople to return to Jerusalem. Alarmed by the protests of Sophronius which threatened to destroy all his patient efforts toward the reunion of the Monophysites, Sergius convoked the Home Synod of Constantinople. There it was decided that though all actions, divine and human, in Christ are to be attributed to one sole agent, the Incarnate Word, there should be no numbering of activities. To Cyrus at Alexandria Sergius dispatched the *Psephos*, which instructed Cyrus not to permit talk of one or two activites in relation to Christ. Rather, the teaching should be that the only Son, Our Lord Jesus Christ, does what is divine and human and that all activity of God and man proceeds from the sole Incarnate Word without division or confusion. Talk of one activity seemed to abolish the two natures hypostatically united in Christ; talk of two activities, to indicate that there could be in Christ two acts of will, one opposed to the other. Rather, the Fathers have taught that at no moment could the flesh animated by reason accomplish any natural movement contrary to the assent of God the Word who is hypostatically united to it, for the flesh acts in the manner and measure in which God the Word has willed. For Christ the human composite was always and in all things under the divine motion of the divinity of the Word Himself.

But the life of an ecclesiastical politician is not an easy one, and Sergius' careful plans were soon upset. To everyone's surprise, in Jerusalem Sophronius was elected patriarch. As a monk he had bowed to Sergius' pleas to remain silent about the activities of Christ; as patriarch he felt compelled to speak the truth as he saw it. He held a synod at Jerusalem in 634 which defined the doctrine of two wills and operations. Further, he sent his synodical profession of faith to Pope Honorius, Sergius and his fellow patriarchs. In the Christological section of his letter accepting the Tome of Leo as coming from St. Peter, the works of Cyril as coming from St. Mark, he expounded the doctrine of the unity of person and duality of natures, and then turned to the problem of operations. For Sophronius the duality of operations results from the duality of the natures and their properties: "As in Christ each nature preserves its properties inviolate, so each form works, in communion with the other, what is proper to itself." Since the being of the natures is distinct, it followed that the operations are also distinct. To deny the duality of operations could lead to the fusion of the natures, for by means of operations, natures are discerned; differences of operation enable us to realize the diversity of substances. When Dionysius spoke of a theandrical operation, he did not present it as the only operation in Christ, but as a new operation, added to the two others, comprising the actions in which the divinity and the humanity are exercised at the same time. But even though insisting that there are in Christ two operations, Sophronius insisted equally that there is in Him only one agent: "We maintain that all the speech and energy of Christ, whether divine and heavenly, or human and earthly, proceed from one and the same Christ and Son, from the one compound and unique hypostasis which is the incarnate Logos of God, who brings forth naturally from Himself both energies unseparated and unmixed, according to His natures: according to His divine nature, by which He is consubstantial with the Father, the divine and ineffable energy; according to His human nature, by which He became consubstantial with us men, the human and earthly, the energy being in accordance with the nature to which it belongs." But Sophronius nowhere speaks of two wills, even though Sergius had already spoken of one will. As yet the controversy had not turned precisely to this point. He does observe that Christ did not undergo necessarily and unwillingly the motions and passions of human nature, even though He underwent them naturally and humanly.

At Constantinople, Sergius had anticipated that once Sophronius was patriarch, news of developments in the East would soon reach Rome. So before Sophronius' synodical letter reached Rome, Pope Honorius had received a letter from Sergius. The patriarch informed the pope of the events that had transpired in the East. He told Honorius that he had enjoined Cyrus of Alexandria to avoid discussion of one or two operations because this was thought an innovation in doctrine and scandalized many. Especially talk of two operations would lead many to assume in Christ two wills contrary to each other, while the Fathers teach that the humanity of Christ always performed its natural operation just when and how and inasmuch as the Word willed, at all times and in all things moved and directed by the divinity of the Word. Rather, we should confess with Leo that from one and the same Incarnate Word all divine and human energy proceeds indivisibly and inseparably.

Not fully understanding the state of the question in the East, Honorius responded favorably to Sergius' letter. He made three points. First, we should avoid speaking of one or two operations; these are new and scandalous disputes about words. It would be Nestorian to speak of two operations; Eutychian to speak only of one. Scripture attests to the fact that Christ is the one working agent of the divinity and the humanity and that He worked in a great many ways. Neither the Apostles nor the Fathers spoke of one or two operations. The question should be left to the philosophers and grammarians or best left in silence. Secondly, Jesus Christ, who is one person, has performed both divine and human works through the concourse of two natures; the same Christ has worked in His two natures both divinely and humanly.

Thirdly, we must hold the unity of Christ's will, for while the Word truly took our nature, He did not take our vitiated nature; He took our flesh but not the law of flesh repugnant to that of the spirit. There was in Christ no will tending in a direction opposed to the law of the spirit. Christ's words: "I came down from heaven, not to do my own will, but the will of Him who sent me" (Jn 6:38) and "Father, not what I will, but what you will" (Mt 26:39) do not reveal a will differing from the Father's but merely the economy of the humanity which He had assumed, to give us an example upon which to model our willing submission to God. In a second letter to Sergius, after having received Sophronius' synodical profession of faith, Honorius repeated the doctrine of his first concluding that it was better to speak of one operator and two operating natures. He added that he had so informed Sophronius of Jerusalem and Cyrus of Alexandria.

With the pope apparently won over to his view, Sergius continued to press his policy on the East. He prepared an edict, the *Ecthesis*, in 636 which Heraclius signed in 638 to define the policy of the Church. After explaining the general doctrine of the Trinity and the Incarnation, it treated specifically the question of operations and wills in Christ. Every operation, divine or human, is ascribed solely to the Incarnate Word. But rather than numbering the operations, we should teach that there is but one Christ who works both divine and human effects. It concludes, as did the *Psephos*, that, following the holy Fathers, we confess one will of Our Lord Jesus Christ, the true God, for at no time did His rationally quickened flesh, separately and of its own impulse, and in opposition to the suggestion of the hypostatically united Word, exercise its natural activity, but it exercised that activity at the time and in the manner and measure in which the Word of God willed it.

Thus the discussion was moved from a single action to the source of action, the will. From the Greek term "one will," this position became known as Monothelitism. The change in the terms of the discussion also added fuel to the flames of controversy. Little could be found in the Gospels, the Fathers and the Councils about one operation or two operations in Christ, but a great deal could be found about Christ's will. For the will of Christ was near the center of the New Testament, at the heart of the passion narratives. Interpretation of the texts quoted by Honorius became the crux of the controversy from now on. And the works of the Fathers provided abundant matter for interpretation.

In the East, most of the bishops accepted the *Ecthesis*. Sophronius of Jerusalem died in 638 to be succeeded by a Monothelite patriarch; the patriarchs Macedonius at Antioch and Cyrus at Alexandria favored the imperial profession of faith. A council at Constantinople held just before Sergius' death approved the *Ecthesis*, and a second held by his successor, Pyrrhus, in 639, followed suit. There would be opposition in Rome and the West as the successors of Honorius, who died in 638, came to realize the full impact of the matter. For what Sergius and the emperor had decreed was that there is in Jesus Christ only one will and one truly free and spontaneous activity, the divine activity and will. Granting the existence of a human nature, its activity is completely subordinate to that of the divine; the humanity in the power of the Word is merely a docile instrument which He uses and which is devoid of any initiative of its own.

3. Muslim Invasion

Just as the protest of Sophronius began to unravel Sergius' laboriously woven religious settlement, other factors tore the newly reknit fabric of Heraclius' Empire to shreds. In the very year, 622, that he had launched his great campaign against Persia, an obscure religious reformer, Mohammed by name, fled from Mecca to Medina in the heart of Arabia, a journey revered by Muslims as the Hegira, which ushered in the Islamic era. By his death in 632 Mohammed had given to the Arabs a new faith recorded in the Koran and based on the belief in one all-powerful God, Allah, and on the religious duties of prayer, fasting, almsgiving and pilgrimage. On the foundation of this new faith he had begun to organize the hitherto disparate idolatrous tribes of central Arabia into a single dynamic nation. Under Mohammed's father-in-law, the Caliph Abu Bakr and his commanding general Khalid, the Arab armies began to probe the defenses of their northern neighbors, the Byzantines and Persians, weakened by their twenty year struggle. By 634 Arab raiders struck into Syria and in the next year Damascus fell. When the Byzantine army rushed to the defense of Syria, it was disastrously defeated in 636 at the River Yarmuk. All the laboriously restored southeastern provinces of the Empire, Roman-dominated for 700 years, lay open to this new and terrible enemy. In 638 Antioch was overrun; in 639, Caesarea in Palestine. The aged patriarch Sophronius long led the resistance at Jerusalem, but finally, just before his death, the city opened its gates to Abu Bakr's successor, the Caliph Omar, in 638. Only Ascalon and Gaza on the Palestinian coast held out to 640. In 639 Arab armies drove into Egypt and after the fall of the fortress of Babylon, at the apex of the Nile delta, the Patriarch Cyrus negotiated the surrender of Alexandria in 642. In 641 it was Mesopotamia's turn; in 642, Persia's. By 647 the Muslims reached the borders of Roman Africa but fell back, regrouping their forces for a second attack which established Kairouan in 670 as the outpost for the final assault on Carthage in 698. By the death of Heraclius, 641, only Asia Minor, enclaves in the Balkans, Italy and North Africa remained under Byzantine control

Save for Rome, Constantinople and a reduced Antioch, the other ancient patriarchal sees — Alexandria and Jerusalem — were lost to the Empire. In the first years of the conquest, the Muslims did not seek to make converts. They levied a general tribute and a poll tax on the Christians, bade them wear a distinctive garb and refrain from building new churches, displaying the cross in public, ringing church bells and riding horses. Since all Christians were treated equally by the Muslim overlord, pressures to conform to an imperially prescribed standard of orthodoxy were lifted. Monophysites and Nestorians were free to pursue their own beliefs. In Egypt, Benjamin (d. 662) was restored to the patriarchate of Alexandria; Copts, using their own language until the imposition of Arabic in 705, continued the local administration acting as scribes, tax collectors and magistrates. From Syria under the Jacobite patriarch John I (d. 648) Monophysites spread their faith into Arab-controlled Mesopotamia and Persia, and many prospered as merchants. In Armenia the Monophysite church under its Catholicos remained rigidly opposed to Chalcedon and to reconciliation with the Byzantines while serving as the one unifying factor in Armenian life. In conquered Persia, the Nestorians, their beliefs settled in the Book of Union of Mar Babai the Great (d. 628), actually flourished under Muslim rule. Accorded special favor by the Muslims, Nestorian Christians were valued as physicians, teachers and interpreters, and many amassed large fortunes. From Ctesiphon, the patriarch, with some ten metropolitans, organized far-flung missionary activity, establishing bishoprics, schools, libraries and hospitals. Nestorian missions were established in central Asia among Turks, Tartars and Mongols, in the Indies and on the southern coast of India, and the Segan-Fu stone discovered by seventeenth-century Jesuits testifies to the arrival of Nestorians in China in 635. Orthodox Christianity in the East gradually shrank to the confines of the Byzantine Empire, Greek in language, theology and culture under the patriarch of Constantinople.

Across the Slavic-occupied Balkans, Rome stood in a Byzantine enclave separated from the other enclaves of Genoa, Naples and Ravenna, seat of the exarch or governor, by the Lombard kingdom and its satellite duchies, orthodox Catholics after the reign of Rothari (d. 652). Here the pope still regarded himself as the subject of the Byzantine emperor, his regnal years dated papal documents, his effigy was stamped on Roman coins. Contacts by the pope with Germanic kingdoms were infrequent, but all these kingdoms were now largely orthodox Catholic. Visigothic Spain abandoned Arianism to become orthodox under King Reccard I (d. 601), and the church was governed by the primate at Toledo assisted by his bishops frequently assembled in council in the primatial city. In Frankland, the kingdom slipped into decadence after the death of King Dagobert (d. 639), but the Anglo-Irish missionary activity fostered by Irish monk Columban (d. 615) established fervent monastic centers in an otherwise barbarous land. In England, seven petty Anglo-Saxon kingdoms contended for dominance, as a Greek, Theodore of Tarsus (d. 690), consecrated archbishop of Canterbury by the pope, organized the Church on a Roman diocesan model. Barbarous by Byzantine standards, learning in these kingdoms was largely Latin, fostered by the likes of Gregory, bishop of Tours (d. 594) in France, Isidore, archbishop of Seville (d. 636) in Spain and the Englishman Venerable Bede (d. 735), monk of Jarrow in Northumbria.

4. Western Response

Though geography, political organization, language and culture were threatening the unity of the Catholic Church, separation between East and West was not complete. The Persian and Arab invasions had compelled large groups of Greek monks to take refuge in Byzantine Africa, Sicily and mainland Italy. These men were able to spread an appreciation of Byzantine theology in the West. Among these the greatest was the monk Maximus, a member of a noble family of Constantinople allied to the family of Heraclius himself. Six years older than the emperor, he served as first secretary to Heraclius before becoming a monk. His was a wandering life, first to Cyzicus on the Bosporus where he became a close friend of the bishop there. By 628 he had fled the Persian invasion to Carthage in Africa. There, in contact with the highest civil and ecclesiastical circles of the Empire, he took up the struggle against Monothelitism begun by his mentor Sophronius. His was the finest mind engaged in the great Christological controversy over Monothelitism. In fact, comments John Meyendorff, "It remains impossible ... to understand the whole of Byzantine theology without becoming aware of Maximus' synthesis."

Here we will have to be content with a brief discussion of his Christology as it bears upon the Monothelite controversy. For Maximus the Incarnation was the central factor in man's deification: "that the whole people might participate in the whole God, and that in the same way in which soul and body are united, God should become partakable of by the soul, and, that by the soul's intermediary, by the body, in order that the soul might receive an unchanging character and the body immortality; and finally that the whole man should become God, deified by the grace of God become man, becoming whole man, soul and body, and becoming whole God, soul and body, by grace." Thus Christ is the meeting point of God's reaching out to mankind and of mankind's God-given tendency toward the divine. Human beings possess an order of nature established by God; they tend toward God as the ultimate good of their nature. But this inner natural order exists according to a mode brought about by the exercise of free will. Through the fall of primal man the mode of human existence has been modified and is now in opposition to the inner drive of human nature. The perfectly human mode of existence consonant with human nature is restored only in Christ.

If the natures in Christ are really two, then the operations of those natures must also be two. For activity, operation is essential to an existent being. Only through operations can natures be discerned and distinguished. Natures and operations are thus necessarily and ineluctably connected. If there are two natures really existent in Christ, there must be as well two really existent operations. Moreover, every being possesses a necessary appetite for good appropriate to its nature. In human beings the good of nature is freely reached. As a consequence of the primal sin, humans acquired a gnomic will which chooses, hesitates, ignores the real good. Gnomic will gives to action its moral quality, its mode of existence, and proceeds not from nature but from person. By reason of sin, humans now make free choices of merely relative goods, goods not in accord with the law of their nature. The gnomic will is to be distinguished from the natural will uncontaminated by sin, free will at its highest, liberty which always chooses the real good without possibility of sin. The Word took to Himself a natural will, for according to the age-old rule of the Fathers, what is not assumed is not redeemed. Christ had a fully human natural will. But He could have no gnomic will. Gnomic will is always linked to sin and since Christ is sinless, He can have no will ignorant, hesitant and in conflict with Himself. His human will adheres without doubt or hesitation to its perfect good. He has only natural will, both human and divine, which with sovereign freedom always chooses the appropriate good. Christ has therefore two natures, two operations, two wills really proceeding from the divine and human natures but always in harmony because the single divine Person assures their goodness of choice. In human beings salvation and deification consist in bringing the gnomic will, through redemption in Christ, into conformity with the innate drive of our natural will toward God. In the Incarnation Christ has revealed the deepest fact about humanity, said Maximus, "as man he accomplishes in all truth the true human destiny that he himself had predetermined as God, and from which man had turned: he unites man to God."

For the Emperor Heraclius the Islamic conquests meant the collapse of his life-work. After the battle of Yarmuk, he gave up the cause as lost and withdrew to Asia Minor. There he remained for a time filled with a morbid dread of crossing the sea to Constantinople. At last when disturbances in the capital made his presence imperative, he crossed over on a ship's deck covered with earth and foliage. At his death in 641 after great suffering, he left the crown jointly to his sons by two wives, Constantine III and Heraclonas. The faltering Empire was further distracted by factions divided in their support of the co-emperors. But Constantine died later in the year and the people turned against the boy-emperor Heraclonas and his unpopular mother, Martina. By order of the Senate Heraclonas and his mother were deposed, the decision sealed by cutting off Martina's tongue and Heraclonas' nose, the first instance in Byzantine history of the oriental custom of mutilation as a sign of incapacity to hold office. The young son of Constantine III, Constans II, was made emperor. Constans' reign was marked by further incursions by the Arabs and the loss of Byzantine naval supremacy in the Mediterranean, but the Arab advance was halted by internal dissension between rival caliphs, Muawya in Syria and Ali, Mohammed's son-in-law, in Arabia, and the subsequent removal of the capital of the Islamic Empire to Damascus. A momentary peace between the Arabs and the Byzantines was declared in 659. Free for the moment of anxiety in the East, Constans turned West and managed to halt further Slavic penetration in the Balkans, and gain a shadowy overlordship of the occupying Slavs.

In Italy and in Africa, however, deep dissatisfaction with the imperial religious policy defined by the *Ecthesis* continued. Pope Severinus, Honorius' successor in 638, sent representatives to Constantinople asking for imperial approval of his election. In 640 they returned with news of the *Ecthesis*, but Severinus died before he could deal with this new development. His successor John IV called a synod which condemned the *Ecthesis* before the death of Heraclius in 641. Further, the pope protested the encyclical letter of the patriarch Pyrrhus imposing the *Ecthesis* and defended an orthodox interpretation of Honorius' view of a single will in Christ. Further communication between Rome and Constantinople was disrupted by the dynastic struggle following the death of Heraclius. In the course of that struggle the regent-empress Martina deposed the patriarch Pyrrhus, a staunch defender of Monothelitism, for political reasons. Pyrrhus, at first, tried to maintain his position in Constantinople but then fled to Africa. Here he found a hotbed of intrigue. The imperial exarch of Africa, Gregory, was plotting a coup against the central government such as Heraclius himself had accomplished in 610. It is possible that Pyrrhus saw in Gregory an agent who as emperor could restore him to the patriarchal throne. Since Gregory was orthodox and opposed to Monothelitism, this would entail a change of religious belief. However that may be, in 645 Pyrrhus met Maximus the Confessor in a public debate before the exarch in which he allowed himself to be convinced of the error of Monothelitism. He then proceeded to Rome where he formally recanted his heresy in St. Peter's basilica before Pope Theodore, John IV's successor. He was allowed to assist at the liturgy seated on a patriarchal throne and the pope wrote to the emperor demanding Pyrrhus' reinstatement as patriarch. If Pyrrhus had really pinned his hopes on the success of Gregory's coup against the emperor, he was to be disappointed. Gregory was defeated and killed by the invading Muslims in central Tunisia in 647, and Pyrrhus found himself called to the court of the exarch of Italy at Ravenna. There he recanted his recantation, and once again in the Monothelite camp, continued on to Constantinople. In Rome, a disappointed Pope Theodore condemned him, signing the document, it is said, with a pen dipped in consecrated wine. In Rome opposition to the Monothelite imperial policy grew, especially with the presence in the city of Maximus from 645/6 and Sophronius' disciple, Stephen of Dore who had been active in the election as pope of the Palestinian Theodore who had been consecrated without imperial approval.

Pope Theodore had received a synodical profession of faith from Paul, Pyrrhus' successor at Constantinople, which was orthodox but said nothing of suppression of the hated *Ecthesis*. For three years, Pope Theodore urged a profession of faith from Paul of Constantinople on the subject of Christ's will. When at last Paul formally professed Monothelitism, Pope Theodore excommunicated him. Paul thereupon laid an interdict on the palace of the papal representative and urged Emperor Constans to revise his religious policy with the issue of a new edict called the *Typos* in 648. In the *Typos*, the emperor professed his continuing concern for the purity of the Christian faith and expressed his dismay at the divisions in the Empire caused by those who professed one or two wills and activities in Christ. Thus, inspired by God, he forbade any further discussion of the question. In the future all were to abide by the faith of the Scriptures, the traditions of the five Councils and the formulas of the Fathers, without interpreting them according to personal views. There should be no recriminations for past mistakes in this matter. The *Ecthesis* was suppressed and penalties imposed for transgression of the new imperial edict.

In 649 Martin I, an Italian from Todi in Umbria, succeeded Theodore. Consecrated without imperial approval, partly because there was at the time no exarch resident in Italy, the new pope was strong and energetic, experienced in ecclesiastical affairs, aware of the theology and personalities in the East, where he had served as papal legate. Three months after his consecration he called a synod at the Lateran Palace, the pope's official residence. The synod convened on October 5, 649, with a hundred bishops in attendance, most from suburbicarian Italy but with representatives from the Romagna, Ravenna and Aquileia. At Pope Martin's request Maximus the Confessor was present. Martin, who was a dominant factor in the proceedings, opened the synod with an address relating the history of the whole Monothelite question. Protests against the heresy were presented by Stephen of Dore and the Byzantine monks resident in Rome and in letters from Ravenna, Palestine, Cyprus and Africa. Two weeks later a dossier of documents was read out, including texts of Cyrus of Alexandria, Sergius, Pyrrhus and Paul of Constantinople, and Theodore of Pharan. Then were read out the acts of the Councils which were followed by lengthy comments from Pope Martin and Maximus of Aquileia. Another two weeks later, orthodox texts were compared with Monothelite texts interspersed with comments pointing out the discrepancies between the Monothelite position and the teaching of the Councils and Fathers. The synod closed with addresses by Maximus of Aquileia, Deusdedit of Cagliari in Sardinia and Martin himself. A profession of faith and twenty canons were signed by 105 bishops, including two who had arrived from Lombard territory.

The bishops confessed the faith of Chalcedon and added their belief that our nature is perfect and without restriction, except for sin, incarnate in Christ, God Himself. From two natures, the bishops continued, and in two natures, divinity and humanity, united hypostatically without confusion or division is the one sole and same Savior and Lord Jesus Christ. There are two wills, divine and human, intimately united in one and the same Christ, because through each of His natures He naturally willed our salvation. There are two operations, divine and human, intimately united in Christ because by each of His natures He wrought our salvation. The anathemas repeated this teaching, condemning Theodore of Pharan, Cyrus of Alexandria, the patriarchs Sergius, Pyrrhus and Paul of Constantinople and the imperial edicts, the *Ecthesis* and the *Typos*. All were bidden to accept the teaching of the five holy and general councils.

The decisions of the Lateran Synod were clearly a direct affront to imperial policy, but Martin duly forwarded the acts to the emperor. In the West, it is known that he wrote to Amandus, bishop of Maastricht, and Sigebert, king of the Franks, and dispatched two monks to Africa with instructions to continue from there to inform John of Philadelphia, papal vicar for Jerusalem and Antioch, of the results of the synod. The imperial response is the only one known; it was prompt and brutal. A new exarch, Olympius was commissioned to enforce the *Typos* in Italy and to arrest the pope. When the people's loyalty to the pope frustrated his mission, Olympius sought to exploit Roman dissatisfaction with imperial policy for his own ends before moving to the south of Italy and rebelling against the emperor only to die at the hands of Muslim invaders in Sicily. In 653 a second exarch, Theodore Calliopas, was dispatched to Italy. He succeeded in arresting the pope ill in bed at the Lateran and in transporting him under harsh conditions on a 15 month voyage to Constantinople. There the pope was mistreated, insulted and tried before the Senate for treasonable complicity in Olympius' revolt. He was found guilty and condemned to death. While the emperor watched, hidden behind a lattice, the pope was degraded from office amid the insults of the mob. When the dying patriarch Paul was told of the event by the emperor personally, he exclaimed, "One more crime to answer for at my judgment," and begged the emperor to commute the pope's sentence. After Paul's death, the restored patriarch Pyrrhus, who had abjured Monothelitism in the presence of Pope Theodore, tried to compel Martin to testify that the abjuration had been extorted from him by force. Martin refused to perjure himself and was exiled to the Crimea where he died of ill treatment six months later in 655.

Even before Martin's death, Eugene allowed himself to be elected pope. Peter, who replaced the short-lived Pyrrhus as patriarch of Constantinople, wrote a moderate letter to Pope Eugene who ignored it. An imperial representative was sent west to negotiate improved relations between Rome and Constantinople. Papal representatives in turn arrived in Constantinople at the very time that Maximus the Confessor and a companion were being put on trial allegedly for political crimes. Maximus was exiled to Thrace where imperial agents tried to win him over. But Maximus remained loyal to the decisions of the Lateran Synod which he regarded as a conciliar definition. Later he was dragged back to Constantinople, retried and, according to one account, mutilated by having his tongue and right hand cut off. Exiled yet again to the Caucasus, he died in 662.

That year, Constans, unpopular at Constantinople for his morbid brutality and murder of his own brother, moved his administration to Syracuse in Sicily, visiting the monuments of Rome in 663.There he had the bronze ornaments of the ancient buildings stripped off and sent to Constantinople. Pope Vitalian, reconciled with Constantinople since 657 welcomed the emperor with all due ceremony. In 668, having exasperated the people by his heavy taxation, Constans, living in Sicily, was assassinated in his bath by one of his own chamberlains.

His son Constantine IV (668-685) succeeded to the throne with the help of Pope Vitalian. The new emperor was forced to deal with the increasing assaults by the Muslims who took Cyprus, Rhodes and Cos. In 677/78 they threatened Constantinople itself but were finally repulsed with the use of the famous Greek fire, an inflammable liquid sprayed on the enemy forces.During these years, Constantine had little time for religious affairs. From 667 to 677 successive popes refused to acknowledge successive patriarchs. But in 678 with the Empire at last secure from Muslim attack, the emperor turned to the religious question. He sent a formal letter, the *Sacra*, to Pope Donus asking that representatives be sent to Constantinople from the pope, his bishops and the Greek monasteries of Rome for a discussion of the religious differences between East and West. When the pope delayed answering, the patriarch of Constantinople erased his name from the diptychs. In loyalty to the papacy, which had helped him to the imperial throne, Constantine opposed this move and deposed the patriarch. Since Donus had in the meantime died, the imperial letter was answered by the new pope, Agatho (678-681). He asked for time to consult the Western bishops. Local synods were convened all over the West; one is known at Milan, another at Heathfield in England under Theodore of Tarsus, archbishop of Canterbury. Theodore himself was invited by the pope to join the delegation to be sent to Constantinople. Unfortunately, Theodore, whose expertise would have been valuable, could not make the journey, and the legates were two Roman priests, the Roman deacon John and subdeacon Constantine, both later popes, three Italian bishops, a priest representing the bishop of Ravenna and four Greek monks. The legates were given explicit instructions and carried with them a letter from the pope to the emperor and a letter from the western episcopate signed by 125 bishops.

The pope clearly informed the emperor: "The Roman church has by God's grace never erred from the pathway of the apostolic teaching, nor has it lapsed into heretical novelties, but from the very beginning of the Christian faith has preserved unimpaired that which it received from its founders, the princes of the Apostles." He then laid down the orthodox belief in the two wills of Christ: "We truly confess that just as He has two natures or substances, that is, divinity and humanity, unconfusedly, indivisibly and unchangeably, so too He has two natural wills and two natural operations, as perfect God and perfect man, one and the same Lord Jesus Christ. . . ."

5. Council of Constantinople III

The legates arrived in Constantinople on September 10, 680. Constantine ordered his new patriarch of Constantinople, George, and the patriarch of Antioch, Macarius, to assemble their bishops. The emperor had decided to turn the meeting of bishops into an ecumenical council. On November 7, 680, the Council of Constantinople III opened in a great domed room, the Trullus, in the imperial palace with only some forty-three bishops present. The emperor himself opened the Council and presided over the first eleven sessions. The Council would meet in eighteen sessions separated by long intervals until September 16, 681.

The papal legates began by demanding that the clergy of Constantinople explain their teaching of Monoenergism and Monothelitism. At the emperor's invitation, George of Constantinople and Macarius of Antioch responded that they taught only doctrines defined by the councils. There followed the reading of the acts of the Councils of Ephesus, Chalcedon and Constantinople II. In the acts of Constantinople II the legates objected to the inclusion of a letter of Menas of Constantinople to Pope Vigilius which had been much used by Sergius in propagating his doctrines. The archivists of the patriarchal library examined their text of the acts and discovered that the handwriting and pagination of the letter differed from the rest of the text. The letter was rejected as a forgery. In the fifth and sixth sessions Macarius of Antioch introduced three large volumes of extracts from the Fathers supporting his position. Upon examination, the legates objected that many of the texts were corrupted or twisted out of context. Whereupon the emperor ordered that the three volumes be sealed in the presence of the imperial commissioners and the legates. The next day in the seventh session the legates produced their own collection of texts which was also sealed. In the eighth session George of Constantinople testified that a comparison of the texts presented by the legates with those in the patriarchal library convinced him of the existence of two wills in Christ. The bishops of his patriarchate agreed and requested authorization of the emperor to restore the pope's name to the diptychs.

Macarius of Antioch, however, refused to accept two wills in Christ because this was in his view Nestorianism. In response to a question by the emperor, Macarius said that he would rather be torn to pieces than accept two wills in

Christ. The volumes of extracts presented by Macarius were then brought in and the archivists proved that the texts had been mutilated and misinterpreted. In the ninth session the Council concluded that Macarius and his disciple Stephen had deliberately falsified the patristic extracts. They were forthwith deprived of all priestly authority. In the tenth session the patristic texts presented by the legates were declared authentic and the bishops of the Orient and priests of Constantinople presented an orthodox statement of their faith. In the eleventh and twelfth sessions Macarius was put on trial before the Council. All his letters and writings were examined and some were shown to be heretical. After he acknowledged the authenticity of the documents, he was deposed and the emperor was requested to designate a new patriarch for Antioch.

At the thirteenth session the condemnation of Sergius, Cyrus, Pyrrhus, Paul, Peter, Theodore and Honorius was discussed and the synodical letters of Sophronius of Jerusalem were declared orthodox. The fourteenth session saw the seating of the new patriarch of Antioch, Theophanes, a Sicilian. On the Sunday of the octave of Easter the legate Bishop John of Porto celebrated mass in Latin before the emperor and the patriarch. On this occasion Constantine IV abolished the taxes the pope paid to the emperor at his enthronement and the obligation to have his election ratified by the imperial governor at Ravenna.

Two bizarre incidents marked the fifteenth and sixteenth sessions. The priest Polychronius, a follower of the condemned Macarius, offered to raise a dead man as a proof of the orthodoxy of Monothelitism. A profession of faith was laid on the dead man's chest while Polychronius whispered in his ear. When the attempt failed, Polychronius was degraded from the priesthood. Then a simple-minded priest Constantine was allowed to present his muddled view of the controversy that Christ had abandoned His human will on the Cross as He entered into glory; he found himself condemned for his views. Finally, in the seventeenth session the final touches were added to the definition which was solemnly promulgated in the last session, September 16, 681, and signed by 174 bishops. As the Emperor Constantine IV signed last of all, the bishops shouted their acclamations.

In their Definition of Faith the bishops, after praising the emperor's zeal for orthodoxy in calling the Council, solemnly accepted the decisions of the first five ecumenical councils and recorded their adherence to the Creeds of Nicaea and Constantinople I. They then listed those "suitable instruments for the working out of the [devil's] will." Despite previous efforts of George of Constantinople to avoid condemnation of his predecessors, Sergius, Pyrrhus, Paul and Peter, all patriarchs of Constantinople from 610 to 666, were anathematized. The bishops evened the score by condemning Pope Honorius (d. 638). There is no evidence in the acts that the legates opposed this measure, although the long summer's delay between the fifteenth and sixteenth sessions may perhaps have been devoted to a discussion of this condemnation. Added to the condemnations were Theodore of Pharan and Cyrus of Alexandria, two of the first Monoenergists, and the last Monothelites, Macarius of Antioch and his disciple Stephen. The bishops then accepted the letter of Pope Agatho and the 125 Western bishops to the Council as consonant with the Council of Chalcedon, the Tome of Leo and the letter of Cyril of Alexandria.

They proceeded to rehearse the doctrines of Chalcedon and Leo's Tome:

> Following the five holy Ecumenical Councils and the holy and approved Fathers, with one voice defining that our Lord Jesus Christ must be confessed to be very God and very man, one of the holy and consubstantial and life-giving Trinity, perfect in Deity and perfect in humanity, very God and very man, of a reasonable soul and human body subsisting; consubstantial with the Father as touching his Godhead and consubstantial with us as touching his manhood; in all things like unto us, sin only excepted; begotten of His Father before all ages according to his Godhead, but in these last days for us men and for our salvation made man of the Holy Spirit and of the Virgin Mary, strictly and properly the Mother of God according to the flesh; one and the same Christ our Lord the only-begotten Son of two natures unconfusedly,

unchangeably, inseparably, indivisibly to be recognized, the peculiarities of neither nature being lost by the union but rather the proprieties of each nature being preserved, concurring in One Person and in one subsistence, not parted or divided into two persons but one and the same only-begotten Son of God, the Word, our Lord Jesus Christ.....

Then, coming to the heart of the matter, they declared that in Christ there are "two natural wills and two natural operations indivisibly, inconvertibly, inseparably, inconfusedly." These two wills "are not contrary the one to the other. . . but his human will follows and that not as resisting and reluctant, but rather as subject to his divine and omnipotent will. . . . For as his flesh is called and is the flesh of God the Word, so also the natural will of his flesh is called and is the proper will of God the Word." They added that "as his most holy and immaculate animated flesh was not destroyed because it was deified but continued in its own state and nature, so also his human will, although deified, was not suppressed, but was rather preserved...." They then applied the teaching of Leo the Great to the matter:

> We glorify two natural operations indivisibily, immutably, inconfusedly, inseparably in the same our Lord Jesus Christ our true God, that is to say a divine operation and a human operation, according to the divine preacher Leo, who most distinctly asserts as follows: 'For each form does in communion with the other what pertains properly to it, the Word, namely, doing that which pertains to the Word, and the flesh that which pertains to the flesh.'
>
> For we will not admit one natural operation in God and in the creature, as we will not exalt into the divine essence what is created, nor will we bring down the glory of the divine nature to the place suited to the creature.

This they balanced with the teaching of Cyril of Alexandria:

> We recognize the miracles and the sufferings as of one and the same [Person], but of one or of the other nature of which he is and in which he exists, as Cyril admirably says. Preserv-

ing therefore the inconfusedness and indivisibility, we make briefly this whole confession, believing our Lord Jesus Christ to be one of the Trinity and after the incarnation our true God, we say that his two natures shone forth in his one subsistence in which he both performed the miracles and endured the sufferings through the whole of his economic conversation and that not in appearance only but in very deed, and this by reason of the difference of nature which must be recognized in the same Person, for although joined together yet each nature wills and does the things proper to it and that indivisibly and inconfusedly.

The bishops concluded: "wherefore we confess two wills and two operations, concurring most fitly in him for the salvation of the human race." The decisions of the Council were embodied in an imperial edict hung up in the atrium of Hagia Sophia and on December 23, 681, promulgated to all the bishops of the Empire.

A letter was prepared to be sent to Pope Agatho but news of his death on January 10, 681, reached Constantinople before the departure of the legates. The letter was readdressed to his successor, Leo II. Macarius and the bishops deposed with him insisted on accompanying the legates to Rome to plead their cause before the pope. At Rome their condemnation was ratified and they were interned in a monastery. Leo II approved the definition of the Council and had it translated into Latin and sent for subscription to the bishops of the West. The Church was finally at peace and remained so to the death of Constantine in 685.

6. Aftermath

Constantine IV was succeeded by his son Justinian II, aged sixteen. Invested with supreme power in adolescence, the new emperor was headstrong and reckless. But he was determined to ape the career of his great namesake Justinian I, even imposing the name Theodora on his Khazar wife. Monothelites still existed in Constantinople and in the Empire, while the Jacobites and Copts within the Islamic

Empire resolutely rejected the definition of Constantinople III. When George of Constantinople died the emperor put in his place Theodore who had been deposed for his unwillingness to compromise with Rome and who, unknown to the emperor, cherished Monophysite sympathies. In order to emphasize his adherence to Constantinople III, Justinian II organized a solemn procession of ecclesiastical and civil dignitaries who carried in triumph the original copy of the acts of the Council. Six sumptuous copies were made of the original and sent to the Pope for his signature before being circulated to the patriarchs of the East. Moreover, the emperor showed his good will toward the pope by remitting taxes he owed to the imperial treasury for lands in southern Italy. At the death of Theodore a lay official of the imperial court, accustomed to abject obedience to the imperial will, was made patriarch of Constantinople.

Just as Justinian I had codified a thousand years of Roman civil law in his great *Corpus Juris Civilis*, so Justinian II determined to codify canon law. The new code was not to be confined to the Empire alone but was to bind the Christians of the world. Accordingly, in 692 a Council, which was later named the Quinisext, was called in Constantinople to reform ecclesiastical law neglected in the fifth and sixth councils and apply it to the changed circumstances caused by the Germanic and Islamic invasions. Present at the Council were the four Eastern patriarchs, the papal ambassadors resident in Constantinople and some 211 bishops of the East. The Council was intended to be ecumenical, for places were left at the ends of the acts for the signatures of the pope, the bishop of Ravenna, and the bishops of Illyricum, all citizens of the Empire. In the end the Council agreed on 102 canons. The first canon contained a profession of faith and a declaration of acceptance of the six ecumenical councils, repeating the condemnations of Constantinople III, including that of Pope Honorius. The second confirmed the canons of ecumenical and provincial councils, including only one from the West, a council of Carthage. Much of this legislation was sound, but the basis for future trouble was soon laid.

The Council accepted all 85 so-called Apostolic Canons which actually dated only from the fourth century. In the West only the first fifty of these canons were regarded as authentic. The East also diverged from the West in allowing deacons and priests to live with their wives. Liturgically, the Council ordered, contrary to Western usage, that during the weekdays of Lent the full Mass was not to be celebrated but only the Eucharist distributed. The Saturday fast during Lent, practiced at Rome, was forbidden. Finally, the Council signified its acceptance of the twenty-eighth canon of Chalcedon declaring the Church of Constantinople equal in power to that of Rome but second to it in honor.

The resident papal ambassadors signed the canons, and the emperor confidently expected the pope to accept them. All copies which were to be circulated to the patriarchs and filed in the imperial archives were sent for his signature to Pope Sergius, a Sicilian born of a family fled from Antioch. Sergius adamantly refused to sign or to accept his copy of the canons. Especially he rejected the canon on the marriage of the clergy, refused to accept the authenticity of all the Apostolic Canons, and denounced the prohibiton of the Saturday fast. Justinian II proposed to deal with the unexpectedly recalcitrant pope as had Justinian I. He ordered two of the pope's advisors arrested, one of whom was the former legate to Constantinople III. When Pope Sergius remained uncowed, the emperor sent a commissioner to arrest the pope himself. The militias of Ravenna and Rome rose to defend the pope, and the commissioner was forced to flee for his life to papal protection. He returned from Rome empty-handed.

Before the emperor could respond to this insult, a coup d'état deposed him for his cruelty, avarice and arbitrary use of power. The general Leontius was proclaimed emperor and had Justinian II hauled into the Circus where his nose was cut off and his tongue mutilated. Then he was sent into exile. With his going, the Empire fell into disorder, and after a series of romantic adventures, Justinian II succeeded in regaining his throne with the help of the Bulgar Khan in 705, a golden nose masking his scarred face. The patriarch who had supported the usurper Leontius was blinded and sent to Rome. Then Justinian II wrote to Pope John VII, a Greek by birth, asking him to review in synod the canons of the Quinisext and indicate his objections. Before John VII could comply, he died, to be replaced by Pope Constantine in 708. As the emperor carried out his long-delayed revenge on Ravenna for having protected Pope Sergius against his orders, Pope Constantine proceeded by slow stages to Constantinople. In Constantinople the imperial crown prince welcomed the pope with all ceremony and took him across the Bosporus to Nicomedia to meet with his father. The exact result of the conference is not known, but it seems that the pope and emperor resolved their differences and the Canons of the Quinisext were not applied in the West.

During Justinian's rule and that of his son, the Empire shrank further as Armenia in eastern Asia Minor and all North Africa were lost to the Arabs. Justinian himself was overthrown a second time, and he and his family massacred by an Armenian general who made himself emperor under the name Philippicus. The new emperor was staunchly Monothelite and refused to enter the imperial palace in Constantinople until a tablet commemorating the Council of Constantinople III was taken down. The orthodox patriarch was deposed; Pope Constantine was sent the head of Justinian II and ordered to see to the teaching of Monothelitism in all theological schools; the original copy of the acts of Constantinople II was burned. All the bishops — Sergius and Honorius included — condemned in 681 were restored to the diptychs. Pope Constantine refused the edict, Justinian's severed head, and approval of the new emperor. Instead, he organized a procession to St. Peter's commemorating the six ecumenical councils. Fortunately, for the peace of the Church, Philippicus, incompetent in dealing with the Bulgars, the Arabs and religious policy, was overthrown and blinded. The new emperor Anastasius II proclaimed his adherence to Constantinople III and sent his profession of faith to the pope. The patriarch too took an oath testifying to his orthodoxy before the papal ambassador. Peace once more reigned in the imperial Church, and the Christological controversies were at last ended.

7. *Chronology*

610-641   Emperor Heraclius; Sergius, patriarch of Constantinople.

625-638   Pope Honorius I.

628   Heraclius victorious over Persians; Cross restored to Jerusalem.

632   Death of Mohammed.

633   Cyrus of Alexandria signed Pact of Union with Copts.

636   Defeat of Byzantine army in Palestine.

638   Publication of *Ecthesis* imposing Monothelitism on East; fall of Jerusalem as Sophronius of Jerusalem lay dying; fall of Antioch.

641   Death of Heraclius; accession of Constans II; Pope John IV condemned Monothelitism.

642   Fall of Alexandria.

647   Imperial *Typos* imposed silence on all parties.

649   Pope Martin I in Roman Synod condemned Monothelites and *Typos.*

653   Byzantine governor sent Martin to Constantinople under arrest.

655   Pope Martin I died in exile.

662   Maximus the Confessor died in exile.

668   Assassination of Constans II; accession of Constantine IV.

678-681   Pope Agatho.

678   Constantine IV opened negotiations with Agatho.

680   Roman and provincial synods prepared for reconciliation.

680-681   Council of Constantinople III; eighteen sessions from November 7 to following September 16.

682   Pope Leo II, Agatho's successor, confirmed the Council and promulgated decrees.

692   Quinisext Council ordered by Justinian II.

Canons rejected by Pope Sergius.

710   Pope Constantine at Constantinople reconciled with Justinian II.

713   Emperor Philippicus resurrected Monothelitism. At his death Christological controversies ended.

8. Select Bibliography

The period of the Monothelite controversy is not well covered in English. The political background is developed by G. Ostrogorsky, *History of the Byzantine State* (New Brunswick, 1957). The most recent full-scale ecclesiastical history of the age is H. Jedin, editor, *History of the Church*, Volume II (New York, 1980). The best theological treatment is J. Meyendorff, *Christ in Eastern Christian Thought* (St. Vladimir's Seminary, 1975). Useful too are J. Pelikan, *Spirit of Eastern Christian Thought* (Chicago, 1974), and H. A. Wolfson, *Philosophy of the Church Fathers* (Cambridge, MA, 1956). The part played by the papacy is outlined by T. Jalland, *The Church and the Papacy* (London, 1944). The documents of the Council are translated by H. M. Percival, *The Seven Ecumenical Councils*, Volume 14 of *Nicene and Post-Nicene Fathers* (New York, 1900).

8

The Council of Nicaea II, 787

1. Beginnings of Iconoclasm

With the death of Justinian II in 711 the hundred year old dynasty of Heraclius came to an end. For the next six years usurpers rose and fell: Philippicus who attempted to restore Monothelitism in 713, Anastasius II who adhered to Constantinople III in 715, Theodosius III a tax official who hesitated to accept the crown in 717. His unwanted crown was soon snatched from him by Leo, the military governor of western Asia Minor, the largest and most important of the imperial provinces. Leo III has been called the Isaurian but was in fact a native of Germanicia in northern Syria. Raised in northern Greece, he came to Justinian II's notice in 705 when he sent 500 sheep from his family estate to supply the army campaigning against the Bulgarians. He rose rapidly through the ranks of the bureaucracy and reigned as emperor from 717 to 740. At his accession he had to face the ferocious siege of Constantinople by the Muslims on land and sea. For a year the outcome hung in the balance, but finally with help from the famous Greek fire, bad weather, famine in the Muslim ranks and his own resolute leadership, Leo repelled the Muslim attack, a victory which ranks with the defeat of the Muslims in the West by the Frankish mayor Charles Martel in 732. By the end of his reign he had driven the Muslims from Asia Minor and reorganized its provinces, providing a solid foundation for the Empire's security. Victory over foreign enemies and order within the Empire cemented the loyalty of army and people to Leo and the dynasty he founded.

Leo's synopsis and revision of Justinian's Code of Civil Law, the *Ecloga,* reveals something of the spirit of the age in its curious combination of Christian values—extension of the rights of women and children and the strengthening of the bonds of marriage—and a coarsening of culture in its savage criminal penalties—chopping off noses, tongues and hands, blinding, burning off hair, punishments unknown to the earlier Code. The prologue to the Ecloga reveals too the emperor's view of his powers. He is confident in his possession of absolute authority under God. Echoing the First Letter of Peter (I Pet. 5:2), Leo sees God handing sovereignty to him in order that he tend the faithful flock. There are no two swords or two powers governing the earth; there is only one, the emperor himself. There is no question of Emperor and Patriarch sharing the direction of God's people, for there is no intermediary between God and the emperor who is the sole earthly interpreter and executor of the divine will. He is the new Moses, a second Solomon. Says S. Gero, "It needs but a little stretch of the imagination to suppose that he could also come to regard his role as that of Hezekiah or Josiah *redivivus,* divinely appointed to cast out the idols from the house of the Lord."

In 726 Leo opened the struggle to overthrow the ubiquitous sacred images of the Byzantine world; the result was the Iconoclast Controversy which would convulse the Empire for over a hundred years. Christian opposition to sacred pictures was nothing new; indeed E. Kitzinger reminds us that "it is necessary to think more in terms of a continuing conflict, which finally erupted into an explosion" set off by the action of Leo III.

In the early Church, Christians had ringing in their ears the denunciations of graven images in the Old Testament and rearing up before their eyes the idols of the pagan Greco-Roman world. Only by about 200 did Christian art make its appearance and by the fourth century were churches filled with cycles of Christian painting. Only by the second half of the fourth century did Christian authors begin to speak in positive terms about pictorial art. But alongside this development ran a current of strong opposition. Eusebius of Caesarea (d. 340) replied to a request by Constantia, the Emperor Constantine the Great's sister, for an image of Christ with astonishment. Christians do not need, he replied, any artificial image of Christ for Christ's historical image, the form in which He underwent the humiliation of the Cross, has been superseded by His divine splendor, his humanity has been amalgamated with His divinity. This splendor cannot be depicted in lifeless colors. Rather Christians must look forward to that moment when we meet Him face to face in the glory of the age to come. Behind Eusebius' view lay the Christology of Origen for whom, since the unique historical event is only transitory and unimportant, the historical Incarnation is to be regarded merely as a moment in the revelation of the Divine Word. Even in the days of Christ's earthly life, He could not be depicted as He truly is but only in a wholly inadequate image accommodated to the gaze of the fleshly minded. After His resurrection His body was assumed into His divinity and cannot be distinguished from it. Later in the fourth century Epiphanius of Salamis would argue that Christ's humanity is so profoundly elevated and immersed in the divine essence that it is impossible to discern it as simple humanity. He cried, "How will one describe in painting the incomprehensible, inexpressible, unthinkable and undescribable, whom even Moses could look upon." In the sixth century the Monophysite churches of Syria contained few sacred images.

In the West too Gregory the Great (d. 604) had to rebuke Serenus, bishop of Marseilles, for tearing down sacred images since, said the pope, they are a means of leading the illiterate to a knowledge of the truths of faith. The pope also wrote to a hermit who had requested sacred images from him: "I know that you do not seek the image of our Savior that you may worship it as God, but by bringing to mind the Son of God you may keep warm in the love of Him whose image you desire to have before you. We bow before it not as before divinity but we worship Him of whom we are reminded by the picture that shows His birth or His throne."

In the East in the period after Justinian I, the attitude toward images as means of education or as memorials gave way to something very different. Perhaps because of the insecurity of the times, people looked on the images as links to the realities of the spiritual world offering them help and protection. People longed more and more for the palpable presence of spiritual powers to cope with their anxiety. Images were moved from the walls of the churches into private homes where icons depicting Christ and the saints became objects of private devotion which escaped the direction of church authorities. With incense burning before them, they became the objects of ritual genuflections and prostrations. The story is told of a hermit who always left a candle burning before his icon of the Virgin. In his absence the Virgin tended the candle and he found it always alight no matter how long his absence. In 656 a conference attended by Maximus the Confessor ended with the kissing of the icons which had watched over the proceedings. The people's enthusiasm for icons was so great that the most revered image of Christ at Camuliana was carried in procession to raise funds for a church and village destroyed in a barbarian raid. Stories circulated of statues bleeding when maltreated by unbelievers, of dry wells giving water when an icon was lowered into them, of cures being wrought by means of dew or oil adhering to the icon. Especially revered was the picture of Christ supposedly sent by the Lord Himself to the recently converted King of Edessa. According to the story the picture was made miraculously when Christ pressed His face to a cloth after an artist could not capture His likeness. Other miraculous images of the Lord included the impression of His chest and hands on the column to which He was tied during His scourging preserved in a church in Jerusalem. The government itself encouraged the devotion to the icons as Emperor Heraclius carried an image of Christ before his armies in the Persian Wars and the Patriarch Sergius had the Virgin's image painted on the walls of Constantinople to repel the besieging armies of 626. Even as Leo III himself defended the city against the Muslims in 717/18, images of Christ were carried about to repel attacks.

The church itself began to promote the use of images for doctrinal reasons. In the eighty-second canon of the Quinisext Council of 692 it was decreed that Christ was not to be portrayed in merely symbolic form as a lamb but in human form, "so that we may perceive through it the depth of the humiliation of God the Word and be led to the remembrance of His life in the flesh, His passion and His death, and of the redemption which it brought to the world." It has been argued that this development was hastened by the attitude of the people toward images of the emperor. In both pagan and Christian times, the imperial portrait had long been displayed at all official government functions, civil and military. The portrait represented the sacred person of the emperor, even more, it made him present vicariously at the function. By the sixth century the attitude toward imperial portraits was carried over to the icons. A Coptic preacher argued, "For if the image of the Emperor of this world, when painted and set up in the marketplace, becomes a protection to the whole city, and if violence is committed against any one, and he takes hold of the image of the Emperor: then no one will be able to harm him, even though the Emperor is naught but a mortal man; and he is taken to a court of law. Let us, therefore, my beloved, honor the icon of our Lady the true Queen, the holy Theotokos, Mary...." The Emperor Justinian II himself revolutionized Byzantine coinage by placing the image of Christ for the first time on his coins with the inscription, King of Kings.

Only in the course of the sixth century was there a really systematic attempt to develop a Christian theory of images. The work of Pseudo-Dionysius which figured in the Monothelite controversy provided a base on which to construct a theory: "The essences and orders which are above us...are incorporeal and their hierarchy is of the intellect and transcends our world. Our human hierarchy, on the contrary, we see filled with the multiplicity of visible symbols, through which we are led up hierarchically and according to our capability to the unified deification, to God and divine virtue. They, as is meet to them, comprehend as pure intellects. We, however, are led up, as far as possible, through visible images to contemplation of the divine." Pseudo-Dionysius did not apply his theory to art, but others would soon do so. Hypatius of Ephesus wrote in the sixth century to a fellow bishop: "We leave material adornment in the churches . . . because we conceive that each order of the faithful is guided and led up to the Divine in its own way and that some are led even by these [material decorations] toward the intelligible beauty and from the abundant light in the sanctuaries to the intelligible and immaterial light." This chain of being can be traced downward as well. In the sixth century Leontius of Neapolis defended Christian images against Jewish objections, arguing that "the image of God is man, who is made in the image of God, and particularly that man who has received the indwelling of the Holy Spirit. Justly, therefore, I honor and worship the image of God's servants and glorify the house of the Holy Spirit." Thus, though the artist portrays only the house, the bodily shell in which the Spirit dwelt, still this shell, hallowed by the Spirit, reflects its divine inhabitant. This line of thought is taken one step further by the author of the life of St. Symeon the Younger whose image worked wonders because the Holy Spirit which dwelt in him overshadowed the image, incarnating in it miraculous powers. In the case of the image of Christ, comments Kitzinger, "the image had begun to be thought of not simply as a reminder of the Incarnation, but as an organic part, an extension, or even a re-enactment thereof. Slowly concepts had begun to evolve whereby the Byzantine religious image was to become a means of demonstrating the Incarnation not merely as past history but as a living and perpetual presence. The role of the image ceased to be purely didactic and was in the process of becoming sacramental like the Sacrifice of the Mass."

2. Iconoclasm of Leo III

It was against this background that Leo III began a propaganda campaign in 726 against the cult of images. Exactly
what motivated him is not clear. As with all failed move-
ments, the victors destroyed much of the writings of the
vanquished and wrote the history of the period. It is true that
Leo came from northern Syria where Jacobite Monophysitism unfavorable to religious images had eclipsed imperial
Chalcedonianism. But it seems certain that when Leo
entered the imperial service he was an orthodox Chalcedonian, and many sources attest to his support of Chalcedonians within and outside of the Empire, though some of his
supporters showed a discernible Monophysite tendency.
Northern Syria was under Muslim control and Leo was
himself a Semite who knew both Syriac and Arabic. In
723/24 the Muslim Caliph Yazid perhaps at Jewish urging
had ordered the destruction not only of all Christian icons
but also of all representations of living beings. Yet S. Gero,
author of the latest study of iconoclasm under Leo, thinks
"that there is little concrete support in the sources in favor of
direct Jewish or Muslim influence on Leo and early Byzantine iconoclasm in the 720's." It is true also that three Byzantine bishops in Asia Minor—Constantine of Nacolia, Thomas of Claudiopolis and Theodosius of Ephesus—revealed
iconoclastic tendencies even before Leo opened his campaign. But here again Gero argues that it cannot be proved
that these bishops had contact with the emperor prior to 726
or influenced his subsequent policies. "In the final analysis,"
Gero claims, "Byzantine iconoclasm, in its first phase, was
not Jewish, Muslim, or Anatolian, but it was indeed an
imperial heresy, born 'in the purple,' in the royal palace. . . .
When all is said and done, the key to understanding the
origin of Byzantine iconoclasm is still the person of emperor
Leo himself." There is no clear evidence that Leo based his
opposition to sacred images on Christology; the only reason
attributed to him in the sources is "a biblically inspired anti-
pathy to idolatry."

When the propaganda begun in 726 did not bring about

the expected results, Leo decided on an overt act and ordered the destruction of the icon of Christ over the bronze doors of the imperial palace. Some women overturned the ladder of the official engaged in the desecration, and a riot ensued in which several palace officals were killed. Those responsible were put under arrest and condemned to the lash, mutilation and exile. During this period Germanus, patriarch of Constantinople, took up the cause of religious images. He based his case on the Incarnation: "In eternal memory of the life in the flesh of Our Lord Jesus Christ, of His passion, of His saving death and the redemption of the world, which result from them, we have received the tradition of representing Him in His human form, that is, His visible theophany, understanding that in this way we exalt the humiliation of God the Word." For Germanus, it is possible to make an image of the "only Son who is in the bosom of the Father," because He "deigned to become man." It is not the image of the "incomprehensible and immortal Godhead" that the Christian artist represents but the image of his human character testifying by this that God "really became man in all things," sin alone excepted. Germanus from the first conceived the images as witnesses against the merely apparent Incarnation of the Word: "since the only Son ... deigned to become man, we make the image of His human form and of His human aspect according to the flesh ... thus showing that it is not in a purely imaginary way that He put on our nature." Just as the image represents the reality of the human in Christ, so it represents the reality of our faith: "For since we consist of flesh and blood, we are impelled to confirm by sight what we are wholly convinced of in the soul."

When news of the emperor's policy of iconoclasm reached Pope Gregory II in Rome, he responded with amazing vehemence, though still a citizen of the Empire. Gregory told Leo: "You know that the dogmas of holy church are not the concern of emperors but of pontiffs, who ought to teach securely. The pontiffs who preside over the church do not meddle in affairs of state, and likewise the emperors ought not to meddle in ecclesiastical affairs...." The Pope reproached the emperor for his inattention to the affairs of Italy which allowed the Lombards to expand their territory, occupying Ravenna, seat of the Byzantine government in the peninsula. Gregory practically dared Leo to attempt to arrest him; were he to try, "the Roman pontiff will withdraw a few miles into the Campania; then you may go and chase the wind." Boldly Gregory threw down the gauntlet: "If you do send anyone to cast down the image of St. Peter, we protest to you that we shall be innocent of the blood that will be shed. The responsibility will fall on your head..." An ominous rift was opening between the pope at Rome and his sovereign in Constantinople. However, despite this, Gregory refused to support a movement in Italy to select a native emperor in protest at Leo's fiscal policies. He loyally held Rome for the Empire against the Lombard king Liutprand and continued to send taxes to Constantinople.

The most powerful opponent of iconoclasm was John of Damascus (675-749). Born of a rich Christian family of Damascus, the political capital of the Muslim Caliphate, he succeeded his father as the chief representative of the Christians at the Islamic court. He gave up this office to become a priest and monk at the monastery of St. Sabas near Jerusalem. Between 726 and 730 he wrote three important works defending the veneration of sacred images. Basic to his defense is the Christological argument: "If we made an image of the invisible God, we would certainly be in error, but we do nothing of the sort, for we are not in error if we make the image of the incarnate God, who appeared on earth in the flesh, and who, in his ineffable goodness, lived with human beings and assumed the nature, quantity, shape and color of flesh." Not only can Christ be pictured but even spiritual beings, other than God, for they are not absolutely simple and uncomposed but are finite and limited to space. John argues that Christians no longer live under the Old Law with its limitations but in the new age of grace in which the tradition of the Church authorizes sacred images. Images are found everywhere: in God exists the image of the world which He creates; the world and humankind are the images of God. To argue that something merely material should not be honored is to fall into Manicheism, conceiving matter as evil. The body and blood of Christ, His cross, the liturgical vessels, all material, can be the objects of honor and reverence. Yet certain distinctions must be made: adoration in the strict sense must be rendered only to God, but veneration is paid to persons and things of special dignity and excellence. Among things venerable are the sacred images which are means of instruction in the truths of faith, memorials of the triumphs of Christian lives, incitements to lead a good life. More than this, sacred images are in a sense channels of grace: they have about them sacramental power. They impart to the one who venerates them a certain sanctifying power which they receive from the persons represented. From afar in the safety of the Islamic Empire, John warned Emperor Leo that it was not his to decide on the question of images.

As opposition to his policies mounted, Leo made attempts to win over the Patriarch Germanus, but in vain. The patriarch was therefore marked down for deposition. In January, 730, the emperor held a *silentium,* an assembly of senators and high officials, in the imperial palace. The edict outlawing images had been prepared; when Germanus refused to sign it, he was allowed to retire to his home. In his place Anastasius, chaplain to the emperor, was made patriarch. When the new patriarch sent notification of his appointment to the pope, Gregory refused to acknowledge him. The emperor now began the systematic destruction of sacred images; only the Cross was approved as a sacred image. It is difficult to judge how severely the supporters of the images suffered: sources speak of torture, mutilation and beheadings, but no known martyr died during this period. Some inhabitants of Constantinople did flee the city rather than conform to the imperial edict.

In 731, Gregory II died and was succeeded by Gregory III, a Syrian by birth. The new pope convoked a synod at Rome attended by the archbishops of Ravenna and Grado and 93 Italian bishops. The synod excommunicated all those who, despising the ancient custom of the Church, refused to venerate the sacred images and blasphemed, destroyed or profaned them. East and West were again in schism. With some difficulty the pope managed to get notification of the decree of his synod to Leo. Infuriated, the emperor sent a fleet to Italy which was wrecked by storms in the Adriatic. To get his revenge, Leo raised the taxes of Calabria and Sicily, and unwisely confiscated the papal estates in these regions. It may have been at this time that Leo took the even more momentous step of detaching Illyricum, Calabria, Sicily and Sardinia from papal jurisdiction and submitting them to the patriarch of Constantinople. Whether this action was taken now or sometime later, it would long embitter relations between Rome and Constantinople.

3. Constantine V and Council of Hieria

In 740 the death of Leo III brought to the throne his able son Constantine V, a greater enemy of sacred images than his father. Later iconophil historians would blacken his name, calling him Copronymous, in the belief that he soiled the font at his baptism, and Kabillinos, contemptuous of his fascination for horses. High strung, in poor health and homosexual, he still held the loyalty of his people as a states-man, administrator and military commander of first rank. Unfortunately for the peace of the Church he intensified the campaign against sacred images. The year after Constan-tine's accession, Artabasius, governor general of the Armen-ian province, rose in rebellion supported by the orthodox party opposed to iconoclasm. While Constantine in hiding began to rally his troops, Artabasius was crowned by the Patriarch Anastasius and began the restoration of the images. But within a year Constantine routed the usurper and regained Constantinople where he paraded Artabasius blinded along with his sons and had the treasonous Patri-arch Anastasius flogged and seated backwards on a donkey. The emperor geared up iconoclasm once again, destroying icons and plastering over the art on church walls. Only the Cross, scenes of hunting, circus events or gardens full of birds and animals were permitted. At this time St. Stephen the Younger, abbot of a famous monastery in northwestern Asia Minor, counseled his fellow monks to emigrate to the frontier provinces of the Empire to escape the emperor's iconoclastic zeal.

In the West, the popes were worrying less about iconoclasm than about the more immediate pressure of the Lombards on the city of Rome. Gregory III's successor Zachary remained loyal to Constantine, initially refusing to support the usurper Artabasius. It was Zachary who at this time approved the overthrow of the Frankish Merovingian dynasty by Pepin, the all powerful mayor of the palace, who was anointed king by the papally sponsored apostle to the Germans, St. Boniface, thus allying the papacy with the rising Carolingians. The fall of Ravenna to the Lombards for the second time in 751 and their advance on Rome in 752 as Zachary lay dying transformed the situation in Italy.

In the East Constantine strengthened the governmental organization begun by his father, and taking advantage of the Abbasid seizure of the Caliphate pushed back the Muslims in Asia Minor, even recapturing the dynasty's city of origin, Germanicia in northern Syria. The emperor now began a policy of transplanting inhabitants from the newly reconquered regions to the interior of the Empire, especially in the thinly populated Balkans. This had grave religious consequences as Monophysites and other heterodox sects carried their faiths into the heart of the Empire. Above all, the army of Asia Minor remained staunchly loyal to the victorious emperor and his iconoclast program.

Under his own name, Constantine issued a doctrinal statement outlining the iconoclast argument. Unlike his father, Leo III, he based his position on Christology. He made no explicit mention of the Chalcedonian "in two natures" but spoke of Christ as one *prosopon* or person out of two natures. The only proper image of Christ would be one that was of the same essence as its prototype. But Christ has one *prosopon* compounded inseparably of human and divine nature. If an image of Christ pictures only his human nature it severs that nature from the divine nature and is a false image of Christ. Any attempt to picture both natures, human and divine, in an image, is an attempt to reduce the divine to limits, to circumscribe the divine, something which is impossible. The conclusion is that Christ cannot be pictured. The only real image of Christ is the one which He Himself gave us, the true image not made by hands, the Holy Eucharist.

Not content with this personal confession of faith, Constantine convoked a general council to define iconoclast doctrine. It met on February 10, 754, in the palace of Hieria just north of Chalcedon. Present were 338 bishops of the East under the presidency of Theodosius of Ephesus, one of the original iconoclasts, and Sissinius of Perga. None of the patriarchs, much less the pope or his legates, were present; in fact, the see of Constantinople was vacant at the time and was filled by imperial appointment only at the end of the Council. For seven months the Council discussed the problem of sacred images. In August, 754, the bishops voted their final decree, called the *Horos,* preserved in the acts of the Council of Nicaea II.

Calling their Council holy and ecumenical, the bishops observed that it was Satan who first tempted humans to worship creatures instead of God, but that the Mosaic Law and the prophets undid this ruinous course. In order to save humankind God sent His Son who turned us from the worship of idols to the worship of God "in spirit and in truth." The message of Christ left with the Apostles has been preserved in the Church by the Fathers and the six ecumenical councils. The faithful emperors impelled by the Holy Spirit have summoned the bishops that in council they might institute "a scriptural examination into the deceitful coloring of the pictures which draws down the spirit of man from the lofty adoration of God to the low and material adoration of the creature...." In accordance with decrees of the six previous ecumenical councils and under the guidance of the Holy Spirit, the bishops declared: "we found that the unlawful art of painting living creatures blasphemed the fundamental doctrine of our salvation—namely the Incarnation of Christ, and contradicted the six holy synods. These condemned Nestorius because he divided the one Son and Word of God into two sons, and on the other side, Arius, Dioscurus, Eutyches, and Severus because they maintained a mingling of the two natures of the one Christ." Following these councils, "no one may imagine any kind of separation or mingling in opposition to the unsearchable, unspeakable, and incomprehensible union of two natures in the one hypostasis or person." One who makes an image and calls it Christ—a name signifying God and man—foolishly attempts to depict the Godhead which cannot be represented and mingles what should not be mingled. He is therefore guilty of a double blasphemy. One who argues that in depicting Christ he is representing only the flesh of Christ, is attempting to separate that flesh from God the Word and is guilty of Nestorianism. The iconoclast bishops next proposed an argument redolent of Origen and Eusebius:

> For it should be considered that that flesh was also the flesh of God the Word, without any separation, perfectly assumed by the divine nature and made wholly divine. How could it now be separated and represented apart? So is it with the human soul of Christ which mediates between the Godhead of the Son and the dullness of the flesh. As the human flesh is at the same time flesh of God and Word, so is the human soul also soul of God and Word, and both at the same time, the soul being deified as well as the body, and the Godhead remained undivided even in the separation of the soul from the body in his voluntary passion. For where the soul of Christ is, there is also his Godhead; and where the body of Christ is, there too is his Godhead. If then in his passion the divinity remained inseparable from these, how do the fools venture to separate the flesh from the Godhead, and represent it by itself as the image of a mere man?

The only admissible figure of the humanity of Christ, they argued, "is bread and wine in the holy supper. This and no other form, this and no other type, has he chosen to represent his Incarnation."

The bishops also declared that the custom of giving names to images or of consecrating them by prayers is not justified by apostolic or patristic tradition. They concluded with a blanket condemnation of all sacred images:

> Christianity has rejected the *whole* of heathenism, and so not merely heathen sacrifices, but also the heathen worship of images. The Saints live on eternally with God, although they have died. If anyone thinks to call them back again to life by a dead art, discovered by the heathen, he makes himself guilty of blasphemy. Who dares attempt with heathenish art to paint the Mother of God, who is exalted above all heavens and the Saints? It is not permitted to Christians, who have the hope of the resurrection, to imitate the customs of demon-worshippers, and to insult the Saints, who shine in so great glory, by common dead matter.

This was followed by a long list of scriptural quotations and citations of the Fathers. At the end anathemas were hurled against the iconophils, especially Germanus of Constantinople and John of Damascus. The decrees were read out to the people in the forum of Constantinople in the presence of the emperor and his newly appointed patriarch. Iconoclasm was now the defined teaching of the Imperial Church. The Melkite patriarchs in Muslim lands, however, refused to accept these decrees.

For some years after the Council of Hieria, the emperor was fairly moderate in his dealings with the iconophils for fear of weakening the Empire in the face of foreign pressures, especially from the Bulgarians. In these years the emperor's zeal was directed rather against the monks. In 761 two prominent monks died under the lash in the Circus. About this time an imperial edict ordered all subjects to take an oath against images. The Patriarch Constantine led the way, swearing on the relic of the Holy Cross from the pulpit of Hagia Sophia. In 764 one of the leaders of the monastic party, St. Stephen the Younger, was mistreated, imprisoned and finally torn to pieces by the mob in Constantinople. The next year a crowd of monks were forced to don lay clothes, each holding a woman by the hand, and parade before the jeering crowds of the Circus. Shortly after the religious habit was banned altogether. In 766 the Patriarch Constantine, despite his loyalty to iconoclasm, was deposed, exiled and then returned to Constantinople where the following year he was maltreated and publicly beheaded, his head affixed to the doors of the patriarchal palace. His successor quickly destroyed all the icons in the patriarchal palace. Next, not only were images attacked but prayers to the saints were outlawed and their relics were destroyed. The revered relic of St. Euphemia in whose sanctuary the Council of Chalcedon had met, was thrown into the sea and the church desecrated. Around Ephesus, the governor-general Michael Lackandracon unleashed a reign of terror, forcing monks to marry and destroying monasteries and saintly relics. Monastic property was auctioned off as monks had their hair and beards burned off and their nostrils slit. The Emperor congratulated him: "I have found a man after my own heart.' In the midst of these atrocities the Emperor Constantine V was forced by illness to withdraw from the campaign against the Bulgarians and died in 775.

4. Aftermath

In these years momentous events were transpiring in the West. In 754, the very year that the Council of Hieria condemned sacred images, Pope Stephen II, Zachary's successor, despairing of help from the schismatic East against the Lombards, traveled north to Frankland for a conference with the recently crowned King Pepin the Short. The pope granted the king the title of patrician, designating him in some sense protector of Rome. That year Pepin entered Italy, defeated the Lombards and ordered them to surrender the old Byzantine provinces in central Italy to the pope. When Pepin returned home, the Lombards defaulted on their agreement. In 756, Pepin returned, again defeated the Lombards and granted the pope temporal authority over the region around Rome; the donation of Pepin was the nucleus of the Papal State which would last until 1870. The Frankish Pepin not the Byzantine Emperor was now the arbiter of northern and central Italy and protector of the papacy. In 768 Pepin was succeeded by his two sons, but from 771 his ablest son, Charles the Great, Charlemagne, embarked on his thirty-three years of sole rule, culminating in his coronation as emperor by the pope in 800. The religious schism between East and West over iconoclasm had incalculable political and cultural consequences. The papacy turned from its age-old relationship with the emperor at Constantinople to a new alliance with the Carolingian dynasty of Frankland.

At the death of Constantine V, his son Leo IV ascended the throne. Leo had married an Athenian named Irene, a woman of forceful personality, dedicated to the monks and to sacred images. He was successful in his wars with the Muslims and granted a measure of toleration to the iconophils, but his reign was cut short after five years in 780. He left a son, Constantine VI, only ten years old. Power was seized immediately by the Empress-mother Irene as she excluded her young son's uncles from any influence by forcing them to become clerics. As her chief adviser for the next twenty years she chose the eunuch Stauracius. In 781, the empress determined to halt the decline of Byzantine power in the West by negotiating an alliance with the Franks. Ambassadors were dispatched to Charlemagne asking for his young daughter Rotruda's hand in marriage to Emperor Constantine VI. A bargain was struck, and a Byzantine tutor ordered to the Frankish court to teach the future empress eastern customs. In 784, the patriarch of Constantinople, Paul, troubled over the religious divisions in the Church, retired to a monastery to prepare for death and advised the Empress Irene to call a general council to remedy matters. Irene agreed and sent ambassadors to Pope Hadrian to prepare for a council of reconciliation. At Constantinople Irene began her own preparations. She started the search for a new patriarch to lead the eastern episcopate deeply involved in iconoclasm. She fixed finally on a high lay bureaucrat— Tarasius—who agreed with her project and had him consecrated patriarch on Christmas Day, 784. He issued a statement of orthodox faith to the pope and the three Melkite patriarchs in Muslim territory who had never embraced the iconoclasm of the bishops of the Empire. Because of the difficulties of communications, Pope Hadrian's reply reached Constantinople only in 785.

In his letter to Irene, Hadrian agreed to the convocation of a general council. He recalled that Peter had been given the keys of heaven by Christ Himself and had transmitted them to his successors, the bishops of Rome. He recounted the legend that Emperor Constantine the Great had been converted by a vision of Peter and Paul and had been baptized by Pope Sylvester I. Reminding the empress that popes from Gregory II (d. 731) to Stephen III (d. 772) had condemned iconoclasm, he argued for the veneration of sacred images on the basis of the Scriptures and the writings of the Fathers. Therefore, he demanded the condemnation of the Council of Hieria of 754. He demanded as well the return of the papal estates in South Italy and Sicily, seized by Emperor Leo III, and the restoration of papal authority there and in Illyricum. Lastly, he protested the elevation of the layman Tarasius to the patriarchate of Constantinople and his use of the title "Universal Patriarch." Nevertheless, he dispatched as his legates the archpriest Peter and Peter, abbot of the Greek monastery of St. Sabas in Rome. The Melkite patriarchs of Antioch and Alexandria could not attend the projected council but were represented by the monks, John the Chaplain and Thomas, later archbishop of Thessalonika.

Thereupon the Council opened on August 1, 786, in the Basilica of the Holy Apostles in Constantinople with Irene and Constantine VI in attendance. No sooner had discussions begun than a troop of soldiers burst in and threatened to kill the Patriarch Tarasius. Vainly the empress and patriarch tried to restore order as iconoclast bishops shouted "Victory for our side." The Council had to be adjourned *sine die*. But Irene was determined to try again. Her adviser Stauracius began the removal of troops loyal to the memory of the great iconoclast emperors from the capital to the frontier. Troops loyal to the empress were stationed in Constantinople. The papal legates were recalled from Sicily, the Eastern bishops were convoked to Nicaea and at last, 452 years after the first general council, the Council of Nicaea II opened its deliberations.

5. The Council of Nicaea II

Between 258 and 335 bishops, including eight Sicilians and six Calabrians, the two papal legates, the representatives of Antioch and Alexandria were present at Nicaea on September 24, 787, when the Patriarch Tarasius opened the Council. The Patriarch exhorted the bishops to brevity, but in vain, for the ensuing discussions were to prove long and verbose, at an intellectual level far below preceding councils. The first session was occupied with debates over the reinstatement of iconoclast bishops but ended without a decision. On September 26, the letter from Pope Hadrian was verified by the legates, read out to the bishops and accepted as orthodox. Two days later iconoclast bishops were reinstated at the urging of the papal legates and the letters from the absent patriarchs of Antioch and Alexandria accepted. At this point, Bishop Constantine of Cyprus addressed the Council, proclaiming, "I accept images of the saints but I reserve adoration exclusively for the Trinity." This statement would become notorious in the West when it was translated into Latin to mean that the same adoration is to be given to the saints as to the Trinity. On October 1, the bishops discussed a series of biblical texts pertaining to images and a long series of citations from patristic writings. The authentic and the spurious were mixed in about equal quantities. Gregory of Nazianzus was said to have known of an instance in which a prostitute was converted by seeing the image of a saint. The statue supposedly set up by the woman Christ cured of bleeding was cited. A text thought to be from Athanasius mentioned how blood came from an image pierced by a Jew. St. Nicholas of Myra and St. Plato were said to have been recognized in visions because they both looked like their images. The session on October 4 was also spent in the reading of patristic texts; texts of Eusebius of Caesarea, Philoxenus of Mabbough and Severus of Antioch were rejected as heretical. Finally, the Council declared itself satisfied and concluded that images should be restored. The papal legates suggested that an image of Christ should be placed in their midst. This was done amid acclamations for images and the emperor, anathemas against the iconoclasts.

On October 6, the Bishop of Neo-Caesarea began the reading of the *Horos* of the Iconoclast Council of 754 while two bishops refuted it point by point, a long process which covers 160 folios in the edition by G.B. Mansi. The following week the Council's final decree was finished. After it was read out, it was signed first by the papal legates and then by all present amid acclamations, but unlike the acclamations of previous councils the pope was not included. A letter informing Irene and Constantine was dispatched to Constantinople. On October 23 the Council moved to the Magnaura Palace in the capital where Tarasius presented the decree to the imperial pair who approved it amid the usual acclamations.

Though the bishops had been notably long-winded in their debates, they were fairly concise in their decree. Christ, they said, delivered us from idolatrous madness and always continues to sustain His Church, but some, even priests, have gone astray, failing "to distinguish between holy and profane, styling the images of Our Lord and of His saints by the same name as the statues of diabolical idols." The bishops added their acceptance of the previous six ecumenical councils, especially that which met "in the illustrious metropolis of Nicaea," and condemned the arch-heretics anathematized at those councils. Then getting to the matter at hand: "To make our confession short, we keep unchanged all the ecclesiastical traditions handed down to us, whether in writing or verbally, one of which is the making of pictorial representations, agreeable to the history of the preaching of the Gospels, a tradition useful in many respects, but especially in this, that the incarnation of the Word of God is shown forth as real and not merely phantastic. . . ." Following the authority of the Fathers and the traditions of the Church, in which the Holy Spirit dwells, the bishops defined "with all certitude and accuracy that just as the figure of the precious and life-giving Cross, so also the venerable and holy images, as well in painting and mosaic as of other fit materials, should be set forth in the holy churches of God, and on the sacred vessels and on the vestments and on hangings and in pictures both in houses and by the wayside, to wit, the figure of Our Lord God and Savior Jesus Christ, of our spotless Lady, the Mother of God, of the honorable Angels, of all the saints and of all pious people. For by so much more frequently as they are seen in artistic representation, by so much more readily are men lifted up to the memory of their prototypes, and to a longing after them; and to these should be given due salutation and honorable reverence, not indeed that true worship of faith which pertains only to the divine nature; but to these, as to the figure of the precious and life-giving Cross and to the Books of the Gospels and to other holy objects, incense and lights may be offered according to ancient pious custom. For the honor which is paid to the image passes on to that which the image represents, and he who reveres the image reveres in it the subject represented." At the end, appropriate penalties were prescribed for those who refused to obey.

The bishops also voted twenty-two canons which give some insight into the problems affecting the Church during sixty years of controversy. Echoing the Quinisext Council of 692, the bishops decreed acceptance of the Apostolic Canons, the decrees of the six ecumenical councils and of local synods. Rather boldly they decreed that ecclesiastical appointments made by princes are invalid. Bishops are bidden to know the Psalter by heart, read the canons and Scriptures, and live and teach the Commandments of God. Synods are to be held in every metropolitan province once a year. Simony, that is, the buying or selling of church office, was clearly a serious problem and the bishops ordered that it should cease. Moreover, bishops are forbidden to extort anything from monks and clerics. Clerics who are ordained without simony but because of their generosity to the Church are warned not to despise those who are ordained without similar largesse. Bishops who consecrate churches without relics are to be deposed. Bishops and abbots are

bidden to have stewards for their residences and monasteries, not to have women in their service, and not to alienate
the property of their institutions. Clerics are warned to
remain in their own dioceses, to dress with becoming
modesty, and to eat with women in public or private places
only in emergency. Clerics may not serve two churches in
Constantinople itself, but may do so in rural areas. One who
is not duly ordained must not read from the pulpit in the
churches. Several canons deal with the monasteries: those
converted into public houses must be restored; new ones
should not be begun unless there are sufficient funds to
complete them; there should be no double monasteries of
men and women. Monks and nuns are ordered to remain in
their own monasteries and eat apart and in silence. As early
as 722 Leo III had ordered the forcible baptism of Jews; now
Jews who are Christian only in appearance are to be
excluded from the Church; their children are not to be baptized; and they are forbidden to hold slaves. Finally, all
books defending iconoclast doctrines must be turned into
the patriarch's residence in Constantinople.

6. Reaction of the West

Tarasius duly forwarded a letter to Pope Hadrian, not
requesting confirmation of the Council, for the action of the
papal legates had already signified the pope's acceptance,
but simply notifying him of the Council's decisions. There
was no reply from Hadrian for seven years, for the pope
found himself caught in a delicate situation. Though Nicaea
II had reconciled Rome and Constantinople, it met with a
frosty reception in Frankland. The acts of Nicaea II reached
King Charles, Hadrian's ally and protector, in a hopelessly
corrupt Latin translation. So bad was it that it sometimes
gave the very opposite meaning from that intended by the
Greek original. In 790, Charles commissioned the Visigothic
scholar, Theodulf, bishop of Orleans, to undertake a detailed
refutation of the decree of Nicaea II. On the basis of Theodulf's work, Charles notified Pope Hadrian of his rejection

of the Council. Hadrian replied with a defense of Nicaea II, but Charles had Theodulf draw up a statement of the Frankish view of sacred images which was embodied in the official declaration called the *Libri Carolini*. The doctrine of the declaration was clear: only God can be adored; one can never adore sacred images. One cannot give to images the reverence and veneration due to the saints, their relics and the Cross nor even that given to living persons of distinction. The principle that veneration is given to images because of their relationship to the original is false, and it misleads simple people into giving veneration to the image alone. Lights and incense are not to be burned before images. Images can be used to ornament churches, but the whole problem was relatively unimportant for the Franks: "The question whether or not the images were installed [in the churches] in memory of deeds or for decoration does not affect in any way Catholic faith itself since images have hardly any function in the performance of the mystery that involves our salvation." Finally, existing images are not to be marred nor destroyed.

While holding stoutly to the primacy of the Roman Church to which the Frankish Church was proud to be in holy and venerated communion, the *Libri Carolini* attacked the universal character of Nicaea II. Despite the presence of papal legates, the Frankish Church was not represented. The Council of Nicaea "attempted in a presumptuous and imprudent manner to excommunicate all the churches of the world before it had consulted them by letters and in accordance with ecclesiastical customs had asked for their opinion." Therefore, Charles rejected both the Iconoclast Council of Hieria of 754 and the Iconophil Council of Nicaea II. The document is marked throughout by hostility toward the Greeks, especially toward the Empress Irene, "for the weakness of her sex and her instability of mind forbids that she should hold the leadership over men in teaching and preaching." The projected marriage of Rotruda and Constantine was broken off. Hadrian wrote a detailed refutation of the eighty-five propositions drawn from the *Libri* and sent to him, but without changing Charles' mind. Clearly the Frankish king was not going to let a council held under the authority of a Byzantine Empress dictate the faith of his Church. When Pope Hadrian did reply to the Empress Irene, it was to approve the definition of Nicaea II but to threaten excommunication if the papal estates in South Italy and Sicily were not restored and his jurisdiction there and in Illyricum reinstated.

In 794, the Council of Frankfurt called by King Charles primarily to deal with a Spanish heresy in Christology, again dealt with the problem of sacred images. In its second canon the Council ruled: "The question was introduced at the recent synod of the Greeks on the worship of images held at Constantinople. There it was laid down that those who refuse to pay service and veneration to the images as to the divine Trinity should be judged anathema. Our most holy fathers, absolutely refusing that service, held them in contempt and unanimously condemned them." Obviously the Frankish bishops still had no clear idea of the Greek position. However, the Council of Frankfurt did not expressly ratify the *Libri Carolini,* probably out of deference to the views of the pope. Diplomatic relations between West and East deteriorated still further with the coronation by Leo III, Hadrian's successor, of King Charles as emperor on Christmas Day, 800. Constantinople refused to recognize the new title until 812 when Charles extorted eastern acknowledgement by seizing the Byzantine controlled city of Venice. Now there were two hostile empires both regarding themselves as the continuations of the Roman Empire. But the problem of images was shelved for the moment. It was broached with the West again only in 824 when Emperor Michael II sent a mission to Emperor Louis the Pious, Charles's son, to reestablish good relations by agreeing with the Franks to condemn adoration of images but allow them in churches. Pope Eugene II again maintained papal approval of Nicaea II but sanctioned Louis' plan to convoke a synod of Frankish bishops to discuss the question. In 825 either at Paris or outside the city at the royal abbey of Saint-Denis a conference was called under the inspiration of the Archdeacon Hilduin. Despite complicated communications with the pope, nothing definite seems to have come from the attempt. Iconoclasm had a brief final vogue in the actions and writings of Claudius, bishop of Turin in Italy, (d.c. 840). He was opposed privately by the Irishman Dungal working in Italy, and officially by Jonas, bishop of Orleans.

7. Aftermath in the East

Meanwhile in the East, as Emperor Constantine VI came to maturity, he began to resent the power of his mother Irene. Unpopular with the army, Irene was forced into obscurity in 790 but two years later took her place again by the side of her son as co-emperor. Not a great general in the mold of the iconoclast emperors, Constantine lost the loyalty of the army, and then embroiled himself in difficulties with the Church. He put aside his lawful wife and married his mistress, the priest Joseph presiding at the ceremony with the acquiescence of the Patriarch Tarasius. Forsaken by army and Church, Constantine was overthrown by his mother Irene who had him blinded in the very room in which he had been born. Tarasius and Joseph lost support of the leaders of the monastic party, opposed to the emperor's remarriage: the powerful Plato, abbot of the Saccudium monastery and his even more able nephew Theodore, abbot of Studium. But Irene herself was overthrown and exiled in 802 by a palace coup which placed the minister of the treasury Nicephorus (802-811) on the throne.

Orthodox and iconophil, Emperor Nicephorus made his namesake Nicephorus patriarch of Constantinople in 806 after the death of Tarasius. Because emperor and patriarch allowed the reinstatement of the priest Joseph, witness to the remarriage of Constantine VI, neither was fully trusted by Theodore of Studium. Unfortunately for Emperor Nicephorus, the western Emperor Charlemagne's campaign against the Avars of the Transylvanian basin had freed the Bulgarians for action against the Eastern Empire. Their great Khan Krum attacked the East, and Emperor Nicephorus fell in battle, the only emperor to do so since 378; his skull was made into a drinking goblet by Krum. His son too was carried from the field mortally wounded. Michael I (811-813) called Rangabe seized the throne with Theodore of Studium as his chief theological adviser. To regain Venice occupied by Charlemagne, Michael recognized his title as emperor in 812. In terror at the Bulgarian invasion, crowds gathered at the tomb of the iconoclast Emperor Constantine V and prayed for the return of that great military commander. In the midst of the Bulgarian war the weak but amiable Michael I was deposed after his army was defeated, partly because of the desertion of a large contingent from western Asia Minor.

The new emperor crowned by the Patriarch Nicephorus was the leader of the deserters, Leo V (813-820) called the Armenian. Leo was more fortunate than his predecessors. The Bulgarian Krum died unexpectedly, and the Empire secured a truce of thirty years with the Bulgarians. Since the Arabs in the east were occupied with internal problems after the death of the Caliph of Baghdad, Haroun-al-Rashid of Arabian Nights' fame, the Byzantine Empire enjoyed some years of peace. Emperor Leo now restored iconoclasm. The leaders of the orthodox party were dealt with summarily: the Patriarch Nicephorus was removed and Theodore of Studium exiled. John the Grammarian laid the groundwork for a new doctrinal statement. At a council held in Hagia Sophia in Constantinople in 815, Nicaea II was repudiated and the decrees of the Iconoclast Council of 754 declared the faith of the Empire. But in 820 Leo V was assassinated in front of the high altar of Hagia Sophia.

The murdered Leo V, the Armenian, was replaced by Michael II (820-829) founder of the Amorian dynasty, a rough and illiterate soldier but endowed with common sense, energy and prudence. He allowed the former Patriarch Nicephorus and Theodore of Studium, the iconophil leaders, to return to the capital. But he refused to allow the return of the sacred images. Forbidding all discussion of sacred images after the iconophils balked at negotiations, the emperor refused to recognize either Nicaea II or the Iconoclast Councils of 754 and 815. After Theodore of Studium appealed to Rome as the highest of the Churches of which Peter was the first bishop, Michael in 824 opened talks with the western Emperor Louis the Pious, Charlemagne's son, but, as we have mentioned, nothing came of the discussions, and Michael continued a policy of moderate iconoclasm. He had to face a usurper in the east supported by iconophils, but helped by the Bulgarians he held on to his throne. He was less successful, however, against the growing Muslim threat; Crete fell in 826, and Sicily was invaded the next year. The Christian East was slowly contracting, when Michael died in 829.

In these years of renewed iconoclasm, the standard bearers of the iconophil cause were the monk Theodore the Studite and the Patriarch of Constantinople Nicephorus. Theodore was born in Constantinople in 759 and was received as a monk in the Studite monastery by his uncle Plato who later resigned as abbot to make way for his talented nephew. Both uncle and nephew opposed the Patriarch Nicephorus in the conflict over the divorce and remarriage of Emperor Constantine VI, and Theodore was twice exiled. During the reign of Emperor Leo V, he led the resistance to iconoclasm. In his treatise, *On the Holy Icons,* he argues that if one says that Christ cannot be portrayed it would follow that is because He lacks a genuine human nature as the Docetist heretics held or that his human nature is absorbed into His divinity as the long-condemned Monophysites maintain. Theodore insists that when Christ is pictured, it is His *hypostasis* which is portrayed not His divine or human nature. The properties of the individual man Jesus, which subsist in His *hypostasis,* can be portrayed. Just as all predicates are attributed to the one person, so it is the person who is portrayed. It is the one Christ who after the resurrection appeared as man, sharing food with his disciples and who before the resurrection walked on water and was transfigured. So Christ can be the prototype of an image precisely because of His humanity which can be circumscribed and pictured even though it subsists in His divine person. Image and prototype differ in essence but share the same likeness and name. It is not the material essence of the image which is reverenced but rather the like-ness of the prototype appearing in the image. In the case of the saints, this reverence is not the adoration due to God but the veneration due to holy persons, relics and icons. The Eucharist is not an image but the reality of Christ's body and blood. Allowed to return to the capital under Emperor Michael II, for his continued defense of the icons, Theodore was condemned to semi-exile where he died in 826.

Though never fully trusted by Theodore the Studite because of their differences over the remarriage of Emperor Constantine VI, Nicephorus was a resolute foe of icono-clasm. As a civil official he had represented the emperor at the Council of Nicaea II and served as Patriarch of Constan-tinople from 806 until his deposition by Emperor Leo V in 815. Nicephorus rejected the Origenist notion that the deifi-cation of Christ's humanity involved its dematerialization. He insisted on the concrete humanity of Christ who really experienced to the full the human situation. Nicephorus even went beyond most other theologians to emphasize that Christ truly experienced ignorance through His humanity. Since Christ is fully human, possessing a true human body, He can be pictured. "Where in the world," he asked, "has an uncircumscribed body ever been heard of? Especially as cir-cumscription is a condition *sine qua non* of bodies. For as a body does not exist without place or time, thus it does not exist without circumscription." Thus, "...the humanity of Christ if bereft of one of its properties is a defective nature, and Christ not a perfect man or rather not Christ at all, but is lost altogether if He cannot be circumscribed or repre-sented in art." Exiled for his opposition to imperial icono-clasm, Nicephorus followed Michael II to the grave in 829 in a monastery which he had founded as a layman.

Michael II's son, Theophilus, succeeded without difficulty in that year. Educated by iconoclast teachers and a lover of Islamic aniconic art, Theophilus soon unleashed iconoclasm in its full vigor. The prisons filled with iconophils; monks again had to flee their monasteries. A celebrated painter who continued to paint sacred images was beaten and impri-soned. When he persisted in his trade, his hands were burned. Two monks who supported orthodoxy had icono-clast verses burned into their foreheads. The radical icono-clast, John the Grammarian, replaced the moderate patriarch in 837. By 839 ominously Amorium, seat of the dynasty, fell bloodily to the Muslim armies. In 842 Emperor Theophilus died, on his death bed begging his entourage to continue his policies.

Power passed into the hands of the Empress-Mother Theodora, regent for the child Michael III. Though the dead emperor's brother pressed for the restoration of the images, Theodora hesitated to reverse her beloved husband's icono-clast policies. Still she allowed the inconoclast patriarch to be replaced by the iconophil Methodius. The new patriarch professed to believe Theodora's protestations that her hus-band Theophilus had repented of iconoclasm on his death bed and agreed not to condemn him. Finally in 843, the Patriarch Methodius declared sacred images lawful and condemned iconoclasm. The one hundred and seventeen year old struggle was over. The First Sunday of Lent was declared the Feast of Orthodoxy, still celebrated by the East-ern Church.

In conclusion it might be well to summarize the conse-quences of the long iconclast Controversy. Politically, it was a factor in the alienation of the West from the Eastern Empire at a critical moment. The popes in Rome were under pressure from the encroaching Lombards and feared that the conquest of Rome by these Germans would reduce them to mere court chaplains. Opposed as they were to iconoclasm, the popes could expect no help from the emperor at Con-stantinople, busily stripping the icons from the churches. Thus Pope Zachary gave Pepin of the Franks moral support in his effort to win the crown from the do-nothing Mero-vingian kings in return for military help against the Lom-bards. Pope Stephen would go further to accept temporal control of the old Byzantine provinces in central Italy, thus founding the Papal States claimed by the popes until the Lateran Treaty with Mussolini in 1929. In 800 Pope Leo III crowned Charlemagne emperor of the West, creating a new defender of papal authority who turned out to be as ready to dictate theology to the Church as his eastern counterparts.

Artistically, iconoclasm arrested progress and destroyed countless ancient treasures. Had iconoclasm become the official teaching of the Church the western world would never have witnessed the glorious achievements of its figured sacred art. It would have been immeasurably poorer artistically. After the iconoclast interlude, Byzantine art rose to new heights and continued to exert strong influence on the West, inheritors of the geometric interlace and stylized animals of Germanic art. But the theological tendency to see the icon as a reflection of the reality portrayed had its effect on artistic style. Icons came to be considered exact and true portraits of their prototypes, thus leading Byzantine artists to repeat endlessly the stereotyped images of Christ and the saints.

Ecclesiastically, the monks' resolute defense of sacred images in the face of imperial and episcopal pressures enhanced their standing among the laity. Monastic churches filled with icons concentrating the spiritual powers of their prototypes became places of vital mediation between the divine and the human. And the monks themselves became the focus of the holy in the world.

Theologically, the controversy was really an attempt to recover the meaning of Christ's humanity. The old Antiochene Christology which had striven to do full justice to Christ's human nature was in danger of being submerged beneath an exaggerated Cyrillian Christology in Monophysitism and Monothelitism. Imperial Iconoclasm tended to approach God only as an intelligibly apprehensible abstraction or to reduce the importance of Christ's humanity to the thirty or so years He lived among us. But iconophil theologians reasserted the permanent importance of Christ's humanity. He is God become man and always remains so even when exalted to the Father's right hand. Jesus, divine and human, was and is the way to the Father. The sacred images of Christ, portraying him as truly incarnate, truly reflecting their divine and human prototype, are a perpetual reminder of that fact.

8. *Chronology*

717-740   Emperor Leo III the Isaurian.

717/18   Siege of Constantinople by Muslims.

726   Beginning of Iconoclasm; John of Damascus begins work, d. 749.

730   Intensification of Iconoclasm and deposition of Iconophil Patriarch Germanus.

731   Condemnation of Iconoclasm by Pope Gregory III.

At this time perhaps, confiscation of papal estates in South Italy and Sicily and withdrawal of papal jurisdiction there and in Illyricum.

751   Fall of Ravenna to Lombards; Pope Zachary approves of Pepin as King of Franks.

754   Pope Stephen negotiates with King Pepin of Franks.

740-775   Constantine V.

754   Iconoclast Council of Hieria.

756   Donation of Pepin, foundation of Papal States.

768   Charlemagne, King of Franks.

772-792   Pope Hadrian I.

780   Irene co-emperor with son Constantine VI.

787   Council of Nicaea II; Patriarch Tarasius president. *Libri Carolini.*

794   Council of Frankfurt condemns adoration of images.

797-802   Irene sole emperor after blinding son.

800   Charlemagne crowned Emperor of West by Pope Leo III; rules until 814.

802	Irene deposed; Nicephorus I succeeds.
811	Emperor Nicephorus I killed by Bulgarians.
814-841	Emperor Louis the Pious, son of Charlemagne.
815	Leo V the Armenian holds Iconoclast Council; Patriarch Nicephorus deposed.
820-829	Moderate Iconoclasm of Michael II the Amorian.
826	Death of Theodore of Studium.
829-842	Intensification of Iconoclasm by Theophilus I.
843	Regent Theodora supports restoration of icons; Feast of Orthodoxy.

9. Select Bibliography

Contrary to what the reader might expect, this period is well covered in English. G. Ostrogorsky, *History of the Byzantine State* (New Brunswick, 1969) is a valuable political narrative. The most complete but somewhat dated work on the whole question is E.G. Martin, *A History of the Iconoclastic Controversy* (New York, 1930). A masterful survey is E. Kitzinger, "The Cult of Images in the Age before Iconoclasm," *Dumbarton Oaks Papers,* 7 (1954), 83-150. Useful too are G.B. Ladner, "Origin and Significance of the Byzantine Iconoclastic Controversy," *Medieval Studies,* 2 (1940), 127-149; and his "The Concept of the Images in the Greek Fathers and the Byzantine Iconoclastic Controversy," *Dumbarton Oaks Papers,* 7 (1953), 1-34; G. Florovsky, "Origen, Eusebius and the Iconoclastic Controversy," *Church History,* 19 (1950), 77-96; N.H. Baynes, "The Icons before Iconoclasm," *Harvard Theological Review,* 44 (1951), 93-106; H. von Campenhausen, "The Theological Problem of Images in the Early Church," in *Tradition and Life in the Church,* pp. 171-200 (Philadelphia, 1968); P. Brown, "A Dark-Age Crisis: Aspects of the Iconoclastic Controversy," *English Historical Review,* 346 (1973), 1-34. The conclusion of this chapter relies heavily on P. Henry, "What Was the Iconoclastic Controversy About?" *Church History,* 45 (1976), 16-31. Defense of Iconoclasm may be found in M.V. Anastos, "The Argument for Iconoclasm as Presented by the Iconoclastic Council of 754," in *Late Classical and Mediaeval Studies in Honor of A.M. Friend,* pp. 177-188 (Princeton, 1955) and "The Ethical Theory of Images Formulated by the Iconoclasts in 754 and 815," *Dumbarton Oaks Papers,* 8 (1954), 153-160. Full-scale monographs are P.J. Alexander, *The Patriarch Nicephorus of Constantinople* (Oxford, 1958) and S. Gero, *Byzantine Iconoclasm during the Reign of Leo III* (Louvain, 1973) and *Byzantine Iconoclasm during the Reign of Constantine V* (Louvain, 1977). The theology involved in the controversy is well treated in J. Meyendorff, *Christ in Eastern Thought* (St. Vladimir's Press, 1975) and J. Pelikan, *The Spirit of Eastern Christendom 600-1700* (Chicago, 1974). For art see C. Mango, *The Art of the Byzantine Empire 312-1453: Sources and Documents* (Englewood Cliffs, 1972). A symposium covering all aspects of the controversy is edited by Anthony Bryer and Judith Herrin, *Iconoclasm* (Birmingham, England, 1977). A useful short history of the Age of Charlemagne is H. Fichtenau, *The Carolingian Empire* (New York, 1964). The difficult question of the *Libri Carolini* is best handled by A. Freeman, "Theodulf of Orleans and the *Libri Carolini,*" *Speculum,* 32 (1957), 663-705 and "Further Studies in the *Libri Carolini,*" *Speculum,* 40 (1965), 203-289. The definitions of the Councils of Hieria and Nicaea II are newly translated in D.J. Sahas, *Icon and Logos* (Toronto, 1986).

9

Epilogue

According to the Roman Catholic Code of Canon Law, an ecumenical council is an assembly of bishops and other specified persons, convoked and presided over by the pope, for the purpose of formulating decisions concerning the Christian faith and discipline, which decisions require papal confirmation. The persons entitled to participate in an ecumenical council are the cardinals, patriarchs, archbishops and bishops, the abbot primate and abbots general of the monastic congregations, the superiors general of the exempt orders and abbots and prelates of special jurisdictions. However, it is abundantly clear from the history of the first seven ecumenical councils that this neat definition has not always applied. Rather, the first seven ecumenical councils were all called by the emperor, the vote of the papal legates not subsequent approval signified papal adherence to conciliar decrees, all five patriarchs had to be present in order that a council be truly ecumenical and councils were sometimes only designated ecumenical by the action of subsequent ecumenical councils. This untidy process and other subsequent misunderstandings have greatly complicated the count of ecumenical councils. Today Roman Catholics accept twenty ecumenical councils; the Orthodox and some Protestants only seven.

Complication set in during the century following the Council of Nicaea II. In 869-870 a council was called by Emperor Basil I to deal with the legitimacy of Photius, the controversial patriarch of Constantinople. The council was opened by the legates of Pope Nicholas I and the eastern patriarchs but with only twelve bishops in attendance. The final acts which condemned Photius as a usurper and recognized Ignatius as the legitimate patriarch of Constantinople were signed by 110 bishops dragooned by the emperor. Ten years later Emperor Basil I again called a council to deal with the still controversial Photius. This time the papal legates, the patriarchs and 380 bishops recognized Photius as legitimate patriarch and abrogated the decisions of the council of 869-870. The council of 879-880 called itself ecumenical, but even Photius himself did not accept it as on a par with the seven recognized ecumenical councils. The general consensus of the eastern church was that there were only seven strictly ecumenical councils. In the fourteenth century, after the great quarrel in the East over the form of mystical prayer called Hesychasm, the supporters of Hesychasm recognized the council of 879-880 which restored Photius as the eighth ecumenical council and the wholly eastern synod of 1341, which approved Hesychasm, as the ninth ecumenical council. But this was not generally accepted by either the East or the West. In the aftermath of the attempts to reunite Eastern and Western Churches in schism since 1054, some Greek Uniates recognized the unionist Council of Lyons II of 1274, the synod of the Patriarch Bekkos of 1277 which proclaimed the reunion of Lyons and the Council of Florence of 1438-1439 as ecumenical councils. But this Uniate sentiment was not shared by the majority of the Orthodox East who continued to recognize only seven ecumenical councils.

In the West only seven ecumenical councils were accepted until the pontificate of Pope Gregory VII (1073-1085). However, during the Investiture Controversy as canon lawyers searched for precedents to support papal efforts to wrest control of the Church from lay patrons, they discovered canon 22 of the anti-Photian council of 869-870 which forbade laymen to influence clerical appointments. Gradually this council came to be recognized in the West as the eighth ecumenical council. At the Council of Florence of 1438-1439, the ecumenical status of the Council of 869-870 was discussed. Though the Greek Orthodox refused to accept it while the Latin West insisted on it as ecumenical, the question was not resolved.

In 1602 the great Roman Catholic historian Cardinal Cesare Baronius accepted the Council of 869-870 as the eighth ecumenical council and labeled Photius a dangerous enemy of the Western Church. Canonists and historians in the West varied in their count of ecumenical councils. These variations were swept aside by Cardinal Robert Bellarmine in his monumental Counter Reformation polemic *De Controversiis* (1586-1593) which called the anti-Photian Council of 869-870 the eighth ecumenical council and added the four Lateran Councils, the two Councils of Lyons, the Council of Constance and numbered the Council of Florence the sixteenth ecumenical council. To do this he denied the need for the presence of all five patriarchs to make a council fully ecumenical.

During the pontificate of Pope Paul V, a papal commission in 1595 decided that the Council of Florence should be the sixteenth council. To this was added the Lateran Council V (1512-1517) and the Council of Trent (1545-1563). In the nineteenth century the Vatican Council I and in the twentieth Vatican Council II became the nineteenth and twentieth ecumenical councils.

However, the Orthodox Churches still accept only the first seven councils as truly ecumenical. All subsequent councils are rejected as non-ecumenical because either they dealt with purely disciplinary measures and did not make dogmatic definitions like the Councils of 869-870 and 879-880 or they were not attended by all five patriarchs like all subsequent councils. Perhaps in the interests of better relations with the Orthodox and Protestants, the time has come to reconsider the whole question and accept with them only the first seven great councils as the truly ecumenical pillars of the faith.

Glossary of Theological Terms

Adoptionists—theologians who sought to ensure monotheism by describing Jesus as a man gifted by the Father with divine powers. Paul of Samosata and his followers, called Paulianists by the Council of Nicaea I, are usually styled Adoptionists or dynamic monarchians.

Alexandrians—school of theologians centered in Alexandria in Egypt whose tendency was toward the spiritual interpretation of Scripture and the insistence on the full divinity of Christ.

Angel Christology—an early popular attempt to express the transcendence of Christ by describing Him as the greatest of the angels as in the *Shepherd of Hermas*.

Anomeans—Arian theologians who held that the Son is unlike (*anomoios*) the Father. Aetius and Eunomius were their leaders.

Antiochenes—school of theologians centered in Antioch in Syria whose tendency was to the historical interpretation of Scripture and insistence on the full humanity of Christ.

Aphthartodocetists—followers of the Monophysite Julius of Halicarnassus who taught that from the first moment of the Incarnation the body of Christ was by nature incorruptible (*aphthartos*), incapable of suffering and immortal, but that Christ by a free act of the will accepted suffering and death.

Apollinarianists—faction led by Apollinaris of Laodicea, a staunch Nicene, who maintained that the Divine Logos functioned as the mind of Christ who possessed a sentient human body.

Arians—faction led by Arius of Alexandria who proposed that the Son of God was created by the Father from nothing as an instrument for the creation and salvation of the universe; not God by nature this highest of creatures received the title Son of God on account of his foreseen righteousness.

Communicatio Idiomatum—an interchange of properties, is the theological principle that though the human and divine natures of Christ are distinct, the attributes of the one may be predicated of the other because of their union in the one Person.

Communio—bond of faith and love, strengthened by the Eucharist, uniting the local Christian communities and the entire Church at a level deeper than a union of common purpose and expressed in charitable works, letters of recommendation and communication among bishops.

Donatists—schismatics largely in North Africa who insisted on a holy church in which the unworthiness of the minister invalidated the sacraments he conferred; thus they broke with Caecilian of Carthage on the grounds that his consecration involved a bishop who had handed over sacred books to the Roman authorities during the persecution of Diocletian.

Enhypostaton—term proposed by Leontius of Byzantium signifying that the full human nature of Christ subsists only within the single Divine Person or hypostasis.

Eusebians—large body of conservative bishops led by Eusebius of Nicomedia and Eusebius of Caesarea who opposed the Creed of Nicaea I as favoring Sabellianism and who preferred to distinguish the Son from the Father as image from prototype, the Son being united to the Father through knowledge and love.

Gnosticism—a complicated religious movement which claimed a secret knowledge (gnosis) revealed to the Apostles capable of freeing the spiritual element in humans from the evil of the body in which it was trapped by a primal mischance among the higher beings emanating from the Father and of restoring it to its original heavenly home.

Homoeans—theologians led by Acacius of Caesarea who asserted that the Son is only like (*homoios*) the Father.

Homoeousians—party opposed both to the Arians and the term homoousios which they thought blurred the distinction between Father and Son, insisting instead that the Son is of like substance (*homoiousios*) with the Father.

Homoousians—those supporting the term homoousios, of one substance, used by Nicaea I to express the relation of the Son to the Father. The term was suspect because of its ambiguity and its use by Gnostics and Paul of Samosata.

Hypostasis—Greek term adapted to theological use meaning individual reality or person. The Cappadocian Fathers standardized eastern Trinitarian theology by insisting on the formula three hypostases or persons in one ousia or substance.

Hypostatic Union—the substantial union of the divine and human natures in the one divine person of Jesus Christ.

Iconoclasts—those who supported Emperor Leo III (717-41) and his successors who outlawed the use of sacred images and ordered their destruction.

Iconophils—those who supported the use of sacred images.

Macedonians—those who denied the full divinity of the Holy Spirit; their name seems to have been derived mistakenly from Macedonius of Constantinople, deposed in 360. Called also Pneumatomachians or fighters against the Holy Spirit.

Monarchians—theologians who attempted to safeguard monotheism by viewing Father, Son and Holy Spirit as a succession of modes or operations of the single Godhead. Thus they are sometimes called Modal Monarchians. Sabellius is usually regarded as this theory's prinicipal proponent. Monarchians are sometimes termed Patripassians because of their contention that the Father suffered with the Son.

Monoenergism—doctrine that there are two natures in Christ but only one mode of activity.

Monophysites—proponents of the view that there is one divine nature of the Incarnate Word. They refused to accept the definition of Chalcedon arguing that it was Nestorian.

Monothelites—adherents of the doctrine that there is only one will in the God-man.

Montanists—apocalyptic followers of Montanus of Phrygia in Asia Minor who preached the imminent coming of the Holy Spirit already manifested in the sect's own prophets and prophetesses. The African Tertullian was attracted to the sect because of its penitential rigorism.

Nestorians—followers of Nestorius of Constantinople who insisted that in Christ there were two objectively real hypostases or concrete subsistent beings joined in one prosopon of union or one external undivided appearance. For Nestorius Mary should not properly be called Mother of God or Theotokos but rather Christotokos or Mother of Christ, the prosopon of union.

Novatianists—rigorist schismatics led by the Roman priest Novatian who was orthodox in his Trinitarian theology but broke with Pope Cornelius by insisting on more rigorous treatment of those who had lapsed in the Decian persecution.

Ousia—theological term which signifies positive, substantial existence, that which subsists. The Cappadocian Fathers insisted on the formula, one ousia but three hypostases in the Trinity.

Patripassians—See Monarchians.

Paulianists—See Adoptionists.

Person—See Hypostasis.

Photinians—followers of Photinus, bishop of Sermium, pupil of Marcellus of Ancyra, who denied the pre-existence of Christ but admitted the Virgin birth and His superhuman gifts.

Pneumatomachians—See Macedonians.

Principle of Accommodation—rule of the Eastern Church that the ecclesiastical rank of a bishopric is based on the civil importance of its city.

Sabellians—See Monarchians.

Substance—See Ousia.

Theopaschites—defenders of the formula, "One of the Trinity was crucified." Acceptance of the formula signified repudiation of Nestorianism.

Theotokos—See Nestorians.

Index of Names and Subjects

Index of Names and Subjects

333